Estee Kafra's
COOKING INSPIRED

BRINGING CREATIVITY AND PASSION
BACK INTO THE KITCHEN

THE BEST OF

Design and Layout: RB CREATIVE
www.rbcreativedesign.com

Distributed by:
Feldheim
208 Airport Executive Park
Nanuet, NY 10954

www.feldheim.com

Printed in China

To the staff at Mishpacha Magazine, who believed in me, Kosher Inspired, and Kosher Scoop from the very beginning. Thank you in particular to Eli Paley, Avi Lazar, Nina Feiner, Nomee Shaingarten, Shana Friedman, Hila Paley, Bassi Gruen, and Chanie Nayman. You settle for nothing less than the best, and your passion for excellence is apparent in all you do. You guys are truly an "inspiration."

My partner, Dassi, who ensures that Kosher Scoop runs efficiently and smoothly, keeping it the fastest growing kosher website out there. Not everyone can say that their partner is their good friend, and I don't take that lightly.

Daphna Rabinovitch, writer, editor, and mentor...thanks for all your help and support, and for always going that extra mile.

Andre Reichmann, your talents grace the pages of this book, enhancing them with your beautiful imagery and vision. Thank you for so generously opening your archive to me.

Rivki Bakst of RB Creative: once again, you have turned raw material into a masterpiece. It's been a real pleasure working with you, as always.

To my family and friends—you know who you are, you know what you have done—and for that I thank you all. You are the driving force behind everything I do.

PHOTO CREDITS

Photography and styling by Estee Kafra

Exclusive of:

Pages 12, 58, 108, 187, 234 - André Reichmann

Pages 116, 127, 137, 150, 190, 216, 226, 227, 233, 290, 307, 308, 318, 323,329, 352 - Amit Farber and Daniel Lailah (Mishpacha)

Pages 53, 54 - Shana Parnes

KOSHER SCOOP is quickly becoming the fastest growing website for kosher recipes and all the latest and greatest in kosher cooking. When *Mishpacha Magazine* (a leading Jewish magazine) recognized the popularity of the kosher food in today's market, it launched the all-new food magazine *Kosher Inspired* with Estee Kafra as its editor. Instantly recognized as a huge hit, *Kosher Inspired* morphed into an online kosher recipe site, known today as Kosher Scoop. The Kosher Scoop community and fan base is growing quickly, with readers returning daily for the reliable recipes that draw inspiration from both classical, traditional Jewish cooking and current, popular trends.

Boasting some of the best kosher food writers and award-winning photographers of our time, the wealth of information available on Kosher Scoop (KS) keeps its readers coming back for more. With a wide range of recipes for every holiday, special occasion or just everyday dinner, there's inspiration to be had for every cook. And with professional articles on topics as diverse as seasonal cooking and healthy living, plus recipes for people with food sensitivities, KS readers turn to the site as a resource for help both in and out of the kitchen. Readers can also watch our informative videos, utilize our fantastic recipe box feature, participate in ongoing contests, and upload and share their favorite recipes with all their friends.

This book is a small sampling of the creative and reliable recipes that can be found on our site. Here you have a small taste of the variety and quality of the recipes and their professional authors who have an important representation in this book. We believe that the combination of recipes and articles from our talented staff lends the site the diversity and interest that keeps our readers satisfied. At Kosher Scoop we often write stories based on a particular ingredient, so for easy reading in this book we have grouped together recipes that are based upon staple ingredients, such as eggs, berries and ground meats.

We're proud to be a part of so many Jewish holiday tables, as our traditional and contemporary recipes prove themselves time and time again as welcome additions to Shabbat and holiday dinners. We'd like to take this opportunity to thank our loyal and committed fans for taking the time to read, respond to, and comment on our weekly e-mag newsletter. Thanks for being so enthusiastic, participating in our contests, and for sending us your warm words. You're the driving force that inspires us to keep KosherScoop.com the number one source for kosher recipes.

Wishing all of you the very best,
Estee

WHY I WROTE THIS BOOK

I have kids: adorable, good-hearted, funny, cranky, picky, really mostly regular kids. And even though I'm a professional recipe writer, I found myself doing the same thing that moms all over the world are doing—cooking only "safe" meals for my kids, meals that I knew they would eat, that wouldn't cause too much grumbling, and that were more or less healthy.

But as wonderful as meatballs and pizza are, I began to realize that I was doing my family a disservice. Instead of expanding their horizons, I was limiting their exposure to the incredibly bountiful world we live in; I was creating a bunch of picky eaters (whose wives would never forgive me!). Not only that, my kids' constant grumbling coupled with my lack of enthusiasm, were turning our dinnertime into something I wanted to avoid. I believe that intertwining family time with mealtime holds a certain strength and I wanted to share that with my children. That wasn't going to happen with all the negativity. Something had to change.

Basil from my herb garden.

I started talking to my kids about the amazing ingredients available to us. I planted my herb garden, got the kids involved, and pointed out every time I used home-grown herbs. Summer fruits came into season, and it was as if we'd won the lottery. My positivity started to rub off. I was showing my kids the small things that inspired me and in turn, they began noticing and pointing out the small things that inspired them.

On my part, this positive thinking added thrill and spice to my cooking. For my kids, it translated into a new enthusiasm for tasting new foods. This wasn't a major upheaval but rather a subtle shift in approach. We have an unspoken understanding: I cook new things, they try new things. (Well, usually. On the nights when that just doesn't work, there's always cereal.)

I wish I could say that no one complains during dinner anymore. I wish I could say that my kids sit like angels, finish their dinner, clear the table, and then run off to play. That will probably never happen. But that's OK. We may have macaroni or fish sticks for dinner (yes, that happens here, too), but on the whole, our family approach—our living inspired—has opened up new worlds for us.

INSPIRATION

Food is one of our most primal needs, and so for most of us, cooking is a basic, everyday chore. But food represents much more than the way in which we satisfy our cravings and keep ourselves alive. It is the way we nurture both ourselves and the people around us. I believe we can take this everyday act and elevate it into an experience of creativity, mindfulness, and meaning. In order to make the most of the world we live in, we need to open our hearts and minds to the inspiration all around us, to the myriad experiences and items that can shape our everyday lives. That's Cooking Inspired.

Inspiration can come from anything and everything around us—from a neighbor, a season, a sale, an occasion, an ingredient. The key, though, is to be cognizant and mindful of this circle of inspiration. Once you open your mind to it, suddenly you'll find inspiration everywhere. You'll find that you have developed a heightened sense of awareness to the era of abundance and opportunity we find ourselves in.

CONNECTION

No one's going to argue that the Friday night meal isn't one of the highlights of the Jewish week. But while it's hard for anything to match the appeal of chicken soup or brisket, the essence of the meal is so much more than the matzah balls you serve. The people you eat with and the conversations that flow are all essentials parts of the big picture. The traditions and customs that are maintained and created form an essential stronghold that keeps the Jewish people continuing from strength to strength.

Eating is not just about the food itself, but about the relationships forged before, during, and after the meals. Everything—the people you cook for, the focus on nutrition, the flavors you create, and the recipes you have from previous generations—is part of a bigger picture. Are you cooking from memory, from an old, worn, and splattered recipe

card of your grandmother's, or from a glossy-paged magazine showcasing the latest food trends? Are you making your husband's favorite dinner for his birthday, or baking the cookies your son just can't live without?

As you cook, you perpetuate your family's "food history"… but you're also creating your own history, adding pages to the manuscript of your family's life. It is a legend passed from one generation to the next, following traditions while passing on ideas and ideals.

Once we've reframed it in this way, cooking food and feeding others has suddenly been transformed from a mundane and tedious chore to something bigger: to an act filled with purpose. It's up to us to keep the trees of family, community, and tradition alive. And so, when cooking, we can make a choice. We can mutter under our breath as we serve up some nice Jewish guilt with the standard, safe chicken and potatoes… or we can try looking at the task with a fresh perspective, viewing it as a source of ideas and inspiration.

AWARENESS
Everywhere you go, everyone you meet, everything you read, is potential for new inspiration. Your five senses are constantly accosted by myriad sights, as well as countless colors, smells, and sounds that cause you to snap to attention. Paying heed to the vibrant world that surrounds you will open up a whole new world of cooking possibilities. Noticing that the oranges are on sale or that sweet peas are in season can be enough to inspire a quick orange and radicchio salad or a sweet pea side dish. If you keep your mind open to all of the possibilities available to you, and tune in to the steady stream of stimulating ideas that surround you, meal preparation will turn from a chore into an adventure; a recipe becomes a venture into uncharted territory.

GRATITUDE AND POSITIVITY
This heightened awareness of the world around you can and will help you develop an open and inspired frame of mind. When you're seeking the good, the beautiful, the positive in each situation, that mind frame will have a positive effect on so many different aspects of your life. Instead of thinking, "I really deserve better," or "I'm too overwhelmed to see beyond this mountain of laundry," you'll be filled with a sense of positivity and appreciation for God, Who created all this for you. When you're in a positive frame of mind, you can prevent negative emotions from ruling over you. You feel ready to accomplish, to conquer, to create.

CREATIVITY

That positive frame of mind allows you to notice and internalize all the gifts God sends you on a daily basis, opening a well of creativity inside of you—and that quality just so happens to be an important part of being a really great cook.

First, a disclaimer: creative cooking does not have to be time-consuming cooking. You may think that trying new ingredients or cooking with the seasons must mean more work, but on the contrary—when using fresh and seasonal ingredients, it takes less time to make your food sing. Usually, a few simple ingredients and some basic techniques are enough to do the trick—and when you've done it long enough, this sort of cooking becomes second nature. You'll know that, when blanched properly, French green beans need nothing more than a sprinkling of some coarse sea salt. When roasted, carrots, fennel, and beets need just some olive oil, salt, and pepper to enhance their natural flavors. It's all about knowing a few simple techniques, getting to know which foods pair well together…and then letting your imagination run wild.

For some people, the joy of cooking comes from the gratification they receive from following a few simple steps in a recipe and creating something new, from taking a few basic raw ingredients and transforming them into a fluffy, light, buttery cake. And really, the very act of cooking is creative. But when you are resourceful, imaginative, and passionate, you're taking that creativity to a whole new level, infusing your cooking or baking with your enthusiasm and vision. If your mind is open to new ingredients, new combinations, and new techniques, then your creativity will come into play, affecting the recipes you choose, the meals you plan, and even the way you present your food. You may choose to try one new ingredient a month or to encourage your children to notice the beautiful bounty everywhere. Whatever you choose, you'll be opening your eyes and your mind to the awesome world that God created; you'll be keeping your life meaninGFul, interesting…and inspired.

GET TO KNOW YOUR KITCHEN:

BASTING is a culinary technique that moistens the surface of roasting foods such as meat, chicken or vegetables using pan drippings, stock or another liquid. In addition to preserving moisture and preventing the food from drying out, basting adds flavor. If basting with pan juices, use a bulb baster to suction up the juices and then release the liquid over the food item. If basting with a separate liquid, use a basting brush to coat the cooking food with the liquid.

BLANCHING immediately stop the cooking process, which helps attain a vegetable's ideal texture, color and flavor. To blanch, bring a pot of salty water to a rapid boil over high heat and prepare a bowl filled with ice water. Cook the vegetables in the boiling water for a few minutes to move them just past their raw state. Drain the boiling water and immediately place the vegetables in the ice water to stop the cooking process.

BRAISING is a method of cooking ideal for tougher cuts of meat and other foods. Similar to stewing, it is used for whole joints. To braise, add a small amount of oil to a heated frying pan until heated. Add seasoned meat or vegetables to the hot pan and quickly brown all sides, which adds color and flavor. Add a small amount of liquid to the pan (about half-way up the height of the food), cover, and cook at a low temperature, either on top of the range or in the oven for a long period of time until the food is tender. Braising is a slow-cooking method and can take from 45 minutes to 6 hours to cook.

CARAMELIZING slowly cooks a vegetable over a low flame so that the water in the vegetable evaporates, the sugars begin to break down and the vegetable thus browns. Vegetables with low water and high sugar content are the best candidates for caramelizing. Most members of the onion family, including leeks, and vegetables such as carrots, fennel and peppers, are delicious when caramelized. To caramelize an onion, for example, heat a pan over medium heat, add a little bit of oil and then continue to heat. Add sliced or chopped onions, and cook, stirring often, until the onions turn a deep-brown color.

GRILLING is a dry heat method of cooking foods directly over charcoal, gas or electric heat, usually uncovered. Because a grill cooks with high-temperature dry heat, choose tender meats to grill and marinate them beforehand to help them retain moisture. The best foods for cooking on a grill are meats and poultry, although firm fish and vegetables are also delicious. When grilling, first bring the grill to a high heat. Place the marinated food directly on the grates. Once one side is cooked, flip over to cook the second side. Cooking time varies according to the food being prepared. When grilling steak, to create the appealing cross-hatched grill marks, turn the meat 90° halfway through the cooking of each side.

PROOFING allows a yeast dough to rise before baking. First dissolve the yeast in warm water (approximately 110–115ºF) and add sugar, as per recipe. The yeast, if active, should foam and smell like bread. To proof, cover the dough and leave it to rise in a warm (approximately 80ºF) location.

ROASTING is a dry-heat cooking method (no liquids) used to cook uncovered foods in an oven. Tender pieces of meat work best for roasting. To roast meat, place seasoned and lightly oiled meat into an oven preheated to 450ºF. Lower the heat to 325ºF and cook until desired doneness. Tent the meat with foil after removing from the oven and wait 10-20 minutes before carving to retain the juices. To roast vegetables, which brings out their sweet flavors, cut vegetables into uniform pieces and season. Lay out on a baking sheet in a single layer and place on the middle rack of an oven preheated to 400ºF. After 10 minutes, stir the vegetables; repeat, returning them to a single layer. Remove from oven when done.

SEARING is the process of quickly cooking the outside of a food, usually meat, using high heat to brown it on all sides, thus caramelizing its sugars and sealing in the juices. Searing may be done in the oven, under a broiler or on top of the range. After allowing the meat to sit at room temperature for 30-60 minutes, heat oil in a pan set on a high flame. Add the meat, and turn over when browned, repeating on all sides. Continue cooking meat using your method of choice.

STIR-FRYING is a quick method of cooking that originated in Asia. Small pieces of uniformly-cut food are quickly sauteed over high heat in a wok or a skillet while being constantly stirred. After heating a frying pan on high heat, add oil, followed by other aromatics once it's hot. First add into the wok those foods / vegetables that require longer cooking times, followed by the remaining foods, keeping in mind their approximate cooking times. When food is about two-thirds cooked, add sauce. Cover and steam until done.

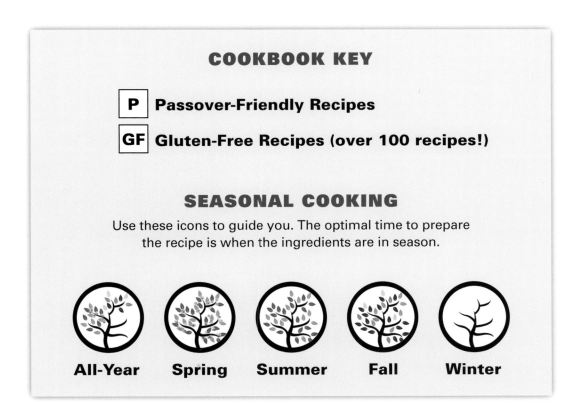

COOKBOOK KEY

P **Passover-Friendly Recipes**

GF **Gluten-Free Recipes (over 100 recipes!)**

SEASONAL COOKING

Use these icons to guide you. The optimal time to prepare the recipe is when the ingredients are in season.

All-Year **Spring** **Summer** **Fall** **Winter**

See, smell,
listen, feel,
and taste...
the world

FIVE SENSES

A whiff of fresh basil, *endless towers of bright, red tomatoes,* THE SMOOTH SKIN OF FIRM FRAGRANT MANGOES. **Glistening silver skin against perfectly pink salmon, SALTY CHEESE,** *endless blue skies.* **The scent of freshly baked bread, the aroma of dark roast coffee,** wind howling through the trees. *ICY COLD STRAWBERRY SMOOTHIES IN A TALL GLASS.* **The sweet tang of pink grapefruit,** THE FUN SOUND OF KERNELS POPPING, ***the pervasive aroma of fresh cinnamon buns.*** MINCED GARLIC SIZZLING IN HOT OLIVE OIL, **the sweet heat of chili peppers, JUICY BLACK OLIVES IN BRINE. Sun-kissed grapes hanging on a vine, *the happy sounds of satisfaction.***

APPETIZERS
off to a good start

Empanadas

While empanadas may have their origin in Spanish cuisine and are wildly popular in Latin America and Mexico, the flavors I chose here are definitely more Middle Eastern. That sort of makes these a cross breed, don't you think? I have a feeling that even the Spanish would agree that they are delicious.

1	**Tbsp oil**
2	**onions, finely diced**
1	**lb ground beef or lamb**
½	**tsp ground cumin**
½	**tsp ground coriander**
½	**tsp Kosher salt**
½	**tsp freshly ground black pepper**
1	**recipe savory crackers (see page 44)**

Egg Wash:
1	**egg, lightly beaten**
	Kosher salt, sesame seeds for sprinkling

❭ Preheat the oven to 400°F. Line a baking sheet with parchment paper.

❭ Heat the oil in a large shallow skillet set over medium-high heat. Add the onions; sauté for about 3 minutes or until soft. Add the beef, breaking up any lumps with a fork. Cover the pot. Cook for 15 minutes or until the meat is cooked through, stirring every few minutes to make sure the meat is not sticking. Add the spices and cook for 2 more minutes.

❭ Roll out the cracker dough into a large, ⅛"-thick sheet, and cut into 16 small squares. Place each square into an empanada press, add about 1 Tbsp of the meat filling and close. You can also make triangle bourekas, or any other shape you desire. Transfer to the prepared baking sheet.

❭ Brush with the egg wash. Sprinkle with the Kosher salt and sesame seeds.

❭ Bake in the center of the preheated oven for 12 minutes.

Makes 16 empanadas.

COMMENTS

I ordered an empanada kit online which contained 3 different sized presses. This recipe will work with all sizes but the amount of filling required will obviously vary.

Authentic Liver Pâté

Don't worry, most of the fat in this recipe is actually drained off, and you won't regret the time it takes to put it together. The results are well worth it!

2	lb chicken livers, broiled
2	cups chicken fat (schmaltz)
2	tsp Kosher salt
1	tsp freshly ground black pepper
1	cup sweetened applesauce
2	Tbsp fat drippings

> Preheat the oven to 250°F.

> Place the chicken livers in a small baking pan, smear with the chicken fat and cover the pan. Bake for 30 minutes. This will soften the chicken livers. Place a strainer over a large container, place the cooked livers in the strainer and drain the fat from the liver, reserving the excess fat.

> Transfer the liver to the bowl of a food processor fitted with the metal "S" blade. (If there are any parts that are very burnt or hard, remove them.) Cream on high speed until smooth. You can move the food processor from side to side to help it mix well. Add the salt and pepper.

> Once smooth, add the applesauce and cream again. While the machine is still running, add 2 Tbsp of the drained fat and emulsify for 10 to 15 minutes or until it forms a creamy consistency. Set a fine mesh sieve over a container or bowl and press the liver through in small batches, using the back of a ladle or a spoon to help push the liver through.

Makes 16 servings.

COMMENTS

Occasionally, I have the distinct honor of hosting a "siyum" (a celebration commemorating the completion of a portion of Talmud) for my husband's learning group. I like to try different ideas but I need to think "guy food." Grainy mustard, sweet pickles, crisp crackers and caramelized onions – every one a tantalizing accompaniment to the liver pâté. On Shabbat, I like to serve the pâté with esrog jam (see page 56) or a fig or wine jam. The tangy sweetness of the jam is a wonderful contrast to the smooth, earthy liver.

Ceviche

In life, one never can predict where certain events will lead, and from what and where one can draw inspiration. On a regular Tuesday afternoon, whilst doing some quick errands, I ran into my favorite fish store to pick up some turbot for dinner. While Ross was cutting my dinner-sized portions and I was wondering how I was going to cook them, the store phone rang, and I couldn't help but overhear the order that came in. Someone (who happens to be my cousin) was ordering "tilapia cut for ceviche." My curiosity was piqued. I asked my friendly (and ever patient) fish store man what ceviche [suh-vee-chey, chee] meant, and how it was prepared. He explained it was a dish that originated in Mexico, and the fish was "cooked"–or cured–in a citrus juice.

I was intrigued and did a quick dinner turnaround, asking him to cut the fish I was buying into small pieces, too.

Next phone call went to my cousin who had put the order through, and she enthusiastically told me that it was a favorite in her family and a big hit with dieters too. I made it that night and was excited about this new, quick and efficient method of preparing fish. It became a staple and eventually I began adding other ingredients to make it into a full meal. I tried to keep true to the Mexican origins of the dish and added some fresh and bright flavors, with instant success and almost no fat whatsoever.

Russian-Style Ceviche

ESTEE KAFRA **GF**

The flavors in this dish really complement each other. I used salmon, which is my favorite, but experiment with other fish as well.

1	lb salmon, sea bass or tuna, finely diced
3-4	lemons, juiced
2	purple beets, unpeeled and cleaned
2	Tbsp olive oil
	Kosher salt and freshly ground black pepper, to taste

¼	cup tahini
3	Tbsp fresh flat-leaf parsley, chopped
1	scallion, chopped

> Combine the fish and lemon juice in a bowl, making sure the fish is completely submerged in the juice. Cover and refrigerate for 1 to 2 hours, or until the fish is opaque.

> Meanwhile, preheat the oven to 400°F.

> Rub the beets with 1 Tbsp of the oil; sprinkle with salt. Place in a small pan and cover well. Roast for 1 hour. Cool slightly. Peel and dice; let cool completely.

> Strain the fish, discarding the lemon juice. Transfer the fish to a serving bowl. Gently stir in all of the remaining ingredients, mixing well. Let sit for 10 minutes at room temperature before serving.

Makes 6 servings.

Mexican-Style Ceviche

ESTEE KAFRA **GF**

If you want even-sized pieces, it's best to cut the fish while partially frozen, or ask the fishmonger to do so, if you prefer.

2	lb tilapia fillets, finely diced
1	cup freshly squeezed lime juice
½	cup English cucumber, finely diced
¼	cup diced celery, finely diced
½	cup seeded tomato, chopped
2	scallions, chopped

¼	cup fresh cilantro, chopped
	Kosher salt and freshly ground black pepper, to taste
2-3	Tbsp taco sauce, optional
1	tsp hot sauce, optional
1	serrano chile, finely chopped, optional

> Combine the fish and lime juice in a bowl, making sure the fish is completely submerged. Cover and refrigerate for approximately 2 hours or until the fish is opaque.

> Strain the fish, discarding the lime juice. Place the fish on a plate lined with a double layer of paper towel to soak up any excess lime juice. (If you really like an acidic note to your ceviche, skip this step.) Transfer the fish to a serving bowl. Gently stir in all of the remaining ingredients. Let sit for 10 minutes at room temperature before serving.

> Serve on salty crackers.

Makes 12 servings.

Pickled–Beet Deviled Eggs

Devilled eggs are always among the first attractions to disappear at a party. They have an old-school charm and are fun to make, handle, and eat. The shot of fuchsia from the beet-pickling makes these even more festive.

3	cups water
1	cup distilled white vinegar
1	small raw beet, peeled and sliced
1	small shallot, sliced
1	tsp granulated sugar
1	Turkish (or ½ California) bay leaf
½	tsp Kosher salt
12	hard-boiled large eggs, peeled
1	tsp caraway seeds, toasted and cooled
⅓	cup mayonnaise
1	Tbsp grainy mustard
1	Tbsp flat-leaf parsley, finely chopped
	Salt and pepper, to taste

❯ Bring the water, vinegar, beet, shallot, sugar, bay leaf and salt to a boil in a 2-quart saucepan. Reduce the heat and simmer, covered, for about 20 minutes or until the beet is tender. Uncover and cool completely. Transfer the beet mixture to a non-reactive container; add the eggs. Marinate in the refrigerator, stirring once or twice, for about 2 hours or until completely chilled.

❯ Finely grind the caraway seeds in a grinder.

❯ Remove the eggs from the beet mixture and pat dry; discard the beet mixture. Halve each egg length-wise and remove the yolks. Mash the yolks with the mayonnaise, mustard, parsley and half of the caraway seeds. Season to taste with salt and pepper. Divide evenly among the egg whites. Sprinkle with the remaining caraway seeds.

❯ Eggs can be marinated in the refrigerator in an airtight container for up to 3 days. Eggs can be filled and refrigerated for up to 2 hours before serving.

Makes 12 servings.

Bistro Mushroom Salad

This salad has a few steps but it's all done in the same pan, and is really simple to make! It's best served at room temperature and is beautiful as an appetizer but can obviously be served as a salad for any meat meal as well.

¼	cup extra virgin olive oil
3	large portobello mushrooms, stemmed and sliced
6	shiitake mushrooms, stemmed and sliced
6	cremini mushrooms, stemmed and sliced
½	cup button mushrooms, stemmed
3	Tbsp red wine
	Kosher salt and freshly ground back pepper
2	heads baby bok choy, stem removed
8	pastrami slices
6	romaine lettuce leaves, cut up
	Sprigs of fresh flat-leaf parsley

Dressing:

⅓	cup balsamic vinegar
⅓	cup olive oil
3	Tbsp granulated sugar
1	tsp garlic powder
¼	tsp Kosher salt
¼	tsp freshly ground black pepper

> Heat half of the olive oil in a large saucepan set over medium-high heat. Add all of the mushrooms and sauté for about 2 minutes or until the mushrooms have softened. Add the wine, sprinkle with salt and pepper and sauté for 3 minutes. Remove the mushrooms to a bowl and set aside.

> Add the bok choy to the pan and sauté for under a minute, just until the bok choy turns a bright green. Remove and set aside. Add the remaining oil to the pan. Add the pastrami; cook for about 20 seconds, just until the edges begin to curl.

> Dressing: Combine all of the ingredients for the dressing in a bowl, mixing well until combined.

> Assemble by creating a small pile of the romaine lettuce on a plate. Layer with the bok choy, cover with an assortment of mushrooms and top with the pastrami. Drizzle the salad with the dressing and garnish with parsley sprigs.

Makes 6 to 8 servings.

Crostini

small bites of goodness

Grilled Avocado Crostini

When shopping at my local grocery store, I stumbled upon red chili peppers in frozen cubes. They sat in my freezer for a while, until I needed an emergency barbecue party appetizer. They added just the right amount of heat to our favorite way of eating avocado.

1	**long whole-wheat or multigrain baguette**
2	**cubes frozen garlic (or 1 large clove garlic, minced)**
2	**Tbsp + 2 tsp extra virgin olive oil**
2	**cubes frozen chili peppers**
2	**ripe avocadoes**
½	**lemon**
	sea salt
	fresh chives

> Preheat a grill pan or outdoor grill to medium-high.

> Slice the baguette on the diagonal; set aside. Place the garlic cubes and 2 Tbsp of the extra virgin olive oil in a bowl. Using the back of a spoon, mash together to create a paste. In another bowl, combine the chilli peppers with 1 tsp of the extra virgin olive oil.

> Brush one side of each baguette slice with the garlic paste. Place the bread, garlic side down, on the grill. Grill until toasted and the edges are just beginning to blacken. Turn the bread over and brush with just a touch of the hot pepper paste. Remove from the grill.

> Meanwhile, cut the avocados in half and remove the pit. Brush the remaining oil over the cut side; place, cut side down, on the grill. Grill for just a minute, until warmed through. Cool slightly and cut into chunks. Transfer the avocado to a bowl. Squeeze the lemon over the avocados to prevent discoloring. Spoon the avocados on top of the bread slices and sprinkle with sea salt. Garnish with chives.

Makes 8 servings.

COMMENTS

For this recipe, you can also toast the baguette slices. After they have been brushed with the garlic oil, lay them flat on a greased cookie sheet. Bake them in a preheated 400°F oven for 8 to 10 minutes or until the edges just begin to brown.

Inspired Salmon Salad

I served this at a few parties recently and it was always enthusiastically received. I placed three crostinis on a plate, lining them up evenly. I topped one with the Inspired Salmon Salad, another with the avocado topping from page 27 and on the third I piled a simple mix of finely chopped tomatoes, some chopped, fresh basil, olive oil and salt and pepper. Neat, simple and refreshing. But what I really love about this recipe is its versatility. Sure, it's great for parties. But it's also a dream folded into an omelette, served on a bagel with cream cheese or just scooped with veggies and crackers for an elegant, light lunch. It's delicious every time.

2	cups dry white wine
1	Tbsp shallot, minced
1	lb skinless salmon fillet, cut into 1" pieces
3	oz smoked salmon, cut into ¼" pieces
½	cup (or more) mayonnaise
2	Tbsp fresh chives, thinly sliced
2	Tbsp drained capers
1	Tbsp (or more) freshly squeezed lemon juice
	Fine sea salt and freshly ground white pepper
1	baguette, thinly sliced, toasted

❯ Bring the wine and shallot to a boil in a small saucepan set over high heat. Reduce the heat to low; add the salmon fillet. Gently poach for 5 minutes or until the center of the salmon is barely opaque. Using a slotted spoon, remove the shallot from the poaching liquid. Remove the salmon. Discard the poaching liquid. Transfer both the salmon and shallot to a large bowl. Cover and refrigerate until completely cooled.

❯ Add the smoked salmon, mayonnaise, chives, capers and lemon juice to the salmon and shallot. Mix gently with a spoon just until combined (salmon will break up a little, but do not overmix or a paste will form). Season to taste with salt, pepper and more mayonnaise and lemon juice, if desired. The salmon mixture can be refrigerated for up to one day.

❯ Serve cold with toasted slices of baguette.

Makes 8 servings.

COMMENTS

To make elegant salmon molds, line 8 x 4-oz ramekins with plastic wrap, making sure that the plastic wrap hangs over the sides of the ramekin by about 2". Spoon the salmon mixture into the ramekins, filling about ¾-full. Close the packet by folding the plastic wrap over the salmon. Invert a ramekin onto a plate; remove the plastic wrap. Repeat with remaining ramekins. Garnish with fresh chives and serve with toasted pitas, pita chips or savory crackers.

Can be refrigerated in ramenkin "molds" for up to 48 hours.

Crostini

Goat Cheese Crostini with Candied Nuts

A few simple steps culminate in a sophisticated and beautiful presentation. I have served these as appetizers, but they can also double as a delicious dessert.

1	long multigrain French baguette
1	Tbsp butter
2	tsp granulated sugar
2	Bosc pears, thinly sliced (unpeeled)
3	small peaches, thinly sliced
8	oz goat cheese, room temperature
1	cup candied nuts (see recipe below)
	fresh parsley sprigs

Candied Nuts:

1	cup walnut pieces
1	cup granulated sugar

❭ Slice the baguette diagonally to create oval slices. Toast for a few minutes just until browned; set aside.

❭ Meanwhile, melt the butter and sugar together in a heavy saucepan or skillet set over medium heat. Add the fruit slices; cook, turning once, for about 6 minutes or until lightly caramelized.

❭ Spread the goat cheese on the toasted bread. Top with the caramelized fruit and garnish with candied nuts and parsley.

❭ Candied Nuts: Place the walnut pieces and sugar in a heavy saucepan or skillet. Cook, stirring as little as possible, over medium-low heat until the sugar turns an amber color. When all the nuts are coated with the melted sugar, immediately pour onto a sheet of parchment paper. Let cool.

Makes 12 to 16 pieces.

COMMENTS

As I was compiling the recipes for this book, I noticed that there was an unusually large number of recipes containing goat cheese. I like goat cheese–that much is obvious. But I also believe that it is an under-appreciated cheese. It's so versatile, relatively low in fat and delicious to boot! I hope you, too, will become a full-fledged member of the goat cheese fan club.

small bites of goodness

GF ESTEE KAFRA

Potato Latkes

Last year it was our turn to host the annual Chanukah party. I had stacks of these earthy, crispy latkes piled up in my kitchen and decided they deserved a bit of a kick. I figured that horseradish and wasabi would do the trick. Chanukah comes once a year but these latkes are a delicious treat all year-round!!

6	Yukon gold potatoes, peeled
2	tsp Kosher salt
1	tsp freshly ground black pepper
	oil, for frying

› Grate the potatoes into a bowl and stir in the salt and pepper.

› Meanwhile, heat about ½" of oil in a skillet set over medium-high heat. Gently drop heaping tablespoonfuls of the potato mixture into the skillet; flatten slightly with the back of a spoon. Flip over when the first side has turned a golden color. Fry on the second side until golden. Remove and place on a paper towel to soak up any excess oil.

Makes 24 latkes.

Parsley Root and Potato Latkes

Here's a slightly different version of typical potato latkes. The parsley root adds wonderful flavor and is a great idea for those who are watching their carbs.

2	cups Idaho or russet potatoes, grated
2	cups parsley root, grated
2	large eggs
¼	cup flavored breadcrumbs
1	Tbsp fresh flat-leaf parsley, chopped
	freshly ground black pepper and salt, to taste
	oil, for frying

› Place the grated potatoes and parsley root in a colander and press to squeeze out the extra liquid. Pour into a large mixing bowl and add all of the remaining ingredients except for the oil; mix well.

› Heat ½" of oil in a large skillet set over medium-high heat. Gently drop heaping tablespoonfuls of the potato mixture into the skillet. Flatten slightly with the back of a spoon. Flip over when the first side has turned a golden color. Fry on the second side until golden. Remove and place on a paper towel to soak up any excess oil.

Makes 16 latkes.

up

serve with

Fish Topping with Creamy Horseradish Sauce and Wasabi Cream

Horseradish Sauce: Mix together **1 heaping tsp prepared white horseradish** and **½ cup sour cream** until creamy. Drop spoonfuls on latkes.

Lox or Tuna Topping: Form small pieces of **lox** into mini rosettes. Or, to garnish with raw tuna, cut a tuna steak into a square "log" and roll the tuna in a mixture of black and white sesame seeds. Slice into thin strips and place on top of latkes. Place fish over the sauce.

Wasabi Cream: Mix together **½ cup sour cream, 1 Tbsp prepared wasabi sauce** and **½ tsp grated lemon zest**. Serve with latkes.

serve with

Spicy Apple Relish

Place **2 cups apple juice** in a pot and bring to a boil. Immediately reduce the heat to low and add **9-oz dried apple rings, finely chopped, 1 cinnamon stick, 4 cloves** and **½ cup dried cranberries**. Cook, stirring often to prevent the mixture from burning, for 10 to 15 minutes or until the apples have softened. Remove the cinnamon stick and cloves and serve warm or at room temperature.

To see a demo, go to **kosherscoop.com/video**

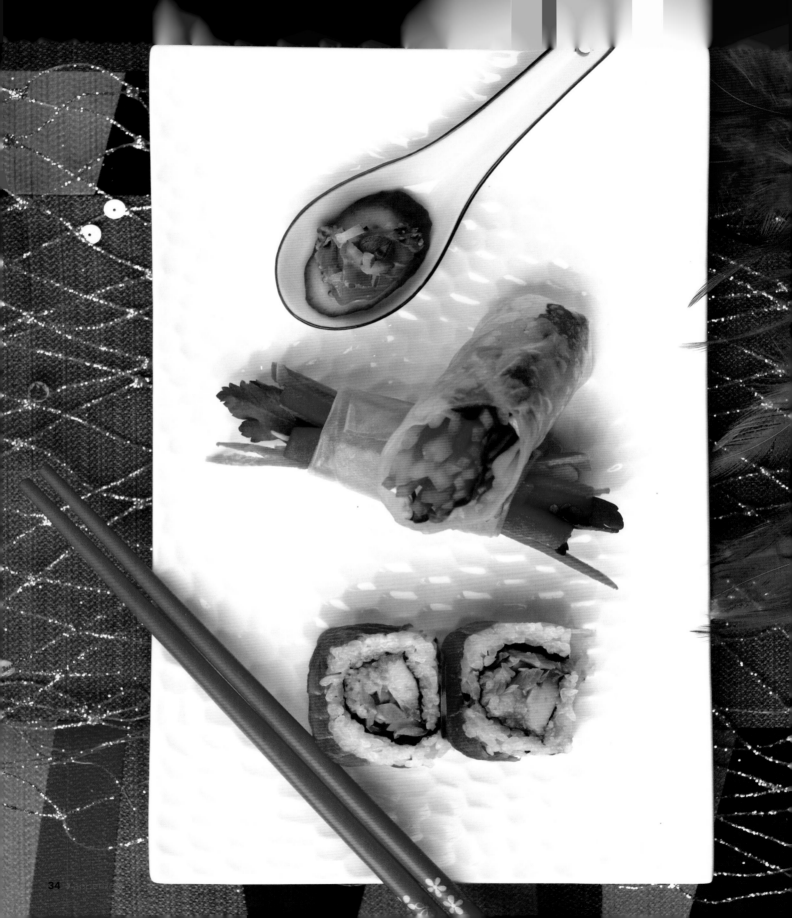

Asian Appetizer

This lineup of beautiful, simple foods makes a refreshing appetizer combination. We bought the sushi and my friend Dina created these gorgeous miniatures that taste as good as they look. This is more of an idea than a full-fledged recipe so, of course, feel free to adapt it and make your own combinations.

1	**red pepper**
1	**orange pepper**
1	**yellow pepper**
1	**carrot, peeled**
10	**rice wrappers**
1	**cup favorite dipping sauce**
1	**bunch fresh flat-leaf parsley**

❯ Using a peeler, peel off the outer skin of the peppers. Using a julienne peeler, create thin strips of the peppers and carrots.

❯ Submerge a rice wrapper in a bowl of lukewarm water. Let soak for 10 seconds or until softened. Place on a flat surface and brush lightly with the dipping sauce. Arrange a few leaves of parsley in the center. Soak another rice paper; place directly on top of the first one. Fold in half and then fold the rounded part up again to create a strip. Place a few pepper and carrot strips in the center, along with parsley leaves and close the wrapper around the vegetables. Cover with a damp paper towel until ready to serve. Repeat with the remaining rice wrappers and vegetables.

Makes 4 to 5 servings.

COMMENTS

This appetizer also looks lovely cut in half on the diagonal.

Create your own savory spoon. Top a slice of cucumber with a dollop of wasabi-flavored mustard. Create a small rosette out of lox or gravlax and place on top of the wasabi mustard. Top with a caper and sprinkle with finely chopped red onion.

Won Ton Duck with Sweet Dipping Sauce

Make sure you defrost the duck completely before beginning. You can freeze these on a cookie sheet and then store them in freezer bags. To reheat, bake at 475° F for 10 minutes. If I do say so myself, these are amazing.

1	duck
2	bay leaves
8-10	black peppercorns
2	cloves garlic, whole
2	Tbsp fresh chives or scallions, chopped
	deli mustard, for spreading
1	pkg egg roll wrappers, approx. 4½" by 4½"
	canola or peanut oil, for deep frying

Dipping Sauce:

1	cup apricot preserves
¾	cup pure maple syrup
6	Tbsp soy sauce
2½	tsp fresh ginger, minced
5	cloves garlic, minced
1	tsp freshly ground black pepper
2	Tbsp scallions or fresh chives, chopped

> Dipping Sauce: Combine all of the ingredients (except for scallions) in a saucepan and bring to a simmer. Remove from heat; pour through a fine mesh sieve to remove any lumps. Add the scallions to the sauce just before serving.

> Preheat the oven to 350°F.

> Place the duck in a baking pan. Add 3 cups of water, bay leaves, peppercorns and garlic. Bake, covered, for 1½ hours. Remove duck from water and cool.

> Remove and discard skin from duck. Remove the meat from the bones. Chop the meat very finely. Place in a bowl with ¼ cup of the dipping sauce and mix well. Stir in the chopped chives.

> Lay an eggroll wrapper flat on a work counter. Wet the center with a dab of good quality deli mustard. Using a paint brush dipped in water or your fingertips, moisten the edges of the wrapper. Place a small mound of the duck filling in the center. Make a purse by gathering the dough around the filling, squeezing the point where the dough encloses it.

> Preheat a wok or deep pot with about 3" of oil to 375°F. Adding the won tons in batches, deep fry for 2 to 3 minutes or until golden. Drain on a piece of paper towel. Serve with the remaining dipping sauce.

Makes about 18 pieces.

Savory Mushroom Squares

These can be cut smaller for hors d'oeuvres or a bit larger to serve as a main dish. The earthiness of the mushrooms and the creaminess of the goat cheese complement each other perfectly.

Caramelized Onions:

1	**Tbsp oil**
4	**Vidalia onions, stemmed and thinly sliced**
2	**tsp granulated sugar**
½	**tsp balsamic vinegar**

Mushroom Filling:

1	**Tbsp oil**
1	**lb button mushrooms, trimmed and sliced**
1	**lb shiitake mushrooms, stems removed and sliced**
	Kosher salt and freshly ground black pepper, to taste
1	**lb puff pastry dough**
1	**clove garlic, crushed**
12	**slices goat cheese**

❯ Caramelized onions: Heat the oil in a large, heavy saucepan set over medium-low heat. Add the onions, sugar and vinegar. Cook, stirring occasionally, for 25 minutes. The onions can be refrigerated for up to 24 hours.

❯ Mushrooms: Heat the oil in a separate heavy saucepan set over medium-high heat. Add the mushrooms, sauté for about 4 minutes or until softened. Strain the mushrooms to discard any excess water. Sprinkle with salt and pepper and set aside.

❯ Preheat the oven to 375°F.

❯ Roll out the puff pastry on a lightly floured work surface to ⅛"-thickness (it should be thin but not thin enough to create holes). Transfer to a parchment paper-lined baking sheet. Smear the dough with the crushed garlic.

❯ Cover the pastry with the onion mixture and then with the mushroom mixture. Arrange the slices of the goat cheese on top, placing them about 2" apart.

❯ Bake in the center of the preheated oven for 35 minutes. Remove the baking sheet to a rack to cool slightly. Cut into desired shapes with a pizza cutter. Serve warm or at room temperature.

Makes 20 large squares.

DIPS & SPREADS

 **P** **GF** ESTEE KAFRA

Herbed Garlic Oil

Thank you to my cousin Mikki for this recipe. It keeps well in the refrigerator for weeks on end and I serve it almost every Friday night. Simply place the oil and a few cloves in a bowl and serve with challah.

20	cloves garlic, peeled
2	tsp ground ginger
1	tsp salt
¼	tsp dried rosemary
¼	tsp dried thyme
¼	tsp dried basil
½	tsp cayenne pepper
	Olive oil

❯ Preheat the oven to 350°F.

❯ Stir together the garlic and all of the spices in a small glass dish that is large enough so that the garlic lies in a single layer. Pour in enough olive oil to entirely cover the garlic, about 1½ cups.

❯ Bake in the center of the preheated oven for 40 minutes. Remove the pan to a wire rack and let cool to room temperature.

Makes 20 to 24 servings.

COMMENTS

I make it in an oven-to-table dish—just refrigerate it after it cools and then keep it on hand for up to 6 weeks.

SAVORY CRACKERS
AND
PURPLE EGGPLANT DIP

Savory Crackers

*Generally, I'm not one to make extra work for myself!
For instance, I don't usually make crackers when there
are so many delicious ones to buy. When I was testing
the recipes for empanadas (see page 17) however, I
had some leftover dough. So I rolled it, cut it and baked
it. The results were outstanding. I served them at my
Shabbat dinner with a few dips and everybody loved
them. Try not to leave out any of the spice ingredients
when you make these; they work so well together.*

½	cup warm water
¼	tsp salt
1½	tsp active dry yeast
2	cups all-purpose flour
¾	tsp freshly crushed black pepper
½	tsp fennel seeds
¼	tsp ground cardamom, optional
¼	tsp onion powder
¼	cup vegetable oil

Egg wash:

1	egg, lightly beaten
	Kosher salt and sesame seeds, for sprinkling

> Stir together the warm water and salt in a small bowl; sprinkle the yeast on top. Cover with plastic wrap and let stand for 10 minutes or until frothy.

> Meanwhile, whisk together the flour and spices in a large bowl. Stir the oil and the yeast mixture into the flour mixture. With your hands, mix together until a soft dough forms, adding more water if necessary to bring the dough together.

> Cover the bowl with a damp tea towel; let rise for 30 minutes.

> Preheat the oven to 400°F. Line 2 baking sheets with parchment paper.

> Transfer the dough to a work surface. Divide the dough into 3 equal-sized pieces. Roll out each section to ⅛"-thickness (if the dough sticks to the counter, coat it with a very thin sheen of oil). Cut into desired shapes; transfer to the prepared baking sheets. Brush with the beaten egg. Sprinkle generously with Kosher salt and sesame seeds. For additional flavor, sprinkle with some black pepper.

> Bake in the preheated oven for 10 minutes.

Makes about 2 dozen crackers.

COMMENTS

Use plain round cookie cutters for round cookies. You could also try heart-shaped cookie cutters, or even irregular-sized rectangles.

Estee's Egg Salad

Double or triple as many times as you need.

4	hard-boiled eggs, peeled
1	red radish
1	heaping Tbsp low-fat mayonnaise
1	tsp gourmet (not sweet) relish
½	tsp grainy mustard (I like to use one with heat)
½	tsp freshly ground black pepper Kosher salt, to taste

❯ Mash the eggs with the back of a fork or a potato masher in a mixing bowl or container.

❯ Using a peeler, peel the radish to create thin slices; add to the eggs.

❯ Stir in all of the remaining ingredients, mixing well.

Makes 4 servings.

Purple Eggplant Dip

Canned or jarred mini purple eggplants are an Israeli staple. I puréed them and got this beautiful colored dip that paired well with the beige-colored tehina and hummus, as well as the green olive tapenade. This dip is about both presentation and taste.

1	can (19 oz) eggplant packed in brine, drained
1	small clove garlic (or 1 cube frozen garlic)
¼	cup mayonnaise (low-fat is fine)
1	tsp freshly squeezed lemon juice
¼	tsp granulated sugar
¼	tsp salt
¼	tsp freshly ground black pepper

❯ Place the eggplant in the bowl of a food processor fitted with the metal "S" blade. Add the remaining ingredients and blend until it's a paste/spread consistency.

Makes 8 to 10 servings.

Egg & Avocado Salad

My family loves this salad. It is healthy and filling. They are happy when I make it and I am happy when they eat it.

1	Tbsp low-fat mayonnaise
1	tsp freshly squeezed lemon juice
¼	tsp garlic powder
1	avocado, cut into chunks
3	hard-boiled eggs, peeled, cut into quarters
1	cup cherry or grape tomatoes, halved
½	tsp Kosher salt Freshly ground black pepper, to taste
½	small red onion, thinly sliced

❯ Stir together the mayonnaise, lemon juice and garlic powder in a bowl to create a dressing; set aside.

❯ Gently combine the avocado, eggs and tomatoes in a bowl. Add the dressing, mixing lightly until coated. Sprinkle with the salt and pepper and top with the sliced onions.

Makes 2 servings.

COMMENTS

Add chopped, fresh flat-leaf parsley for a nice flavor and beautiful color.

 **P** **GF** ESTEE KAFRA

Colorful Guacamole

¼	red onion, finely diced
2	avocados, diced
2	heirloom tomatoes, diced (approx 6 oz)
½	lime, zested and juiced
1	Tbsp extra virgin olive oil
¼	tsp Kosher salt
	Freshly ground black pepper, to taste

❯ Mix all of the ingredients in a serving dish until well combined. Serve immediately with toasted pita chips.

Makes 8 to 10 servings.

COMMENTS

Dairy option: Add a dollop of sour cream. It's delicious!!

Oma's Tuna Salad

Tuna salad with all the extras!

1	cold cooked potato, peeled
½	onion, chopped
4–5	stalks celery, chopped
1	kosher dill pickle
5	cans (4 oz each) chunk light tuna, drained
½	cup mayonnaise
½	tsp freshly ground black pepper

❯ Grate the potato by hand using the larger holes on a shredder; place in a mixing bowl.

❯ Place the onion, celery, and pickle in the bowl of a food processor fitted with a metal "S" blade. Pulse the mixture a few times, just until the vegetables are coarsely chopped. Add to the grated potatoes.

❯ Place the tuna, mayonnaise and black pepper into the processor and blend just until smooth. Add to the bowl of vegetables, mixing until well combined.

Makes 8 to 10 servings.

COMMENTS

My grandmother always uses a potato to add bulk and substance to her tuna salad. It also eliminates the need for too much mayonnaise. The potato will be easier to grate after it sits in the refrigerator for a minimum of 24 hours.

Olive Tapenade

Calling all olive lovers, this one is for you. Great as an appetizer for parties, but I actually love it on challah at Friday night meals.

1	can (19 oz) green olives, drained
2	small cloves garlic, peeled
2	Tbsp drained capers
2	anchovies
2½	Tbsp olive oil
½	tsp freshly ground black pepper

❯ Combine all of the ingredients in the bowl of a food processer fitted with the metal "S" blade. Pulse until combined and a smooth paste forms. Refrigerate until serving.

Makes 8 to 10 servings.

COMMENTS

I also use this spread to make an unbelievably delicious homemade pizza. Dollop some of the tapenade on top of tomato sauce and shredded cheese. It adds the incomparable flavor of olives, garlic and anchovies all in one.

 P GF SHANI MALKA

Feta Dip

1	cup low-fat cottage cheese
¼	cup boiling water
1	cup low-fat sour cream
4	oz feta cheese, crumbled
1	Tbsp olive oil
1	Tbsp lemon juice
	Kosher salt
	Freshly ground black pepper

❯ Blend the cottage cheese and water in a blender or the bowl of a food processor fitted with the metal "S" blade until smooth.

❯ Add the sour cream, feta, oil and lemon juice; blend until combined.

❯ Transfer to a bowl and season with salt and pepper if needed. Cover and refrigerate for at least 1 hour or until the flavors have combined.

Makes 8 to 10 servings.

COMMENTS

Add 10 oz thawed and drained frozen spinach with 2 cloves of crushed garlic with the salt and pepper.

 ESTEE KAFRA

French Onion Dip

My favorite dip to serve with thick, ridged chips or fresh potato latkes!

2	Tbsp extra virgin olive oil
1	extra-large Vidalia onion or 2 regular onions, sliced
2	cloves garlic, minced
1	Tbsp onion soup mix (no msg)
½	cup hot water
¼	tsp freshly ground black pepper
8	oz whipped cream cheese, at room temperature
2	cups regular or light sour cream

❯ Heat the oil in a large pot set over medium heat. Add the onions and garlic; cook, stirring occasionally, for 10 minutes or until softened and lightly browned.

❯ Dissolve the onion soup mix in the hot water. Add, along with the pepper, to the pot. Cook for 5 minutes or until the liquid has evaporated. Remove from the heat; let cool slightly.

❯ Meanwhile, mix together the cream cheese and sour cream in a large bowl. Stir in the onion mixture until well combined. I like to smooth the mixture out with a few pulses of an immersion blender. Refrigerate, covered, for up to 3 days.

Makes 4 cups.

COMMENTS

You can add chopped, fresh flat-leaf parsley, chives and/or thyme for added color and flavor.

DAIRY DIP
WITH LEMON
AND CHIVES

Dairy Dip with Lemon and Chives

This is one of my favorite ways to get my family to eat fresh vegetables. Somehow, when there is a delicious dip set auspiciously in the center of a vegetable platter, that plate takes on a whole new meaning. This dip is also fantastic with steamed broccoli.

½	cup sour cream
½	cup mayonnaise
	zest of 1 lemon
1	Tbsp lemon juice
2	Tbsp grainy Dijon mustard
2	Tbsp fresh chives, chopped
¼	tsp each Kosher salt and freshly cracked black pepper

❯ Combine all of the ingredients in a bowl and mix together well. Best when chilled for at least 3 hours before serving.

Makes 10 to 12 servings.

Garlicky Roasted Eggplant and Red Pepper

Eggplant and red peppers! How can you go wrong? This spread is absolutely addictive! You can make it in advance, as it keeps for about 2 weeks in the refrigerator. It freezes well for up to 2 months.

1	eggplant (about 2 lb), peeled and cut into 2"-chunks
1	red onion, peeled and cut into 2"-chunks
2	red peppers, seeded and cut into 2"-chunks
2	Tbsp olive oil
1	tsp salt, or to taste
¼	tsp freshly ground black pepper
1	whole head garlic
2	Tbsp tomato paste

❯ Preheat the oven to 400°F. Line a large baking sheet with parchment paper or aluminum foil.

❯ Combine the eggplant, onion, and pepper chunks in a large bowl. Drizzle with the oil and sprinkle with the salt and pepper. Mix well. Transfer to the prepared baking sheet.

❯ Trim the top off the head of garlic. Drizzle the cut edges of the garlic with a few drops of oil, wrap in foil, and place on the baking sheet next to the vegetables.

❯ Roast, uncovered, in the center of the preheated oven, stirring occasionally, for 40 to 45 minutes or until the vegetables are tender but slightly blackened around the edges. Remove from the oven and cool slightly.

❯ Transfer the vegetables to the bowl of a food processor fitted with the metal "S" blade. Squeeze the roasted garlic cloves out of their skins and place in the processor along with the tomato paste.

❯ Process with quick on/off pulses, until coarsely chopped. Transfer to a serving bowl, cover, and refrigerate to allow the flavors to blend.

❯ Use an ice cream scoop to scoop out individual servings and place in wine glasses. Garnish each serving with a lemon twist or thinly sliced cucumber.

Makes about 8 servings.

GARLICKY ROASTED EGGPLANT AND RED PEPPER

MUSHROOM MOCK CHOPPED LIVER

Mushroom Mock Chopped Liver

This is my favorite version of vegetarian chopped liver — it's perfect for Pesach or all year round! A food processor speeds up the preparation.

2	Tbsp olive oil
2	onions, finely chopped
1	pkg (8 oz) fresh mushrooms, sliced (about 3 ¼ cups)
2	cloves garlic, minced
4	Tbsp walnuts
3–4	hard-boiled eggs, peeled
½	tsp salt, or to taste
¼	tsp freshly ground black pepper
	Bibb lettuce, radicchio or salad greens

❯ Spray a large non-stick frying pan with non-stick cooking spray. Add the olive oil and heat over medium heat.

❯ Add the onions and cook for 6 to 8 minutes or until golden. If the onions begin to stick, add a little water.

❯ Add the mushrooms and garlic and cook, stirring occasionally, for 6 to 8 minutes, or until nicely browned. Remove the pan from the heat and cool slightly.

❯ In the bowl of a food processor fitted with the metal "S" blade, process the walnuts for 10 to 12 seconds or until finely ground. Add the onion/mushroom mixture, eggs, salt, and pepper. Process with several quick on/off pulses, just until combined.

❯ Transfer to a container, cover, and refrigerate until ready to serve or for up to 3 days.

❯ To serve: Scoop into individual Bibb lettuce leaves or radicchio cups or onto salad greens.

Makes 6 servings.

Chunky Middle–Eastern Eggplant Salad

I was sitting at a wedding when I was approached by a girl whom I hadn't seen in a long while. "Are you Estee Kafra?" she asked. "Because if you are, I have a great recipe for you." Thank you B. It is indeed a great recipe and we have made it countless times. If you're not an olive lover, simply leave them out.

1	Italian eggplant, peeled and cubed
1-2	tsp Kosher salt
2	onions, diced
½	red pepper, diced
½	yellow pepper, diced
3	Tbsp extra virgin olive oil
½	cup sliced green olives
2-3	cloves garlic, minced
½-¾	cup tomato paste
1	heaping tsp ground cumin
½	tsp turmeric
¼	tsp freshly ground black pepper
¼	tsp salt

❯ Place the cubed eggplant in a strainer and sprinkle with Kosher salt. Let sit for 20 minutes.

❯ Meanwhile, cook the onions in a large skillet or wok set over medium heat for about 10 minutes or until softened but not brown. Add the peppers and cook, stirring occasionally, for about 8 minutes or until softened. Remove the onions and peppers to a bowl.

❯ Add the olive oil to the skillet (you can also use 2 pans simultaneously). Squeeze the eggplant against the strainer to remove any excess water.

❯ Add the eggplant to the skillet; cook until soft but not falling apart. Transfer the eggplant to the bowl with the onion mixture. Add all of the remaining ingredients, mixing well. Cover and refrigerate until chilled or for up to 5 days.

Makes about 8 servings.

Roasted Garlic Aioli

This tasty and healthy dip is easy to make and will be appreciated by one and all. This recipe doubles or triples nicely for bulk.

4	**cloves elephant garlic**
2	**Tbsp olive oil**
½	**cup mayonnaise**
1	**tsp freshly squeezed lemon juice**
½	**tsp granulated sugar**
½	**tsp Kosher salt, or to taste**

❯ Preheat the oven to 375°F.

❯ Cut the tops off the garlic and place in a small baking dish. Pour the olive oil over. Roast in the center of the preheated oven for about 45 minutes or until soft. Remove from the oven and cool.

❯ Using gloves, squeeze the roasted garlic flesh out of the papery skins into a bowl.

❯ Mix in the mayonnaise, lemon juice, sugar and salt. (You can use an immersion blender to create a smooth consistency.)

Makes 8 to 10 servings.

Esrog Jam

Boiling the esrogim eliminates the bitterness of the fruit. Serve this jam along with crackers and chopped liver. It is sweet with a hint of tartness.

4	**esrogim**
2	**quince, peeled, cored and thinly sliced**
1½	**lemons, peeled and thinly sliced**
1	**lb granulated sugar**

❯ Cut the esrog into quarters and slice very thinly. Remove all of the pulp, setting it aside for another use, if desired.

❯ Bring a pot of water to a boil; add the esrogim. Let cook for 5 minutes and strain. Repeat 2 or 3 more times or until the fruit is no longer bitter.

❯ Combine the cooked esrogim, quince, lemon and sugar in a separate pot set over medium-low heat. Add just enough water to cover the fruit. Cook, uncovered and stirring occasionally, for 2 to 3 hours or until thickened.

❯ Meanwhile, boil your mason jars in a pot of hot water for 5 minutes. Remove with tongs onto a towel. Add warm jam into hot jars and cover tightly. Store in a cool place.

I made enough jam to fill 4 small mason jars.

COMMENTS

An esrog is a fruit that Jews use on Succot, upon which they also make a blessing. Therefore, when the week of Succot is over, there are plenty esrogim to go around. My mother and sisters all dropped off their families' collections, assuming that I was making jam once again. I actually hadn't planned on it but once I was faced with the whole pile of fruit, I wasn't left with much choice. The truth is that I was happy I made the jam. I serve it all year long with liver and crackers. It is a special custom to eat esrog on Tu B'Shvat, the New Year of the trees. It is also deemed to have many hidden powers and many women eat esrog jam during labor, as it has been known to make it easier.

ESROG JAM

COMMUNITY

STANDING IN LINE, *a friend passing by,* yesterday's lecture. *Events we attend,* **IDEAS WE SUPPORT,** the people we turn to in time of need. **Lively music at weddings...** the somber mournful tune of death. Charity bake sale, *cake for the neighbors,* SALAD FOR THE BARBECUE, confections for a Kiddush. *The grocery on the corner,* an elderly neighbor, ACTS OF KINDNESS DONE UNDER COVER OF NIGHT. **Sharing ideas**, listening, really living, everyday. We are a part of those we live with.

all-day BRUNCH

EGGS
get a makeover

Roasted Vegetable Shakshouka

This is one of the many dishes for which I use my Friday roasted veggies (for roasted vegetables see page 256). This is made in an 8" skillet, which yields two servings. You can easily halve it for a single-serving portion. Whichever way you make it, it's low in carbs and high in protein.

1	cup roasted vegetables (see page 256)
½	cup large egg whites
2	large eggs
3-4	Tbsp herbed tomato sauce
	Kosher salt, generous amount of freshly ground black pepper
	Fresh flat-leaf parsley, chopped

❯ Place the roasted vegetables in a large skillet set over medium-low heat; warm thoroughly, about 1 minute. Stir in the egg whites, making sure that the vegetables are well distributed. Cook the eggs for about 30 seconds, until they begin to solidify.

❯ Make two small holes in the vegetable-egg mixture, using the back of a spoon. Place one whole egg into each hole. Make a few more small holes with the back of the spoon and spoon in the tomato sauce. Sprinkle with salt and pepper. Cook, covered, for 3 minutes or until the egg whites have set but the yolks remain runny.

❯ When the whites have set, remove from heat. Sprinkle with parsley.

Makes 2 servings.

Carb–Free Egg Muffins

I keep roasted zucchini and sautéed onions in my fridge when I am trying to lose weight and eat healthfully. It makes these muffins a 2-minute pleasure. They're also a great take-to-work lunch or snack.

4	tsp oil
2	onions, finely diced
4	zucchini, cut into ½" cubes
2	tsp soy sauce
2	cloves garlic, minced

Egg Mixture:

6	large eggs
2	large egg whites
2	Tbsp milk
1	(heaping) Tbsp low-fat mayonnaise
½	cup shredded Cheddar cheese
½	tsp Kosher salt
	Freshly ground black pepper, to taste

❯ Heat 3 teaspoons of the oil in a skillet set over low heat. Add the onions; cook, stirring occasionally, for about 30 minutes or until very soft. If the onions are browning too quickly, add 1 Tbsp of water at a time.

❯ Meanwhile, preheat the oven to 400°F.

❯ Stir together the zucchini, soy sauce, garlic and remaining oil in a bowl, mixing to combine well. Spread on a large parchment paper-lined cookie sheet. Roast for 20 minutes. Let cool for 10 minutes. Reduce the oven heat to 350°F.

❯ Combine all of the ingredients for the egg mixture in a separate bowl. Stir in the onions and roasted zucchini. Spoon into 12 well-greased muffin tins (if your muffin tins are smaller, this mixture will fit 16).

❯ Bake in the center of the preheated oven for 20 minutes or until the tops spring back when lightly touched. Cool for 5 minutes, then use a knife to cut around the edges of the muffins to remove from the pan. Let cool on a plate. If not using right away, refrigerate for up to 2 days.

❯ Best served warm or at room temperature.

Makes 12 to 16 servings.

Baked Potato with Fried Egg and Cheese Sauce

Way before I was even old enough to recognize the concept of comfort food, I knew that this dish, served in a restaurant we used to frequent, was filling, creamy and delicious. I recreated it for my family a few years ago on Passover and it has become a steadfast tradition ever since.

2	baking potatoes
1	tsp oil
4	large eggs

Cheese Sauce:

2	Tbsp butter
2	Tbsp potato starch (or cornstarch)
½	cup milk
½	cup heavy cream or full-fat milk
½	tsp freshly ground black pepper
½	cup shredded Cheddar cheese
¼	cup shredded Monterey Jack cheese

❭ Preheat the oven to 400°F. Wrap each potato in foil; bake for 1 hour or until baked through.

❭ Cheese Sauce: Meanwhile, melt the butter in a heavy saucepan set over medium heat. Whisk in the potato starch for 1 minute. Whisk in the milk and heavy cream. Reduce the heat to low; cook, whisking, for 5 to 7 minutes or until thickened. Stir in the remaining ingredients until well combined and the cheeses are melted.

❭ Heat the oil in a separate large skillet set over medium heat. Add the eggs, cooking sunny-side up. Cook, without disturbing, for 3 to 4 minutes or just until set.

❭ Slice each baked potato in half. Top each half with an egg, yolk side up and a few spoonfuls of the warm cheese sauce.

Makes 4 servings.

COMMENTS

Originally, this dish was served with poached, not fried, eggs, so, if you're a bit more daring, go ahead and give it a try.

Inspired Quiche

The filling for this quiche is a blank canvas, just waiting for you to fill in your palette of flavors. I have included some ideas to act as inspiration, but feel free to mix and match and have some fun. It's hard to go wrong. I suggest using three to four fillings, or else it may overflow!

1	9" pie crust

Filling Base:

2	large eggs
½	cup milk (use soy milk for pareve version)
2	Tbsp all-purpose flour
½	cup regular or low-fat mayonnaise

Add-Ins: Choose one or a few, mix and match!

2	cups shredded cheddar or mozzarella cheese or a combination (I suggest using cheese along with at least one of the suggestions below)
1	cup broccoli, chopped and cooked (or frozen and thawed)
1	can (6 oz) tuna, drained
1	can (6 oz) salmon, drained
2	onions, diced and sautéed
1	lb mushrooms, sliced and sautéed until soft
1	cup frozen spinach, defrosted and squeezed well to remove extra moisture
1	cup tomatoes, chopped
2	potatoes, cooked and cubed
1	cup frozen peas, defrosted
2	Tbsp chives, chopped
2	Tbsp fresh basil, parsley, or thyme, chopped
1	cup cooked cauliflower (or frozen and thawed), chopped
2	large peppers, diced and sautéed just until softened
½	cup leek, chopped
8	cubes goat cheese
6	spears asparagus, steamed and chopped
½	cup edamame beans, steamed

> For "meaty" quiche: 3 chopped hot dogs, along with potatoes, sautéed onions, and chopped fresh parsley.

> Preheat the oven to 350°F.

> Place the eggs in a mixing bowl and beat with a fork. Stir in the milk and flour until well combined. Stir in the mayonnaise until combined. Add your chosen fillings, and pour into the pie shell.

> Bake in the center of the preheated oven for 40 to 45 minutes or until the top is just browning and the center is firm to the touch.

Makes 8 servings.

Maple Pecan Granola

*Simple granola made from natural ingredients is a super way to start the day. Use only 100%
pure maple syrup, not table syrup. You can add your favorite nuts to the recipe as well.*

4	**cups old-fashioned oats (not quick-cooking)**
1	**cup oat bran**
¾	**cup oil**
½	**cup pure maple syrup**
¼	**cup honey**
1	**large egg white, beaten**
1	**tsp pure vanilla extract**
½	**tsp salt**
1	**cup pecans, coarsely chopped**
1	**cup raisins or craisins, optional**

❯ Preheat the oven to 325°F.

❯ Place all of the ingredients except the raisins or craisins in a large mixing bowl. Mix
until well combined. Divide the mixture between 2 parchment paper-lined baking sheets,
spreading evenly in a thin layer. Bake for 20 minutes. Stir the granola to redistribute.
Alternate positions of the trays, switching between the higher and lower oven racks. Bake for
10 minutes more or until the edges begin to brown. The oats may still feel soft but they will
harden as they cool.

❯ Stir in the raisins or craisins, if using, mixing well.

❯ Let the granola cool completely. Store in an airtight container for up to 3 weeks or freeze
for up to 3 months.

Makes 24 servings.

COMMENTS

*For a crunchier granola, cool the granola in a turned off oven with the oven door open once you
have finished baking. Watch carefully to make sure it doesn't burn.*

Simple Pareve Smoothie *Makes 4 servings.*

*Literally throw together the ingredients, take them for a spin in the blender, and you have
a perfect any-time-of-day energy booster that is low in fat and oh, so refreshing!*

Place **1 bag (14 oz) frozen strawberries, 12 oz frozen mango cubes, 8 oz soft tofu, 3
packets (1 tsp each) low calorie sweetener such as Splenda** and **1 cup orange juice**
into a blender. Blend until smooth. Enjoy!

Sesame Hemp Seed Granola

The tahini and the maple syrup bring a caramel-like taste to this morning treat. The tahini also adds some extra sesame goodness. It's delicious with plain yogurt, milk or just by itself.

1	cup pecans	¼	cup extra virgin olive oil
4	cups old-fashioned rolled oats	1½	tsp cinnamon
¼	cup sesame seeds	½	tsp fine sea salt
¼	cup hulled hemp seeds	¼	tsp ground cardamom, optional
½	cup pure maple syrup	8	dates, chopped
¼	cup tahini	8	dried figs, chopped

❯ Preheat the oven to 350°F. Line two rimmed baking sheets with parchment paper. Set aside.

❯ Mix together the pecans, oats, sesame and hemp seeds, maple syrup, tahini, olive oil, cinnamon, salt and cardamom in a large bowl, until evenly coated.

❯ Spread the oat mixture onto the two prepared sheets. Bake for 20 minutes.

❯ Add 4 of the chopped dates and 4 of the chopped figs into each one of the pans and mix well with the rest of the granola.

❯ Let cool. Granola can be stored in an airtight container at room temperature for up to 2 weeks.

Makes 15 to 18 servings (7½ cups).

Breakfast Bran Pancakes

This nutritious list of ingredients produces a light and fluffy breakfast treat. Sometimes, when I am in a rush, I like to make one large pancake in an 8" pan and cut it into triangles. It takes less time and involves less flipping.

1	cup white whole-wheat flour		2	large eggs
1	cup Kamut flour		1⅓	cups 1% milk
⅓	cup granulated sugar		¼	cup oil
2	Tbsp wheat bran		¼	cup chocolate chips, optional
4½	tsp baking powder			Oil, for frying

> Combine the first eight ingredients in a bowl, whisking with a fork until smooth. Fold in the chocolate chips, if using.

> Heat an 8" skillet set over medium heat with enough oil to coat the bottom of the pan. Use a ladle to make individual-sized pancakes or use my time-saving method. Pour about one ladleful of the batter into the pan, tilting the pan until the batter is evenly and thinly spread over the bottom of the skillet, adding more batter if necessary. Cook on one side for 3 to 4 minutes or until small bubbles form on top of the pancake. Flip over and cook for about 3 minutes. The batter will puff slightly during cooking. Invert onto serving plate.

> Cut into wedges and serve warm with pure maple syrup.

Makes 8 to 10 pancakes.

Kamut is a natural, unaltered grain available in many health food stores. You can use regular all-purpose flour of you prefer.

Cranberry Butter Scones

Scones are one of my favorite treats. They are light and fluffy, with a buttery flavor, and are not too sweet to feel like you are eating sinfully. There are endless options for add-ins, making them versatile and fun to make. HOWEVER, scones have to be made right. If not, they are heavy, dense and not very appealing. Here, Chef Sam from Pantry Foods describes his simple technique for the perfect scone.

¾	cup dried cranberries
4¾	cups all-purpose flour
1	Tbsp baking powder
¾	tsp baking soda
½	cup granulated sugar
1¼	tsp salt
1	cup + 1 Tbsp unsalted butter, VERY cold
1½	cups buttermilk
1	tsp lemon zest

Topping:

3	Tbsp unsalted butter, melted (approx)
	Large-crystal sugar or granulated sugar, for sprinkling

❯ Preheat the oven to 400°F. Butter a baking sheet.

❯ Combine the dried cranberries with enough warm water to cover them in a small bowl. Let sit for 10 minutes or until plump. Drain well.

❯ Sift the flour, baking powder and baking soda into a large bowl. Stir in the sugar and salt with a wooden spoon. Cut the butter into ½" cubes and scatter over the dried ingredients. Using a pastry cutter or two knives, cut in the butter until the butter is broken down into small chunks with a few larger, pea-sized pieces. Add the buttermilk, lemon zest and cranberries. Stir just until the dough holds together.

❯ Transfer the dough to a lightly floured work surface. Pat the dough into a rectangle about 18" long and 5" wide and 1½" thick. Cut into 24 triangles. Transfer to the baking sheet. Brush the scones with the melted butter. Sprinkle with the sugar.

❯ Bake in the center of the preheated oven for 25 to 35 minutes or until puffed and lightly golden.

To see a demo, go to **kosherscoop.com/video**

Tomato, Herb and Cheese Galette

A galette is a fancy way of serving quiche with a good excuse to be imperfect.☺

Dough:

1½	cups all-purpose flour
1	tsp baking powder
¼	tsp baking soda
½	tsp salt
½	cup cold, unsalted butter, cut into pieces
⅓	cup buttermilk (approx)

Filling:

2	beef steak tomatoes, thickly sliced
¾	cup fresh breadcrumbs
2	cloves garlic, minced
1	Tbsp each fresh thyme and basil, chopped
¼	tsp freshly ground black pepper
⅓	cup shredded Asiago, Muenster or mozzarella cheese
2	Tbsp grated Parmesan cheese
1	large egg, lightly beaten

❯ Combine the flour, baking powder, baking soda and salt in a bowl or the bowl of a food processor. Using a pastry cutter or on/off pulse motion, cut in the butter until the butter is the size of peas with a few larger pieces. Pour in the buttermilk, tossing with a fork or pulsing, until the dough JUST comes together, adding 1 Tbsp more buttermilk if required. Knead lightly into a disc. Cover with plastic wrap and refrigerate for at least 30 minutes or for up to 3 days.

❯ Preheat the oven to 400°F.

❯ Meanwhile, place the tomato slices on paper towels to soak up extra liquid.

❯ Toss together the breadcrumbs, garlic, thyme, basil and pepper in a bowl.

❯ On a lightly floured work surface, roll out the pastry to a roughly 12"-circle. Transfer to a parchment paper-lined rimless baking sheet. Leaving a 2" border, sprinkle half of the breadcrumb mixture over the dough. Arrange the tomato slices, slightly overlapping, on top of the breadcrumbs. Sprinkle with the Asiago and Parmesan cheeses and then the remaining breadcrumb mixture. Lift the pastry over the filling, pleating and folding the pastry as necessary and using the beaten egg to "glue" the pleats together.

❯ Brush the egg all over the pastry. Bake in the center of the preheated oven for about 25 to 30 minutes or until the galette is golden brown. Let cool for 10 minutes Serve warm.

Makes 6 to 8 servings.

COMMENTS

To make homemade buttermilk, place ⅓ cup of milk and 1 tsp vinegar in a cup. Let sit for 20 minutes.

Pizza Tartlets with Onion Jam and Salad

*This pizza dough is a great one to have on hand–it easily makes one-12"
pizza dough and is great for all occasions. Also wonderful to make on the
grill.*

Onion Jam:

2	Tbsp olive oil
1	large red onion, sliced thinly
2	cloves garlic, minced
2	Tbsp light brown sugar
½	tsp dried thyme
	Pinch of salt and freshly ground black pepper
½	cup red wine

Pizza Dough:

2	cups all-purpose flour
2¼	tsp rapid-rise yeast
2	tsp granulated sugar
¾	tsp salt
⅔	cup very hot water (120°F-130°F)
3	Tbsp canola or olive oil

Topping:

3	cups mixed field greens
1	cup cherry tomatoes, halved
⅓	cup goat cheese or herbed cream cheese
1	Tbsp olive oil

> Preheat the oven to 425°F.

> Onion Jam: Heat the oil in a large skillet set over medium heat. Add
the onion, garlic, brown sugar, thyme, salt and pepper; cook for 10 to
12 minutes or until softened and lightly caramelized. Pour in the wine.
Bring to a boil; reduce the heat to medium and cook, stirring occasionally, for 5 minutes or until the onion has absorbed the wine and
turned deep purple. The mixture can be covered with plastic wrap and
refrigerated for up to 2 days. Bring completely to room temperature
before using.

> Pizza Dough: Meanwhile, combine 1 cup of the flour with the yeast,
sugar and salt in a large bowl. Pour in the water and oil, mixing for
about 1 minute or until well blended. Stir in enough of the remaining
flour, ½ cup at a time, to make a soft dough. The dough should be
able to form a ball but still be slightly sticky. Transfer the dough
to a lightly floured work surface; knead, adding additional flour if
necessary, for about 4 minutes or until smooth and elastic. With
floured hands, divide the dough into 4 equal size pieces.

> Pat or roll each piece of dough into 5" or 6" rounds. Transfer to 2 parchment paper-lined baking sheets. Prick all over with the tines of a fork.

> Bake the pizza rounds in the center of the preheated oven for about 10 minutes or until lightly golden (if a crispy dough is preferred, bake for 12 minutes).

> Topping: In a bowl, toss together the greens, tomatoes and goat cheese. Drizzle with the olive oil.

> Divide the onion jam among the 4 pizzas, spreading evenly. Top with the salad.

Makes 6 servings.

COMMENTS

For a pareve version, omit the goat cheese. If you want to make it a complete meal, spread some soft stir-fried tofu over the pizza.

Sheet Pan Pizza

Pizza needs no introduction, and when it's as tasty as this one, you can't talk anyways...your mouth is too full ☺.

Dough:

1½	cups warm water (110°F)
½	cup + 1 Tbsp extra virgin olive oil
1	Tbsp granulated sugar
5	cups all-purpose flour
4¼	tsp instant or rapid-rise yeast
2	tsp salt

Sauce and Toppings:

1	Tbsp extra virgin olive oil
3	cloves garlic, minced
½	tsp red pepper flakes
1	can (16 oz) pizza sauce
	Salt
1½	cups grated Parmesan cheese (3 oz)
3	cups shredded mozzarella cheese (12 oz)
¼	cup finely chopped fresh basil, optional

> Dough: Combine the water, ¼ cup of the oil and the sugar in a 2-cup liquid measuring cup. Combine the flour, yeast and salt together in the bowl of an electric mixer fitted with the dough hook. Mix on low speed for about 30 seconds or until combined. Increase the speed to medium-low; add the water mixture and knead for about 3 minutes or until the dough is uniform in texture. Transfer the dough to a large greased bowl, cover with plastic wrap and let rise at room temperature for 1 to 1½ hours or until doubled in bulk.

> Evenly coat a rimmed baking sheet with the remaining ¼ cup of oil. On a lightly floured work surface, roll the dough into a 16" x 12" rectangle. Transfer the dough to the prepared sheet and stretch the dough to cover the sheet, pressing it into the corners. Brush the dough evenly with the 1 Tbsp of oil and cover with plastic wrap. Set in a warm spot.

> Stir the garlic and pepper flakes into the pizza sauce. Add salt, to taste.

> Preheat the oven to 450°F. Place an oven rack at the lowest position in the oven.

> Remove the plastic wrap from the dough; using your fingers, make indentations all over the dough. Sprinkle the dough with 1 cup of the Parmesan.

> Bake in the preheated oven for 7 to 10 minutes or until the cheese begins to melt. Remove the sheet from the oven. Leaving a 1" border, spoon the pizza sauce over the pizza. Bake for 7 to 10 minute or until the sauce is deep red and steaming.

> Sprinkle the mozzarella and the remaining ½ cup of Parmesan evenly over the sauce and bake for about 12 minutes or until the cheese is golden brown. Remove the pizza from the oven and let rest for 5 minutes. Sprinkle with basil, if using.

Makes 12 servings.

Whole-Wheat Pizza

Whole-wheat pizza is just as easy to make as regular pizza dough so why not switch it up? Combine **1½ Tbsp honey, 3 cups warm water** and **2½ tsp instant dry yeast** in the bowl of an electric mixer fitted with the dough hook. Add **3 Tbsp extra virgin olive oil, 7 cups whole-wheat flour** and **5 tsp salt**. Knead for about 8 minutes or until a smooth dough is formed. Transfer the dough to a large, greased bowl. Cover with a towel and let stand for 30 minutes or cover the dough with plastic wrap and refrigerate for up to 3 days. Let the dough come to room temperature for at least 30 minutes before rolling out.

White Pizza

White pizza, a light and lovely change from a tomato-based pizza, is so easy to make, especially when you take the short cut of buying premade pizza dough. Simply roll out **1-12 oz package of store-bought regular or whole-wheat pizza dough** into a 12" circle. Transfer the dough to a pizza pan. Spread **2 cloves garlic, minced**, over the dough and top with **1 tsp dried basil**. Spread **½ cup ricotta cheese** over the basil and then sprinkle with an **8 oz bag of pizza cheese**. Bake in the center of a preheated 425°F oven for 15 minutes.

Busy Mom's Creamy Pasta Sauce

In my own private utopia, I always have homemade jarred pasta sauce in my refrigerator, ready and able to be warmed up at a moment's notice. Since I don't actually reside in this utopia, I do in fact have to make it often but this recipe is so simple and delicious that I always double or triple the recipe.

½	**cup butter**
5	**cloves garlic, minced**
½	**cup all-purpose flour**
3½	**cups milk**
2	**cans (each 28 oz) crushed tomatoes with their juice**
6	**Tbsp tomato paste**
	Kosher salt and freshly ground black pepper, to taste
1	**Tbsp dried basil**
4	**scallions, chopped**

❯ Melt the butter in a very large pot set over medium-high heat. Add the garlic and sauté until translucent. Whisk in the flour for 1 minute. Whisk in the milk; bring to a boil. Boil, whisking constantly, for 3 minutes or until thickened and smooth.

❯ Stir in the crushed tomatoes and tomato paste, stirring until smooth. Season to taste with salt and pepper. Cook for 5 minutes. Stir in the basil. Remove from heat. Cool before spooning into freezable containers or into Ziploc™ bags. Refrigerate for up to 5 days or freeze for up to 3 months. Just before serving, stir in the scallions.

Makes 8 cups.

COMMENTS

Once thawed, rewarm the sauce over low heat and stir in 1 to 2 Tbsp of milk or cream.

LAYERS OF GOODNESS

Zucchini Parmigiana

Here, zucchini takes the place of the traditional eggplant. With a wonderful, soft texture, it's bound to be a favorite with kids.

3-4	large green zucchini
	Kosher salt
2	large eggs
1	cup seasoned dry bread crumbs
	oil, for frying
1	jar (26 oz) of marinara sauce
1	lb cottage cheese
12	slices American cheese
1	lb mixed shredded cheddar and mozzarella cheese

› Cut the ends off the zucchini and slice lengthwise into ½" slices. You should have enough slices to cover the area of a 13" x 9" pan 3 times. Lay the zucchini on a baking sheet and sprinkle with salt. Let sit until the zucchini sweats. Pat dry.

› Place 1 egg in a bowl; beat lightly. Place the breadcrumbs in a separate bowl. Dip a zucchini slice in the egg and then in the bread crumbs. Repeat with the remaining zucchini. Heat about ½" of oil in a large skillet set over medium-high heat. In batches, fry the zucchini for about 2 minutes per side or until golden and slightly tender. Halfway through, replace the hot oil with a fresh batch of new oil.

› Preheat the oven to 350°F.

› Spread 1 cup of the marinara sauce over the bottom of a 13" x 9" pan. Line the pan with fried zucchini strips. Mix the remaining egg with the cottage cheese. Pour this mixture on top of the zucchini-lined pan. Line with another layer of the zucchini. Layer the American cheese over the zucchini. Line with another layer of the zucchini. Pour another cup of the marinara sauce over layer of the zucchini. Sprinkle shredded cheese over the marinara sauce.

› Bake, covered, in the center of the preheated oven for 45 minutes. Uncover and bake about 10 minutes or until the cheese is completely melted and starting to turn golden. Let the pan sit for a few minutes until firm. Slice and enjoy!

Makes 12 servings.

COMMENTS

You can bake the breaded zucchini for a low-fat version. Simply lay the slices side by side on a lightly greased cookie sheet. Bake in a preheated 350°F oven for 15 minutes.

Provençal Roasted Vegetable Lasagna

The depth of flavor in this particular lasagna comes from roasting the vegetables, which coaxes out all of their natural sweetness and complexity. Adding the capers, sun-dried tomatoes and olives after the roasting perks up that flavor and adds a welcome acidic note to the sweetness. Whether you choose goat cheese or feta cheese as the accompaniment, both will add a salty creaminess that brings all the comparative notes together. The rice noodles make this is a perfect choice for those in your family who have gluten intolerances.

Roasted Vegetables:
1	red onion, chopped
2	small zucchini, diced
1	eggplant, diced
1	fennel bulb, trimmed and diced
2	Tbsp olive oil
1	tsp dried rosemary, crushed
¼	tsp freshly ground black pepper
⅓	cup julienned sun-dried tomatoes, packed in oil
⅓	cup halved pitted olives
¼	cup capers
12	rice flour lasagna noodles

Cheese Filling:
1⅔	cups part-skim ricotta cheese
2	large eggs
½	tsp freshly ground black pepper
4	cups tomato pasta sauce
1	cup crumbled goat or feta cheese
1½	cups shredded mozzarella cheese

> Preheat the oven to 425°F.

> Roasted Vegetables: Gently toss together the onion, zucchini, eggplant, fennel, oil, rosemary and pepper in a bowl. Spread evenly on a rimmed baking sheet. Roast in the center of the preheated oven for about 35 minutes or until tender and golden. Transfer to a bowl; stir in the sun-dried tomatoes, olives and capers. Set aside. Reduce the oven heat to 350°F.

> Meanwhile, in a large pot of boiling salted water, cook the lasagna noodles for 6 to 8 minutes or until tender but firm. Drain well. Arrange the noodles in a single layer on damp tea towels.

> Cheese Filling: Stir together the ricotta, eggs and pepper in a bowl.

> Arrange 3 noodles in the bottom of a 13"x 9" baking dish. Spread ¼ of the tomato sauce over. Top with ⅓ of the vegetables, ⅓ of the ricotta mixture and ⅓ of the goat cheese. Repeat the layers twice more. Layer with the last three noodles and the last quarter of tomato sauce. Sprinkle the mozzarella over evenly. Cover loosely with foil.

> Bake in the center of the preheated oven for 30 minutes. Remove the foil. Bake, uncovered, for 25 to 30 more minutes or until bubbly and the top is light golden. Let the lasagna rest for 10 minutes before cutting into servings.

Makes 8 servings.

Four Cheese and Mushroom Lasagna

Talk about a heady combination!! Emmenthaler cheese, Parmesan, ricotta AND mozzarella. Combine these cheeses, some mild like ricotta and mozzarella, some wonderfully smoky like the Emmenthaler with the robust earthiness of the porcini mushrooms. It's a marriage made in culinary heaven. Although there are several steps in this dish, the end result is well worth it.

Mushroom Filling:

½	oz dried porcini mushrooms
½	cup hot water
3	Tbsp unsalted butter
8	cups sliced mushrooms (1 lb)
½	tsp salt
¼	tsp freshly ground black pepper
¼	cup fresh flat-leaf parsley, chopped
1½	cups shredded Emmenthaler or Swiss cheese
¾	cup grated Parmesan cheese
1¾	cups part-skim ricotta cheese
1	large egg

Bechamel Sauce:

¼	cup unsalted butter
1	small onion, chopped
3	cloves garlic, minced
½	tsp dried thyme
⅓	cup all-purpose flour
2¾	cups milk
1	cup vegetable broth, preferably low-sodium
¼	tsp salt
15	lasagna noodles, cooked until *al dente*
2	cups shredded mozzarella cheese

❯ Place the porcini mushrooms in a small bowl; cover with ½ cup hot water. Set aside for 15 minutes. In a large skillet set over medium high heat, melt the butter; add the mushrooms, salt and pepper. Cook, stirring, for 10 minutes or until the mushrooms are softened, have started to turn golden and any excess liquid has evaporated. Transfer the mushrooms to a bowl. Drain the porcini mushrooms. Chop coarsely; stir into the sliced mushroom mixture along with the parsley.

❯ Combine the Emmenthaler and ½ cup of the Parmesan cheese in a separate bowl. Stir together the ricotta and egg in a third bowl.

❯ Bechamel Sauce: Melt the butter in a saucepan set over medium heat. Add the onion, garlic and thyme; cook, stirring, for 3 minutes. Whisk in the flour for 1 minute; mixture will be very thick. Whisk in the milk and stock, whisking to break up any clumps. Bring to a boil, whisking constantly. Reduce heat to medium-low and cook, stirring often, for about 10 minutes or until thick enough to coat the back of a wooden spoon. Whisk ¼ cup of the sauce into the ricotta mixture. Pour the remaining sauce over the Emmenthaler Parmesan mixture, whisking until the cheese is melted and the mixture is smooth.

❯ Preheat the oven to 350°F.

⟩ Spread ½ cup of the cheese sauce over the bottom of a 13" x 9" baking dish. Layer with three noodles, ½ cup of the ricotta mixture, ½ cup of the mozzarella and ½ cup of the cheese sauce. Repeat layering once. Cover with all of the mushroom mixture. Repeat layering two more times. Spread the remaining sauce over the top of the last layer of noodles. Sprinkle with the remaining ¼ cup of Parmesan cheese. Cover loosely with foil.

⟩ Bake in the center of the preheated oven for 30 minutes. Uncover and broil for about 3 minutes or just until the top is starting to turn golden brown. Let the lasagna rest for 10 minutes before cutting into servings.

Makes 8 servings.

The deeper
the roots,
the
stronger
the tree

ROOTS

ONE NATION. *Roots deeply planted,* **weathered against the odds.** *Commandments to oblige,* LETTER OF THE LAW, **LAW OF THE LAND.** Beliefs remain steadfast throughout turmoil, *scattered, thrown, dispersed amongst all man.* Pain and triumph, kaleidoscope of cultures, **INFLUENCE OF KINGS,** habits and customs of so many lands. *Markets full of produce,* wagons laden with spices, *exotic ingredients.* Cumin, curry, chili, and nutmeg. *Hot dogs,* **PIZZA,** kung pao beef, *pasta,* falafel and schwarma. *A legacy of tradition,* **AN UNBROKEN CHAIN,** undying strength. One Torah, shared by all.

homemade
BREADS

CHALLAH

the sweet taste of tradition

Water Challah

This recipe is our current family favorite. It couldn't be simpler and it comes out light and fluffy. If you prefer a sweeter challah, add ¼ cup additional sugar.

5½	**cups (approx) warm water**
1	**cup granulated sugar**
3	**Tbsp + 2 tsp active dry yeast**
5	**lb high-gluten (or white bread) flour**
1	**cup + 2 Tbsp oil**
4	**Tbsp Kosher salt**
1	**tsp oil**

Egg Wash:

1	**egg yolk**
1	**Tbsp water**

❯ Place half of the warm water, the sugar and yeast in the bowl of an electric mixer large and strong enough to handle 5 lb of flour and fitted with the dough hook. Let the yeast proof for 15 to 20 minutes or until frothy.

❯ With the machine running, alternate adding the wet and dry ingredients: the flour, oil, and remaining water. Add the salt as a dough begins to form and knead it on medium speed for 7 to 8 minutes or until smooth and sticky but not sticky enough that it clings to your finger when touched. Slowly add more water by tablespoons, if necessary, to achieve this consistency.

❯ Place about 1 tsp of oil in the center of a large bowl. Transfer the dough to the bowl and flip it to completely coat with the oil. Place the bowl in a large garbage bag and knot the bag loosely. Let the dough rise for 1 hour. Remove the dough from the bag; transfer it to a work surface.

❯ Preheat the oven to 350°F.

❯ Take challah, and discard the challah piece according to your custom. Form the remaining dough into desired shapes. Transfer to challah pans or parchment paper-lined baking sheets. Stir together the yolk and water for an egg wash; brush over the dough. Let the dough rise, uncovered, for another 45 minutes to 1 hour or until double in bulk.

❯ Place in the oven and immediately increase the heat to 375°F. Bake for 40 minutes for large challahs and about 25 minutes for smaller challahs.

Makes 5 large challahs.

COMMENTS

You can also make this a whole-wheat challah by substituting half of the flour with regular whole-wheat flour or with white-whole-wheat flour. Because whole-wheat flour is denser than regular flour and absorbs more liquid, you may need to add ¼ to ½ cup more water. Feel the dough and make sure that it's moist and not too dry. It should be a bit sticky.

For a lighter crust, use a whole egg mixed with ½ tsp of water.

Whole–Wheat Herb Pull-Aparts

Less than traditional, more than delicious challah rolls. These rolls are soft and tasty and the topping adds great flavor. This is a smaller recipe, but it doubles nicely.

Dough:

2 ¼	cups very warm water
2 ½	Tbsp active dry yeast
2	Tbsp granulated sugar
2	large eggs
½	cup oil
3	cups whole-wheat flour
2 ½	cups white bread flour
¼	cup granulated sugar
2 ½	tsp Kosher salt
1	tsp oil

Onion Filling (optional):

¼	cup extra virgin olive oil
1-2	large Vidalia onions, diced
2	Tbsp poppy seeds

Egg Wash:

1	egg yolk
1	Tbsp water

Herb and Seed Topping:

2	Tbsp each poppy seeds, sesame seeds, rolled oats and raw sunflower seeds
2	tsp dried thyme
2	tsp za'atar, optional
½	tsp dried rosemary, crushed, optional

❯ Combine the water, yeast and sugar in the bowl of an electric mixer fitted with the dough hook. Let the yeast proof for 15 to 20 minutes or until frothy.

❯ Add all of the remaining dough ingredients, except the 1 tsp of oil, leaving the salt for last. Knead for 5 minutes on medium-high speed.

❯ Place about 1 tsp of oil in the center of a large bowl. Transfer the dough to the bowl and flip it to completely coat with the oil. Place the bowl in a large garbage bag and knot the bag loosely. Let rise for 1 hour.

❯ Preheat the oven to 350°F. Lightly grease 2 round 10" pans.

❯ Meanwhile, make the filling, if using. Heat the olive oil in a large pan set over medium-heat; sauté the onions until they are transparent and just beginning to brown. Add the poppy seeds. Set aside to cool.

❯ Remove the dough from the bag; transfer the dough to a work surface. Cut the dough into 14 equal-sized pieces; roll each piece into a ball shape. If using the onion filling, insert the filling in the center of each roll and cover well with dough. Place 7 balls in each pan.

❯ Alternatively, you can create rolls by rolling out each piece into a rope between your palms and then tying into a single knot. Place each roll into a lightly oiled muffin cup.

❯ Stir together the yolk and water for an egg wash; brush over rolls.

❯ Topping: Combine the seeds and thyme, as well as za'atar and rosemary, if using, in a bowl. Sprinkle over the rolls.

❯ Bake in the center of the preheated oven for 25 to 30 minutes or until golden brown.

❯ Remove the pans to a rack to cool for 5 minutes. Remove the rolls from the pans and let cool completely on racks.

Makes 14 rolls.

Authentic Multigrain Challah

One of the tricks to achieving a chewy, evenly-baked multigrain challah is a good combination of different grains and seeds. I have tested many multigrain flours over the years, and some have been more successful than others. The ones I like the best have a combination of white and whole-wheat flours, cracked wheat, cracked rye and whole flax. Every country has its own options, and you may have to do a bit of experimenting, but it's worth it! You can also use a larger ratio of multigrain flour to white if you don't mind a denser texture. I love to think of all those healthy grains going into my children...and they don't seem to mind, either!

5½–6	cups (approx) warm water
1	cup granulated sugar
4	Tbsp active dry yeast
2½	lb high-gluten (or bread) flour
2½	lb multigrain flour
¼	cup raw sunflower seeds
2	Tbsp wheat bran
1	cup oil
2	large eggs
4	Tbsp Kosher salt

Egg wash:

1	egg yolk
1	Tbsp water

〉 Place 3 cups of the warm water, the sugar and yeast in the bowl of an electric mixer strong enough to handle 5 lbs of flour and fitted with the dough hook. Let the yeast proof for 15 to 20 minutes or until frothy.

〉 With the machine running, and alternating the wet and dry ingredients, add the flours, sunflower seeds, bran, oil, eggs and the remaining water. Add the salt as a dough begins to form and mix it at medium speed for 8 minutes. This will resemble thick oatmeal more than a conventional dough.

〉 Cover the bowl lightly with plastic wrap. Let rise for 1 hour in a warm, draft-free area.

〉 Take challah, and discard the challah piece according to your custom. Spoon the batter into 18 well-greased muffin tins or into 8 small challah pans. Stir together the egg and water for an egg wash; brush over the dough. Let dough rise for another 45 minutes to 1 hour or until it has slightly risen (this dough will not double).

〉 Meanwhile, preheat the oven to 375°F.

〉 Bake in the center of the preheated oven for 30 minutes or until golden brown.

Makes 18 challah rolls or 8 smaller challahs.

Sweet Raisin Challah

What better way to celebrate a happy, sweet new year! We make this challah in its round traditional shape for Rosh Hashanah but it can be a special treat any other time of year. And, by the way, when sliced, this makes awesome toast.

5½	cups (approx) warm water
1¼	cups granulated sugar
4	Tbsp active dry yeast
5½	lb high-gluten (or white bread) flour
1	cup oil
2	large eggs
2	large egg yolks
4	Tbsp Kosher salt
½	cup raisins (preferably golden)

Egg Wash:

1	egg yolk
1	Tbsp water
1	tsp vanilla sugar

Streusel Topping:

7	Tbsp trans fat free margarine
1	cup all-purpose flour
1	cup granulated sugar

❭ Place half of the water, the sugar and yeast in the bowl of an electric mixer strong enough to handle 5 lbs of flour fitted with the dough hook. Let the yeast proof for 15 to 20 minutes or until frothy.

❭ With the machine running, and alternating the wet and dry ingredients, add the flour, oil, eggs, egg yolks and the remaining 2½ cups of water. Add the salt as a dough begins to form and knead it on medium speed for 8 minutes. Slowly add up to ½ cup more water by tablespoons, if necessary, to achieve a smooth and elastic dough.

❭ Add the raisins and knead on low speed for 1 minute, just until incorporated.

❭ Place about 1 tsp of oil in the center of a large bowl. Transfer the dough to the bowl and flip it to completely coat with the oil. Place the bowl in a large garbage bag and knot the bag loosely. Let the dough rise for 1 hour. Remove the dough from the bag; transfer the dough to a work surface.

❭ Take challah, and discard the challah piece according to your custom. Form the remaining dough into desired shapes. Transfer to challah pans or parchment paper-lined baking sheets.

❭ Stir together the egg and water for an egg wash; brush over the dough. Let the dough rise, uncovered, for another 45 minutes to 1 hour or until doubled in bulk.

❭ Meanwhile, preheat the oven to 375°F.

❭ Mix together the streusel ingredients with your fingers until a crumbly consistency forms. Sprinkle on top of the challah.

❭ Bake in the center of the preheated oven, 40 minutes for large challahs and about 25 minutes for smaller challahs.

Makes 5 large challahs.

Gluten-Free Oat Challah

In a regular bread recipe, the gluten acts as a binder and provides the elasticity that you want in a good-quality bread dough. Since there is no gluten in oat flour, something else is required to bind the ingredients together, which is why xanthan gum and starch are added. I've also added tapioca and potato starch to replace some of the oat flour in order to lighten the recipe. Tested and loved by many!

½	cup warm water
2	Tbsp active dry yeast
¾	cup +1 Tbsp granulated sugar
4–4½	cups certified gluten-free oat flour, whisked to remove lumps
1⅓	cups potato starch
⅔	cup tapioca flour (starch)
1	Tbsp xanthan gum
1	tsp Kosher salt
4	large eggs
1	cup seltzer
½	cup oil

Egg Wash:

1	egg
1	Tbsp warm water
	sesame seeds, poppy seeds, dehydrated onion, optional

> Preheat the oven to 350°F. Combine the water, yeast and 1 Tbsp of the sugar in a small bowl. Let the yeast proof for 5 minutes.

> Whisk together 4 cups of the oat flour, potato starch, tapioca flour, xanthan gum, remaining sugar and salt in a large mixing bowl. Make a small well in the center of the dry ingredients. Pour the eggs, seltzer, oil and yeast into the well. Mix just until the ingredients are combined and the dough is smooth.

> Let the dough rest for 2 minutes. If the dough is particularly sticky or loose, add the remaining half cup of oat flour and mix until the dough is smooth.

> Spoon the dough into a braided loaf pan or form small dough balls and place in a standard loaf pan to create the effect of braids. (You can also drop the balls into a muffin pan to make rolls.) Cover the loaf; let rise in a warm draft-free area for 1 hour.

> Stir together the egg and water for an egg wash; brush over the risen loaf. Sprinkle with the sesame or poppy seeds or dehydrated onion, if desired.

> Bake in the center of the preheated oven for 30 minutes, or 20 to 25 minutes for rolls, until the top is golden brown.

Makes 1 loaf or 18 muffin-sized rolls.

Use a braided challah pan to achieve this look.

Seeded Cracked Wheat Bread

I have been making this bread for a long time and am so thankful it makes two loaves as it never seems to last very long. It makes excellent toast and I relish the fact that it has so many healthful ingredients.

2	cups warm water
½	cup cracked wheat or bulgur
2	Tbsp active dry yeast (or 2 packages)
⅓	cup honey
¼	cup oil
½	cup sunflower seeds
⅓	cup shelled raw pumpkin seeds
¼	cup raw flax seeds
1	Tbsp each sesame and poppy seeds
1	Tbsp salt
½	cup spelt flour (or whole-wheat flour)
3¾	cups (approx) bread flour

Topping:

1	egg, lightly beaten
1	Tbsp sesame seeds

❯ Pour the warm water over the cracked wheat in a large bowl. Let stand for 15 minutes. Sprinkle the yeast over. Let stand for 15 minutes or until frothy.

❯ Using a wooden spoon, stir in the honey, oil, sunflower seeds, pumpkin seeds, flax and sesame and poppy seeds and salt. Stir in the spelt flour and 1½ cups of the bread flour. Gradually stir in the remaining bread flour, ½ cup at a time, until a soft, slightly sticky dough is formed.

❯ Transfer the dough to a lightly floured work surface. Sprinkling the surface with extra flour as needed to prevent the dough from sticking, knead the dough for 8 to 10 minutes or until soft and supple and elastic. Place in a greased bowl, turning to grease all over. Cover with plastic wrap and let rise in a warm, draft-free area for 1½ to 2 hours or until double in bulk.

❯ Punch down the dough. Divide in half; shape into rectangles and fit into two lightly greased 8½" – x 5½" loaf pans. Cover loosely with plastic wrap and let rise in a warm draft-free area for about 45 minutes or until double in size.

❯ Preheat the oven to 375°F.

❯ Brush the tops with the lightly beaten egg; sprinkle with the sesame seeds.

❯ Bake in the center of the preheated oven for 30 to 35 minutes or until the breads are golden brown and sound hollow when tapped.

Makes 2 loaves.

Soft New York–Style Pretzels

Just like you might find on the corner of any street in New York. Serve with American-style or honey mustard.

2	**Tbsp granulated sugar**
1	**cup warm water**
2½	**tsp active dry yeast**
2	**Tbsp oil**
½	**cup bread flour**
½	**tsp salt**
½	**tsp dried mustard**
2	**cups (approx) all-purpose flour**
3	**Tbsp baking soda**
1	**Tbsp pretzel salt**

❯ Stir 1 Tbsp of the sugar into 1 cup warm water in a large bowl. Sprinkle the yeast on top. Let stand for 10 minutes or until frothy.

❯ Stir the oil into the yeast mixture. Stir in the bread flour, salt and mustard. Stir in enough of the all-purpose flour until a soft dough forms. Transfer the dough on to a lightly floured work surface. Sprinkling the surface with extra flour as needed to prevent the dough from sticking, knead the dough for 8 to 10 minutes or until soft and no longer sticky. Cover with plastic and let rise for 30 minutes.

❯ Cut the dough into 12 pieces. Roll each into an 18" rope. Form a U shape with 1 rope, then twist the ends together twice. Fold the twisted portion backward along the center of the U shape to form a circle; gently press the ends of the rope onto the dough to seal. Transfer to a parchment paper-lined baking sheet. Repeat with the remaining ropes. Cover the twists and let rise for 30 minutes.

❯ Preheat the oven to 450°F.

❯ Bring a large pot of water to a boil; add the baking soda and the remaining Tbsp of sugar. Boil the pretzels in batches for 1 to 2 minutes per side or until puffed and slightly shiny. Transfer to wire racks, and drain well. Return the pretzels to the baking sheet; sprinkle with the pretzel salt.

❯ Bake in the center of the preheated oven for about 15 minutes or until golden brown and cooked through.

Makes 12 pretzels.

Russian Black Bread

Pumpernickel or rye breads tend to take a little longer to make than most conventional breads since they require a starter. Here, I've streamlined the process to avoid that step but the results are no less wonderful and satisfying. It's important to use fancy molasses and not the blackstrap variety as the latter imparts too strong a flavor.

1	Tbsp granulated sugar		1	Tbsp instant coffee granules
2½	cups warm water		3½	cups bread flour
2	Tbsp active dry yeast		2	cups pumpernickel or rye flour
	(or 2 packages)		1	Tbsp salt
⅓	cup fancy molasses		2	cups all-bran cereal (not flakes)
¼	cup cider vinegar		2	Tbsp crushed caraway seeds
¼	cup oil		1	Tbsp onion powder
1	oz unsweetened chocolate		1	tsp crushed fennel seeds

Topping:

1 egg, lightly beaten
1 tsp caraway seeds

> Stir the sugar into 1 cup of the water in a bowl; sprinkle the yeast over it. Let stand for 10 minutes or until frothy.

> Meanwhile, in a small pot, combine the remaining 1½ cups of water, molasses, vinegar, oil, chocolate and coffee granules. Place over a low heat and heat just until the chocolate is softened and almost melted.

> Stir the warm coffee-chocolate mixture into the yeast mixture along with 1 cup of the bread flour, the pumpernickel flour, salt, all bran, caraway seeds, onion powder and fennel seeds. Stir until well mixed and no streaks remain. Let stand for 5 minutes at room temperature.

> Gradually add the remaining bread flour, ½ cup at a time, until a soft, slightly sticky dough is formed.

> Transfer the dough to a lightly floured work surface. Sprinkling the surface with extra flour as needed to prevent the dough from sticking, knead the dough for 8 to 10 minutes or until soft and supple and elastic. Place in a greased bowl, turning to grease all over. Cover with plastic wrap and let rise in warm, draft free area for about 1 hour or until doubled in bulk.

> Punch down the dough. Divide it in half and shape into rectangles and fit into two lightly greased 8½"–5½" loaf pans. Alternately, shape into 1 large ball and place in a greased 8½" or 9" sprinGForm pan. Cover loosely with plastic wrap and let rise in a warm, draft-free area for about 45 minutes or until double in size.

> Preheat the oven to 350°F.

> Brush the tops with the lightly beaten egg; sprinkle with the caraway seeds.

> Bake in the center of the preheated oven for 45 to 50 minutes or until the breads are golden brown and sound hollow when tapped.

Makes 2 rectangular loaves or 1 large round loaf.

Olive and Sun-Dried Tomato Focaccia

Make sure you use the sun-dried tomatoes that are packed in oil. Their extra moisture works well with the focaccia.

2	tsp granulated sugar
1	cup warm water
1	pkg (2½ tsp) active dry yeast
2	Tbsp olive oil
2	Tbsp honey
2	Tbsp cornmeal
½	tsp salt
2½	cups (approx) bread flour
¾	cup sun-dried tomatoes packed in oil, patted dry, julienned
¼	cup halved olives
1½	tsp dried basil

Topping:

2	Tbsp extra virgin olive oil
1	tsp coarse or Kosher salt

⟩ Stir together the sugar and the water in a bowl; sprinkle the yeast over it. Let stand for 10 minutes or until frothy. Stir in the olive oil, honey, cornmeal, salt and enough of the flour to make a soft, slightly sticky dough.

⟩ Transfer the dough to a lightly floured work surface. Sprinkling the surface with extra flour as needed to prevent the dough from sticking, knead the dough for about 10 minutes or until it is soft and elastic.

⟩ Place the dough in a lightly greased bowl. Cover with plastic wrap and let rise in a warm, draft-free area for about 45 minutes or until double in bulk.

⟩ Preheat the oven to 375°F.

⟩ Punch down the dough. Knead the sun-dried tomatoes, olives and basil into the dough. Let rest for 5 minutes. Transfer the dough to a work surface. Roll the dough into a 15" rectangle. Transfer the dough to an ungreased baking sheet. Cover with plastic wrap and let rise again for 15 minutes.

⟩ Press your finger tips into the dough across the surface to create a dimpled effect. Drizzle the oil over top and sprinkle with the coarse salt.

⟩ Bake in the center of the preheated oven for 20 minutes or until golden and hollow-sounding when tapped on the bottom.

Makes 1 large foccaccia.

Garlic Pull-Aparts

These garlic scented rolls are light as a feather and a perfect accompaniment to any main course, be it chicken, pasta or beef. Try not to place them too far apart on the baking sheet or you will lose the pull-apart effect.

1⅓	cups warm water
2	Tbsp granulated sugar
2	tsp active dry yeast
¼	cup oil
3½	cups (approx) all-purpose flour
2	tsp dry mustard
1½	tsp salt

Topping:

¼	cup olive oil
6	cloves garlic, minced
2	Tbsp mayonnaise

❯ Place the water in a large bowl. Sprinkle the sugar over it. Sprinkle the yeast over the water. Let stand for 10 minutes or until frothy.

❯ Stir the oil into the yeast mixture. Stir in 2 cups of the flour, mustard and salt. Stir in enough of the remaining flour to make a soft dough. Transfer the dough to a lightly floured work surface. Sprinkling the work surface with enough flour to prevent sticking, knead the dough for 10 minutes or until smooth and elastic.

❯ Place the dough in a lightly greased bowl. Cover the bowl with plastic wrap. Let rise in a warm, draft-free area for about 45 minutes or until dough is double in bulk.

❯ Meanwhile, make the topping. Heat the oil in a small skillet set over low heat. Add the garlic; cook, stirring, for 3 minutes or until the garlic is softened and the mixture is very fragrant. Remove from the heat. Whisk in the mayonnaise. Set aside to cool.

❯ Preheat the oven to 375°F.

❯ Punch down the dough. Transfer the dough to a work surface. Divide the dough into 12 equal-sized pieces; shape each piece into a 6"-long, thick breadstick. Place on a parchment-lined baking sheet, spacing ½" apart. You should have two rows. Cover loosely with plastic wrap. Let rise in a warm, draft-free area for 45 minutes. Brush the tops and sides of the breadsticks with the garlic mixture.

❯ Bake in the center of the preheated oven for 20 to 25 minute or until puffed and golden. Serve warm.

Makes 12 breadsticks.

Authentic Bagels

These are light and chewy and simply delicious!

⅓	cup warm water
1½	Tbsp granulated sugar
1	Tbsp instant dry yeast
1	tsp potato starch
4	cups all-purpose flour
1	generous Tbsp Kosher salt
¼	cup oil, plus a bit more for coating
1	large egg
¾	cup warm water

For boiling the bagels:

10	cups water
1	Tbsp granulated sugar
2	tsp Kosher salt

Topping:

Sesame seeds
Poppy seeds
Kosher salt

> Place the ⅓ cup warm water, sugar, yeast and potato starch into the bowl of an electric mixer fitted with the dough hook. Let the yeast proof for 5 minutes. Add the flour, salt, oil, egg, and ¾ cup warm water and knead for 6 to 8 minutes, adding a few more teaspoons of water, if necessary, to bring the dough together.

> Place about 1 tsp of oil in the center of a large bowl. Transfer the dough to the bowl and flip it to completely coat with oil. Cover and let rise in a warm, draft-free area for 45 minutes.

> Punch down the dough. Transfer the dough to a work surface; cut into 12 pieces. Form each piece into a smooth ball. Poke a finger through the center and twirl the ball of dough around your fingers to enlarge the hole.

> Preheat the oven to 425°F.

> Boiling the bagels: Fill a large pot with about 10 cups of water; bring to a boil. Add the sugar and salt. In batches of 3 or 4, drop the bagels into the boiling water—they will expand once they hit the water. Cook on each side for 1½ minutes. Remove from the pot with a slotted spoon, shake off excess water, and place on a greased baking sheet. Sprinkle with the sesame seeds, poppy seeds, or Kosher salt.

> Bake in the center of the preheated oven for 20 to 25 minutes or until golden.

Makes 12 bagels.

Honey Quinoa Rolls

I love making these on Sunday morning so the kids can enjoy them fresh and steaming from the oven. Because quinoa is a protein, I'm happy even if my children eat one of these rolls for dinner with some cucumber sticks and hummus. The kids are thrilled to have "challah" as their meal, so it's a win-win situation for everyone!

1	cup quinoa, rinsed well
¼	cup quick-cooking oats
2¼	cups water
¼	cup milk or soy milk
¾	cup hot (not boiling) water
2	Tbsp granulated sugar
2½	tsp active dry yeast
⅓	cup honey
⅓	cup oil
3	cups white bread flour
1	cup whole-wheat flour
2¼	tsp salt
1	egg yolk, beaten
	Additional quinoa or sesame seeds, for sprinkling on loaf

❯ Combine the quinoa, oats, 2¼ cups water and milk in a small saucepan, and bring to a boil. Reduce the heat and simmer for 15 minutes or until all of the liquid is absorbed. Let cool.

❯ Place the ¾ cup hot water in a large bowl or the bowl of an electric mixer fitted with the dough hook. Sprinkle the sugar and yeast over the water and let stand for 5 minutes or until frothy.

❯ Stir the honey and oil into the yeast mixture, then add 1 cup of the bread flour, salt and the cooked quinoa mixture. Mix by hand or with the mixer on low speed until combined.

❯ Add the remaining bread flour and the whole-wheat flour, kneading for about 10 minutes until the dough is smooth and elastic, removing to a work surface if kneading by hand. The dough should feel slightly sticky, but if it is too wet, add ¼ to ½ cup additional flour, as necessary.

❯ Place about 1 tsp of oil in the center of a large bowl. Transfer the dough to the bowl and flip it to completely coat with the oil. Cover loosely with plastic wrap. Let the dough rise in a warm draft-free area for about 2 hours or until doubled in bulk.

❯ Punch down the dough. Transfer the dough to a work surface. Divide the dough into 18 to 20 small, equal-sized pieces. Shape into balls and place in rows on a parchment paper-lined baking sheet. Alternatively, you can place the balls in sprayed muffin tins. Brush the tops with the beaten egg yolk and sprinkle with the raw quinoa or sesame seeds. Let the rolls rise again, uncovered, for 1 to 1½ hours or until almost double in bulk.

❯ Preheat the oven to 375°F.

❯ Bake rolls in the center of the preheated oven for 25 minutes or until golden brown. Remove from the oven and let cool slightly.

Makes 18 to 20 dinner-sized rolls.

Served with love

NURTURE

Perfect little face, TINY SOFT TOES, the strong bond of love. **Brown paper bags lined up on the counter, steaming bowls of oatmeal to start the day right.** *A sigh of satisfaction,* the look in his eyes, dimples. **Chocolate chip cookies,** hot tea with honey, *fluffy, airy babka.* Comfort food, Mom's chicken soup, **DINNER IS AT FIVE.** *Feeding body and soul.* Come sit down, I made your favorite.

SOUP
served hot

Hearty French Onion Soup

I always wanted to know how to make a good onion soup. It has a sophisticated and elusive feeling about it. Maybe it's the word "French" in the title? ☺ But it's rusticness and wholesomeness somehow make it accessible at the same time. Well, I finally decided one very cold winter day that I was just going to tackle it. I knew I had to caramelize the onions properly, as that is what turns a watery, tasteless onion soup into a rich and flavorful meal. It takes some patience, I do admit, but the smell that accompanies it makes the waiting a pleasant experience as well.

1	Tbsp oil
3	Tbsp butter
3	large Vidalia onions, sliced
3	large Spanish onions, sliced
1	tsp granulated sugar
1	tsp dried thyme
1	tsp Kosher salt
3	Tbsp blending flour
½	cup dry white wine
6	cups vegetable stock
	(or use 1-2 Tbsp onion soup mix, msg free, mixed with water)
2	Tbsp soy sauce
	Kosher salt and freshly ground black pepper, to taste
8	buttered slices of French bagette or large croutons, optional
¼	cup grated mozzarella or Swiss cheese

> Melt the butter and oil together in the bottom of a 4 to 5-quart saucepan or Dutch oven set over medium-low heat. Add the onions, tossing until well coated in the oil. Reduce the heat to low. Cook, covered, for 15 minutes.

> Increase the heat to medium-low. Stir in the sugar, thyme and salt. Cook the onions, stirring frequently, for 30 to 40 minutes until they have turned an even, deep golden brown.

> Stir in the flour until it dissolves. Add the remaining ingredients and cook, covered, for 30 minutes. Season to taste with salt and pepper.

> You can serve the soup like this, or top it with large croutons.

> Preheat the oven to 350°F. Spoon the soup into individual crocks or oven-proof bowls. Place 8 French baguette slices on top of each bowl of soup and cheese on top of the bread. If not using bread, place the cheese directly on top of the soup. Bake until the cheese start to brown.

Makes 8 servings.

COMMENTS

Blending flour has been milled using a special process that provides a granular flour that blends smoothly and easily into wet or dry ingredients. It is my favorite way to thicken sauces, but cornstarch can also be used.

Pumpkin Soup with Parsley–Sunflower Pesto

Every year we go apple picking and schlepp home more apples than we know what to do with. We also always buy a small pumpkin for soup. This is what we made with last year's pumpkin. It was so good that the kids have already threatened to bring home 2 pumpkins next year. Pumpkins may be daunting because of their size, but are really simple to work with if you follow this technique.

1	Tbsp oil (or more)
1	large pumpkin (about 3 lbs)
1	Spanish onion, chopped
1	sweet potato, peeled and cubed
½	tsp ground ginger
½	tsp dried thyme
6	cups chicken or vegetable stock
	(or 1 Tbsp chicken soup mix, msg-free, mixed with water)
	Kosher salt and freshly ground black pepper, to taste

Pesto:

2	cups fresh flat-leaf parsley
¼	cup toasted sunflower seeds
1	very small clove garlic (or half of a big one)
	Kosher salt and freshly ground black pepper
3	Tbsp extra virgin olive oil
	Roasted sunflower seeds, extra-salted, for garnishing

❯ Preheat the oven to 400°F.

❯ Cut the pumpkin in half and scrape out the seeds with a large spoon. Rub the inside of the pumpkin with the oil and place face-down on a cookie sheet. Bake for 35 minutes. The pumpkin will have softened considerably. Scrape out the flesh and transfer to a large saucepan. (If it's too hard to scrape the filling out, return the pumpkin to the oven and bake longer.)

❯ Add all of the remaining ingredients to the saucepan. Pour in just enough stock to cover the vegetables.

❯ Bring to a boil. Reduce the heat and cook over medium heat for 45 to 60 minutes or until the sweet potato is tender. Use an immersion blender or ladle batches into the bowl of a food processor fitted with the metal "S" blade and purée. Season to taste with salt and pepper.

❯ Pesto: Separate the leaves and small stems of the parley from the main stem. Discard the main stem. Place the parsley, sunflower seeds and garlic into the bowl of a food processor fitted with the metal "S" blade.

❯ With the machine running, slowly pour the olive oil into the feed tub, combining the ingredients until the mixture is chopped and pasty. Season to taste with salt and pepper.

❯ Dollop the pesto on top of the soup and garnish with extra-salted roasted sunflower seeds.

Makes 6 to 8 servings.

Wholesome Chunky Vegetable Soup

I personally like chunky vegetable soup, but if you don't want to cube all the vegetables, then simply use a food processor fitted with the steel blade to chop them up.

2	onions, diced
2	sweet potatoes, peeled and cut into chunks
6	stalks celery, cut into chunks
6	large carrots, peeled and cut into chunks
1	red, yellow or green pepper, seeded and cut into chunks
2	parsnips, peeled and cut into chunks
12	cups chicken or vegetable broth
1½	cups dried red lentils, rinsed and drained
1	cup pearl barley, rinsed and drained
¼	cup minced fresh dill (or 3 cubes, frozen or 1 Tbsp dried dill)
1	can (19 oz) baked beans, drained
	Kosher salt and freshly ground black pepper to taste

❯ Place all of the vegetables in a 4-quart or larger slow cooker. Cook on high for 1 hour. Add the broth, plus more water if necessary, to cover the vegetables, along with the dill, red lentils and barley.

❯ Cover and cook on low for 8 to 10 hours or until the vegetables are tender. If desired, you can purée at this point. Add the baked beans about 20 minutes before serving. Season to taste with salt and pepper.

Makes 12 to 14 servings.

COMMENTS

This soup freezes well for up to 3 months. It will thicken as it sits, so be sure to thin with some water while reheating.

My Family's Favorite Soup

There is a version of this soup in my last book, "Cooking With Color." From all of the feedback I've received, I have to say it is one of the most popular recipes. The oats add substance and creaminess, making it filling and wholesome at the same time. This soup takes only minutes to put together which is why it's one of my favorites.

2	**Tbsp oil**
2	**large leeks,**
	white and light green parts only, sliced
5	**large carrots, peeled and cut into chunks**
1	**stalk celery, sliced, optional**
2	**cups frozen peas**
½	**cup quick-cooking oats**
	Kosher salt and freshly ground black pepper, to taste
1	**cup milk (low-fat is fine)**

❭ Heat the oil in a large pot set over medium-low heat. Add the leeks, carrots and celery, if using, and cook slowly for about 10 minutes or until very soft.

❭ Add enough water to cover the vegetables. Bring to a boil. Add the peas and cook for 20 minutes.

❭ Stir in the oats and cook for 5 minutes. Season to taste with salt and pepper. Use an immersion blender and purée. Stir in milk and reheat gently before serving.

Makes 6 to 8 servings.

Fennel and Sweet Pea Soup

Meat adds a hearty flavor to this soup. Add some barley and let it be a whole dinner in one! Personally, if there are peas in the recipe, I know I'll like it.

2	tsp oil
1	large onion, chopped
1	large or 2 small fennel bulbs, chopped
2	tsp finely chopped garlic
1	large piece flanken
5	cups chicken or beef stock
	(water will also do, but stock has more flavor)
1	cup chopped potato
4	cups frozen green peas, divided
2	tsp Kosher salt
1	tsp dried basil
½	tsp freshly ground black pepper
2	cups cooked barley, optional

❯ Heat the oil in a large pot set over medium-high heat. Add the onion, fennel and garlic; sauté for about 5 minutes or until soft. Add the flanken; cook for 8 to 10 minutes or until soft. If the onions start to burn, add ¼ cup of water. Stir in the stock and potato. Bring to a boil. Reduce the heat and simmer, covered, for 30 minutes. Add 3½ cups of the frozen peas, salt, basil and pepper; cook for 20 minutes. Remove the meat and set aside.

❯ Using an immersion blender, purée the soup. Add the remaining peas, meat and barley, if using. Heat thoroughly and serve.

Makes 8 to 10 servings.

Cream of Celery and Asparagus Soup with Savory Herb Croutons

This soup has a soft, mellow flavor that is complimented by the thyme and garlic in the croutons. It can be prepared ahead and frozen, but you may need to give it a few more spins with the immersion blender when reheating.

2	Tbsp extra virgin olive oil
3	leeks, white and light green parts only, thinly sliced
2	bunches (approximately 20 stalks) celery, cut into chunks
1	bunch (approximately 12 spears) white asparagus, peeled
1	small (about 3/4 lb) celery root, peeled and diced
5	cups chicken stock
	Kosher salt and freshly ground black pepper, to taste
½	cup quick-cooking oats
¾	tsp dried thyme

Croutons:

2	Tbsp oil
3	sprigs fresh thyme
3	cloves garlic, minced
1	loaf multigrain bread, unsliced, cut into 1" cubes

〉 Heat the oil in a large pot set over medium heat; add the leeks and cook, stirring occasionally, until softened. Add the celery, asparagus and celery root. Cook gently for about 10 minutes or just until softened.

〉 Add the stock and enough water to cover the vegetables. Season with salt and pepper. Bring to a boil. Lower the heat to medium-low; cook for 45 minutes or until the vegetables are very soft. Purée with an immersion blender. If you are making this ahead of time, freeze or refrigerate the soup at this point.

〉 Bring the soup to a boil and add the oats and thyme. Cook over medium heat for 10 minutes. Purée again with an immersion blender to break up any lumps. Adjust the seasoning and serve with croutons.

〉 Croutons: Heat the oil in a large skillet set over medium-high heat. Add the thyme and garlic and sauté for 3 minutes. Add the bread cubes and brown on all sides. Let cool and add to the soup right before serving.

Makes 8 to 10 servings.

Easy "Meatball" Soup

What a great dinner idea! Low in fat, super tasty and so simple to make. The turkey balls freeze well for advance preparation. If you prefer, the turkey can easily be interchanged with lean ground chicken.

Turkey Meatballs:

2	lb lean ground turkey
2	large eggs
1	Tbsp ketchup
¼	cup breadcrumbs (I prefer flavored)
2	Tbsp fresh flat-leaf parsley, finely chopped
1	small onion, grated
½	tsp Kosher salt, or to taste
¼	tsp freshly ground black pepper

Soup:

3	cups chicken broth
4	carrots, peeled and cut into chunks
4	stalks celery, cut into chunks
1	onion, quartered
½	tsp Kosher salt
	freshly ground black pepper
1	package (8 oz) rice noodles

> Preheat the oven to 400°F.

> Turkey Meatballs: Combine all of the ingredients for the meatballs in a bowl, mixing well. Form into walnut-sized balls and place on a parchment paper-lined cookie sheet.

> Bake in the center of the preheated oven for 15 minutes. Set aside.

> Soup: Fill a 4-quart or larger slow cooker half-way with water and add the broth. Add the carrots, celery, onion, baked turkey meatballs and salt. Season to taste with pepper.

> Cook on medium heat for about 6 hours or until the flavors are well melded. (If your slow cooker does not have a medium setting, cook on high for 2 to 3 hours and then decrease it to low to cook for another 3 to 4 hours.)

> About 10 minutes before serving, soak the rice noodles in a bowl of cold water for 2 minutes. Drain; add the noodles to the slow cooker. Serve in large bowls.

Makes 8 servings.

COMMENTS

Don't use a slow cooker that is smaller than 3-quarts.

Curried Cauliflower and Apricot Soup

While curry may not be an everyday ingredient, the combination of spices, the sweetness of the apricots and the creamy mellow flavor of the cauliflower is outstanding. A sophisticated flavor with unparalleled taste, I suggest you try it.

2	heads cauliflower, coarsely chopped (about 10 cups total)
1	Tbsp olive oil, plus more for coating
1	yellow onion, finely chopped
2	cloves garlic, minced
¼	cup dried apricots, chopped
4	cups vegetable stock
1	Tbsp white wine
2	tsp vinegar
2	tsp yellow curry powder
1	tsp ground cumin
½	cup whipping cream, milk or soy milk
	Kosher salt and freshly ground black pepper

Garnish:

¼	cup dried apricots, thinly sliced, or slivered almonds

> Preheat the oven to 425°F.

> Toss half of the cauliflower with some olive oil in a large bowl. Transfer to a roasting pan. Bake in the center of the preheated oven for 20 minutes.

> Heat the olive oil in a large pot set over medium-high heat. Add the onion and garlic; sauté for 5 minutes. Add the remaining cauliflower, apricots and stock to the pot. Bring to a boil. Reduce heat to medium; stir in the white wine vinegar and spices. Simmer, uncovered, for 25 minutes.

> Remove the cauliflower from the oven; add to the pot. Purée with an immersion blender until smooth.

> Stir the cream into the soup and continue to cook for 10 minutes. Season to taste with salt and pepper.

> To serve, garnish with thinly sliced dried apricots or slivered almonds.

Makes 6 to 8 servings.

Squash Pear Soup

Inspired by winter's first snowfall, when soup is in order and pears are still in season. This soup is listed below with versions for dairy and pareve. The pears add a mellow, sweet taste that compliments the squash really well. If you are freezing this soup, omit the cream or milk and add it after reheating, right before serving.

3	Tbsp butter or oil
2	onions, diced
1	butternut squash, peeled, seeded and cut into 1" pieces
4	pears, peeled and chopped into roughly 1" pieces
4	cups low-sodium vegetable or chicken stock, or enough to cover
1	tsp dried thyme
1	tsp granulated sugar
⅛	tsp each ground nutmeg and cinnamon
½	cup whipping cream, whole milk or coconut milk
	Kosher salt and freshly ground black pepper, to taste

Crispy Ginger Garnish:

1	piece fresh ginger
	oil

> Melt the butter in a 4-quart saucepan set over medium-high heat. Add the onions; cook for 5 minutes or until they begin to soften. Reduce the heat to medium. Add the squash and pears; cook for 10 minutes. Watch to make sure that the mixture doesn't burn. If it starts to dry out, add about ¼ cup of water.

> Pour in enough of the stock to just cover the vegetables and fruit. Add the thyme, sugar, nutmeg and cinnamon. Bring to a simmer. Cook for 15 to 18 minutes or until the squash is fork-tender. Using an immersion blender, purée. Stir in the cream and season to taste with salt and pepper.

> Crispy Ginger Garnish: Slice ginger in half and cut into long thin strips. Heat a frying pan with 1" of oil and add the ginger. Fry just until golden; remove with a slotted spoon. Place on paper towel to absorb excess oil.

Makes 8 to 10 servings.

Roasted Garlic and Potato Soup

This rich and perfumed soup is a cinch to make and can be prepared up to three days in advance. Don't be alarmed by the amount of garlic in it—roasting brings out all of its natural sweetness while gently reducing its bite. There is not a spot of thickener in it; rather the creaminess is entirely due to the potatoes and the richness of the garlic.

4	heads garlic
2	lb Yukon gold potatoes, peeled and chopped
3	Tbsp oil
1	tsp dried thyme
½	tsp Kosher salt
¼	tsp freshly ground black pepper
3	shallots, finely chopped
6	cups chicken or vegetable stock

> Preheat the oven to 400°F.

> Trim the ends off each garlic head. Place each on a piece of aluminum foil large enough to fully enclose the head of garlic. Drizzle 1 Tbsp of the oil over the garlic. Enclose each head with the foil. Place on one side of an aluminum foil-lined baking sheet.

> Combine the potatoes, 2 Tbsp of the oil, thyme, salt and pepper in a large bowl. Transfer to the baking sheet. Bake in the center of the preheated oven for about 45 minutes or until the potatoes and garlic are tender.

> Heat the remaining 1 Tbsp of oil in a saucepan set over medium heat. Add the shallots; cook, stirring, for 3 minutes. Add the potatoes to the saucepan. Squeeze the softened garlic heads out of their skins into the pot, mashing them into the potatoes. Pour in the stock. Bring to a boil. Reduce the heat and simmer, uncovered, for 5 minutes.

> In batches, purée the soup in the bowl of a food processor or blender. (The soup can be covered well and refrigerated for up to 2 days. Thin with ½ cup more stock if necessary.)

Makes 6 to 8 servings.

Mushroom Barley Soup

A hearty and wonderful classic that's beloved by all. Even those on a gluten-free diet can enjoy a bowl or two; this recipe includes great alternatives for the barley.

2	Tbsp olive oil
6	large cloves garlic
1	large onion, cut into big chunks
5	stalks celery, peeled and cut into large chunks
1	large bunch dill, fronds and stems
1½	lb portobello or cremini mushrooms, diced
12	cups water
1¼	cups barley (for gluten-free, use short-grain brown rice or wild rice)
2	large carrots, peeled and diced into ½" pieces
1	large parsnip, peeled and diced into ½" pieces
1	large turnip, peeled and diced into ½" pieces
6	bay leaves
1	tsp dried thyme
	Kosher salt and freshly ground black pepper

> Heat the oil in a wide, heavy pot set over medium-high heat.

> In the bowl of a food processor fitted with the metal "S" blade, finely chop the garlic. Add the onion, celery and dill until coarsely ground. Transfer the ground mixture to the pot and sauté for about 10 minutes or until translucent.

> Add the mushrooms; sauté for about 6 minutes or until most of the liquid evaporates.

> Add the remaining ingredients and bring to a boil. Lower the heat to medium-low and cook, covered, for 1½ hours. Remove the bay leaves. Season to taste with salt and pepper.

Makes 12 servings.

Creamy Carrot and Parsnip Soup

The parsnips in this soup give it an earthy flavor that is well balanced with the creaminess of the coconut milk. Even my pickiest eaters liked it.

1	**Tbsp oil**
2	**tsp chopped garlic**
2	**large leeks, white and light green parts only, finely sliced**
5	**large carrots, peeled and diced (about 1½–2 cups)**
2	**large parsnips, peeled and diced (about 1½ cups)**
5	**cups vegetable or chicken stock**
½	**tsp ground ginger**
	Kosher salt and freshly ground black pepper, to taste
1	**can (14 oz) coconut milk**
2	**cloves garlic, halved**
1	**large sprig fresh thyme**
	Toasted pumpkin seeds

❯ Heat the oil in a large pot set over medium-high heat. Add the garlic and leeks; sauté until soft. Add the carrots and parsnips; sauté for 7 to 10 minutes or until they begin to soften. Add the stock, ginger, salt and pepper. Bring to a boil. Lower the heat to medium; cook for about 20 minutes or until a fork inserted into a carrot can easily break it apart. Purée with an immersion blender.

❯ Meanwhile, in a small saucepan, bring the coconut milk, garlic and thyme to a high simmer. Lower the heat to medium. Cook, stirring occasionally, for 30 minutes.

❯ Breaking off some of the thyme leaves so that they remain in the milk, remove the thyme sprig and garlic. Pour ¾ of the coconut milk into the puréed soup and blend once again until smooth.

❯ When ready to serve, garnish the soup with a spoonful of the reserved coconut milk and some toasted pumpkin seeds.

Makes 8 to 10 servings.

Recipe card (top left):

2 stick ma...
(2c) 2 egg beaten
(4T) 1 t orange ju...
(4T) 3 T vanilla...
all dry ingredients add butter...
Bake 1/2 t - far apart on...
minum foil - cool Thoroughly...
more - 350° 8 - 11 min...
Snap crust is yummy too

egg yolks lightly. Add cond. milk, beat
again. Add lime juice + beat until
smooth. Pour into pie shell. Bake 350 - 5 min...

Recipe card (middle left):

margar...
chopped nut...
...chocolate bits...

Preheat oven to 400°. Rinse chicken and
pat dry. Squeeze juice of orange
quarters over chicken (inside + out). Place
onion + orange pieces over (inside) bird.

Sprinkle salt + pepper + rosemary. Place
chicken in roasting pan + pour water in
pan. Roast 20 min. Reduce heat to
350° and roast 1 hr. * (If using chick...
breasts cooking time is approx. 30 - 40 min. to...
...chicken juice is clear when you pierce
...glaze. Hea...

Family is forever

FAMILY

Shouts of laughter, **shared meals and memories,** no one cooks like Mom. Transcending time and countries and war, **REUNIONS,** still no food like Mom's. **Family dinners,** tastes of times past, *traditions closely treasured.* **BUBBY'S FAMOUS CHEESECAKE,** *Aunt Suzie's favorite salad dressing,* **matzah brie just the way you like it.** LOVED ONES PASSED ON, **emotions and memories evoked through their recipes and songs. THE TABLE WE SET,** *the foods we serve,* all a small part of our family history...*written every day.* **Traditions of love.** Eat, my child.

tossed
SALAD

Pink with Polka Dots Salad

The bright color of this salad makes it a nice addition to a plate or salad bar. It's best to dress it right before serving. The concept for this salad came from a reader-submitted recipe on Kosherscoop.com. I played around with it a bit and I think the combination of fruits and vegetables complements the dressing well. Here is it, all dressed up and ready to go.

1	Tbsp olive oil
1	leek, white and light green parts only, thinly sliced
1	lb sugar snap peas
2	mangoes, peeled and cut into thick, matchstick pieces
½	cup pomegranate seeds
½	cup roasted cashews

Dressing:

½	cup oil
5	Tbsp granulated sugar
2½	Tbsp honey
1	tsp salt
4	tsp balsamic vinegar, preferably white
¼	red onion, finely chopped
½	tsp ground ginger
1	Tbsp poppy seeds

❯ Dressing: Place all of the dressing ingredients, except for the poppy seeds, in the bowl of a food processor fitted with the metal "S" blade. Blend well. Add the poppy seeds and mix well. Set aside.

❯ Heat the olive oil in a large skillet set over medium heat. Add the leek and sauté for 1 minute. Add the sugar snap peas and toss, cooking just until the peas turn a bright green. Remove from the heat and let cool for 10 minutes. Transfer to a serving bowl.

❯ Add the mangoes and pomegranate seeds. Toss with half of the dressing. Add the cashews and serve at room temperature.

Makes 8 to 10 servings.

COMMENTS

The remaining dressing can be refrigerated for up to 2 weeks.

Avocado Panzanella Salad

Although avocados are relatively high in fat (remember, the creamier its flesh, the higher in fat it is), it is full of the good, healthy fats, namely, mono- and polyunsaturated. With that in mind, it's important to use avocados sparingly but still make them an important part of your heart-healthy diet. This recipe depends on day-old bread. If it's too fresh, the bread will turn gummy as it soaks up the deliciousness of the vinaigrette. Slightly stale bread can sop up the juice of the tomatoes and still retain its characteristic texture and shape. It's also terrific made with leftover challah.

6	cups day old French or Italian bread, cubed
4	large tomatoes, cut into ¾" pieces
1¾	cups seedless cucumber, cubed (about ¾ of an English cucumber)
½	cup red onion, sliced
1	avocado, peeled, pitted and cubed
⅓	cup fresh basil, chopped

Dressing:

2	Tbsp red wine vinegar
1	clove garlic, minced
1	tsp Dijon mustard
½	tsp Kosher salt
¼	tsp freshly ground black pepper
⅓	cup extra virgin olive oil

❯ Toss together the bread, tomatoes, cucumber, red onion and avocado in a bowl.

❯ Dressing: Whisk together the vinegar, garlic, mustard, salt and pepper in a separate bowl. Slowly, in a gradual stream, whisk in the olive oil until emulsified. Pour the dressing over the salad, tossing gently until evenly coated. Let stand at room temperature for 20 minutes. Toss again, add the fresh basil and serve.

Makes 6 to 8 servings.

Spinach, Mandarin and Almond Salad

This easy, colorful salad is a winner! Plus, baby spinach is a true convenience food: no need to trim those tough stems and its leaves are tender and tasty. This salad is so beautiful that we put it on the cover of a "Kosher Inspired" issue. Believe me, it tastes just as good as it looks.

1	lb fresh baby spinach leaves, washed and well dried
½	cup red onion, thinly sliced
1	red or yellow pepper, halved, seeded and thinly sliced
½	cup carrots, grated and peeled
½-¾	cup dried cranberries
¾ 1	cup canned mandarin oranges, drained and patted dry
	Kosher salt and freshly ground black pepper, to taste
¾	cup slivered almonds or pine nuts, toasted

Honey Mustard Dressing:

¼	cup extra virgin olive oil
¼	cup honey
¼	cup white or rice vinegar
¼	cup orange juice
2	Tbsp Dijon mustard
	freshly ground black pepper

❯ Combine the spinach with the onion, pepper, carrots and cranberries in a large bowl.

❯ Dressing: Combine all of the dressing ingredients in a jar and seal tightly; shake well. Or, place the ingredients in a mini food processor and blend until smooth. Chill before serving. Dressing can be stored in a jar in the refrigerator for 3 to 4 weeks.

❯ Pour the dressing over the spinach mixture along with mandarins; toss gently to combine well. Season to taste with salt and pepper. Transfer to a large platter or serving bowl and sprinkle with the almonds or pine nuts. Serve immediately.

Makes 6 to 8 servings.

COMMENTS

Variations: Add ½ cup bean sprouts with the mandarins. Or, instead of adding canned mandarins, substitute 2 large, seedless oranges, peeled, halved and thinly sliced. Be sure to trim away any of the bitter white pith.

CHEESE PLEASE

Sweet and Salty Salad

The flavors in this salad work so well together. I was at the cottage when the inspiration for a salad made with sweet potatoes hit and I needed some type of seasoning or spice to give the salad a final kick. I looked through my spices for cayenne pepper or red pepper flakes, but the closest I could find was Montreal steak spice. I sprinkled it on, figuring that at least there would be something for the photo I was taking of the salad. When the picture was done, my family happily elected to be the taste testers. They all loved the Montreal steak spice in the salad and convinced me that I would be doing my readers a great injustice if I changed it.

4	**sweet potatoes**
¼	**cup maple syrup**
1	**bag (10 oz) spinach leaves**
½	**cup crumbled feta cheese**
¼	**cup pecans or walnuts, toasted**
2	**Tbsp fresh flat-leaf parsley, chopped**
⅓	**tsp Montreal steak spice or red pepper flakes**
1	**Tbsp olive oil**

❯ Preheat the oven to 350°F.

❯ Slice the sweet potatos into rounds, about ¼"-thick. Arrange in a single layer on a parchment paper-lined baking sheet. Brush with the maple syrup. Bake in the center of the preheated oven for 20 to 25 minutes or until the potatoes are soft but not dry. Remove from the oven and cool.

❯ Assembly: Place the spinach in a large bowl. Top with the sweet potatoes, feta cheese, nuts and parsley. Sprinkle with the steak spice and gently toss with the olive oil. Serve immediately.

Makes 6 to 8 servings.

Pan-Roasted Pear and Goat Cheese Salad

This salad combines two ingredients I love to use: pears are my go-to winter fruit, with their sweet, mellow flavor and softer texture and goat cheese is a personal favorite.

2	Tbsp light olive oil
3	Tbsp + 1 tsp balsamic vinegar
1	small shallot, minced
½	tsp granulated sugar
4	Bartlett or d'Anjou pears, quartered and cored
¼	tsp Kosher salt
⅛	tsp freshly ground black pepper
1	head romaine lettuce, torn into 1" pieces
1	cup watercress leaves
½	cup goat cheese
½	cup honey-glazed pecans, chopped

❭ Whisk together 4 tsp each of the oil and the vinegar, along with the shallot and sugar in a large bowl. Set aside.

❭ Toss the pears with the salt and pepper in a separate bowl.

❭ Heat 2 tsp of the oil in a large skillet set over medium-high heat. Place the pears in the pan in a single layer, cut-side down, and cook for about 5 minutes or until golden brown. Flip the pears over; cook for 5 minutes, until golden brown.

❭ Leaving the pan on the burner, turn off the heat. Add the remaining vinegar, swirling it in the pan until the vinegar becomes syrupy and coats the pears. Set the pears aside to cool.

❭ Add the lettuce, watercress and pears to the bowl with the dressing, tossing gently until well combined

❭ Sprinkle with the goat cheese and pecans right before serving.

Makes 6 to 8 servings.

Summer Salad

This is a really easy salad to throw together. Actually, that's how this recipe came to be. It was an impromptu gathering of pantry and fridge staples. A very successful meeting, I'd say.

2	blood oranges
1	head romaine lettuce, cut into bite-sized pieces
4-5	leaves radicchio, cut into bite-sized pieces
2	scallions, thinly sliced
4	oz goat cheese, sliced
½	cup granola cereal (I used pecan cranberry flavor)

Dressing:

1	Tbsp orange juice
1	tsp toasted sesame oil

❯ Using a sharp knife, cut away the peel from the oranges, including the pith. Holding each orange over a bowl to catch any juices, remove the orange segments by cutting on either side of the segment, close to the membrane. Set aside.

❯ Combine the romaine, radicchio and scallions in a bowl. Top with the orange segments and the goat cheese. Sprinkle with the granola.

❯ Dressing: Whisk together the sesame oil and orange juice in a small bowl; pour over the salad right before serving.

Makes 4 servings.

Winter Salad

This salad uses ingredients easy to find during the winter season and all year round! The sweetness of the grapes perfectly balances the saltiness of the cheese and the earthiness of the nuts. Simple and accessible, this salad is one of my favorites.

10	oz chopped romaine lettuce
2	Granny Smith apples, peeled, cored, cut into matchstick-size strips
1	cup red seedless grapes, halved
½	cup chopped walnuts, toasted
½	cup crumbled feta cheese, optional

Dressing:

⅓	cup oil
¼	cup mayonnaise
¼	cup maple syrup
3	Tbsp white wine vinegar
2	tsp granulated sugar

> Toss together the lettuce, apples and grapes in a large bowl.

> Dressing: Whisk together all of the dressing ingredients. Use a hand blender if you prefer a smooth finish. Shake vigorously before using.

> Pour about ½ of the dressing onto the salad, gently tossing to coat well. Top with the walnuts and feta cheese, if using.

Makes 6 servings.

COMMENTS

This dressing makes more than is required for this particular salad dressing. It's wonderful to have on hand and can keep in the refrigerator for up to 2 weeks.

Crunchy Snow Pea Salad

This is the type of salad that every cook wants to make: it's simple, yet beautiful and delicious. The citrus flavors are complemented wonderfully by the crisp snow peas and the savory fennel. If you prefer, add 1 cup of torn baby romaine lettuce for a leafy, green version.

3	oranges
1	fennel bulb
1½	lb snow peas (about 5 cups)
2	Tbsp sesame seeds, black if desired
	toasted and crushed hazelnuts, optional

Dressing:

5	Tbsp oil
¼	cup freshly squeezed lemon juice
¼	cup orange juice
2	tsp Dijon mustard
1½	tsp minced garlic
1	tsp toasted sesame oil
1	tsp honey
	Kosher salt and freshly ground black pepper
1	tsp lemon zest

> Using a sharp knife, cut away the peel from the oranges, including the pith. Holding each orange over a bowl to catch any juices, remove the orange segments by cutting on either side of each segment, close to the membrane. Set aside.

> Cut the fennel bulb in half and shave each half into thin pieces using a vegetable peeler.

> Dressing: Combine all of the ingredients for the dressing in a bowl, mixing well until combined.

> Mix the orange segments, snow peas and dressing in a bowl and toss. Add the shaved fennel and sesame seeds and top with hazelnuts, if using.

Makes 6 servings.

COMMENTS

Once you have cut out all the flesh, you can squeeze the orange membranes between your fingers to make the orange juice for the dressing.

Inspired Coleslaw

There is no meal that is not enhanced by coleslaw. While almost every takeout food store sells its own, we like the homemade brand best. There is no real set recipe. I add all kinds of delicious ingredients to dress up this family staple. I like to use the pastrami listed below but get creative and come up with your own customized version.

1	bag (10 oz) coleslaw mix
1	carrot, peeled and finely grated
¼	cup mayonnaise
2	Tbsp vinegar
2	Tbsp freshly squeezed lemon juice
2	tsp finely chopped fresh dill (or 3 frozen cubes)
1	tsp Kosher salt
	zest of 1 lemon
¼	lb sliced pastrami

Optional Add-Ins:

sesame seeds
sliced or slivered almonds, toasted
sunflower seeds
hazelnuts, chopped
apple or pear, thinly sliced
raisins
canned pineapple chunks
fresh parsley or basil, chopped
scallions or chives, chopped
ramen noodles

❯ Place the coleslaw mix in a large bowl; run a sharp knife through it to cut the cabbage into smaller pieces.

❯ Stir in the carrot. Add all of the remaining ingredients and toss well until combined. Let sit for 30 minutes before serving.

❯ Just before serving, pile the pastrami decoratively on top of the salad.

Makes 4 servings.

COMMENTS

There are all sorts of ways to change up coleslaw and add variety. Toasted salted sunflower seeds is our favorite way of adding some crunch. You can also try toasted almonds or hazelnuts, 1 Granny Smith apple cut into matchstick pieces and soaked in lemon juice for 4 to 5 minutes. Chopped scallions add color and flavor. Try adding small pieces of pastrami for a great accompaniment to chicken.

Go with the grain

Roasted Citrus Quinoa Salad

Quinoa is always a healthy and easy side dish. The orange juice in this recipe gives this version a tasty twist. It goes especially well with fish and poultry dishes.

2	**cups raw quinoa, rinsed and drained**
2⅓	**cups water**
1	**cup orange juice**
1½	**Tbsp olive oil**
2	**tsp honey**
1	**tsp Kosher salt**
	pinch freshly ground black pepper, to taste
2	**oranges, peeled and cut into segments**
1	**cup toasted, slivered almonds, pecans, or pine nuts, optional**
¼	**cup fresh flat-leaf parsley, chopped or 2 scallions, finely chopped**

❯ Preheat the oven to 375°F.

❯ Gently mix together the quinoa, water, orange juice, oil, honey, salt and pepper in a 13" x 9" baking pan. Bake, uncovered, in the center of the preheated oven for 30 minutes, stirring once. Cool to room temperature. Add the orange segments, nuts, if using, and the parsley before serving.

Makes 8 to 10 servings.

COMMENTS

To make preparation easier, bake the quinoa ahead. Add remaining ingredients right before serving.

Quinoa Pilaf *Makes 4 servings.*

I wasn't going to include the recipe for my quinoa pilaf in this book, but everybody started requesting it and I kept coming across it at Bar and Bat Mitzvahs–a testament to its popularity and versatility.

Simply sauté a small, chopped Vidalia onion in a bit of olive oil until the onion is translucent. Stir in 1 Tbsp of light brown sugar and then cook them together for about 5 more minutes or until the onion is soft and light brown in color. Transfer the onion mixture to a serving bowl along with 2 cups of cooked quinoa, 2 Tbsp of toasted sunflower seeds and 2 Tbsp of dried cranberries. Drizzle with a little olive oil for a lovely and popular pilaf.

Asian Pasta Salad with Vegetables

When making this for Shabbat or in advance for any occasion, prepare the pasta and vegetables separately and combine before serving. It's best served lukewarm or at room temperature.

1	**lb spaghettini**
1	**bag (1.5 lb) frozen broccoli florets**
½	**cup frozen shelled edamame, defrosted**
3	**scallions, sliced**
2	**stalks celery, thinly sliced**
3	**carrots, peeled and julienned**
1	**can (15 oz) baby corn, cut into bite-sized pieces**
⅓	**cup toasted sesame seeds**

Dressing:

1½	**tsp garlic, minced**
1½	**tsp fresh ginger, minced**
⅓	**cup soy sauce**
2	**Tbsp honey**
2	**Tbsp toasted sesame oil**

> Bring a large pot of salted water to a boil. Cook the pasta for 8 to 10 minutes or until *al dente*. Drain well. Rinse under cold, running water to stop the cooking process.

> Dressing: Place the garlic and ginger in a bowl. Stir in the soy sauce, honey and sesame oil, mixing well.

> Pour the dressing over the pasta, tossing to coat the pasta evenly. Transfer the noodles to a Ziploc™ bag; marinate in the refrigerator for a minimum of 3 hours.

> Bring a large pot of salted water to a boil. Add the frozen broccoli florets and edamame and blanch for 4 to 5 minutes or until the water turns dark green. Strain and transfer to a large serving bowl. Add the remaining ingredients to the bowl. Stir in the pasta, tossing well. Serve at room temperature.

Makes 6 to 8 servings.

Although the salad ingredients make enough for six people, the rice actually yields enough for 12 people, especially if you are plating the salad. If you are serving it in a bowl, as opposed to molding it, then it's a good amount for a rice salad.

You can also layer in stemmed bowls for a nice effect.

The rice and dressing can be made up to 24 hours in advance and stored, covered, at room temperature.

Sushi Salad

I have to admit that sushi salad has not been a part of my recipe repertoire at all. I wasn't sure my family would like it, and I imagined it to be more work than it was worth. Then two things happened that made me reconsider. First, two readers of Kosherscoop.com requested a recipe. Second, I went to my son's school tea and tasted a really delicious version made by my friend Dassi. After that, I decided to make it for Yom Tov and it was unanimously approved by all eleven people around the table. This recipe is inspired by a sushi roll I particularly like, and I chose to plate it individually for a beautiful appetizer. The lemons are the secret to the wonderful flavor.

Sushi Rice:
3½	cups short-grain sushi rice
4	cups water

Sushi Vinegar:
5	Tbsp rice vinegar
2	Tbsp granulated sugar
	pinch salt

Dressing:
¼	cup soy sauce
¼	cup rice vinegar
¼	cup toasted sesame oil

Salad:
1½	cups surimi
½	lemon, very thinly sliced (leave peel on)
1	Bosc or Bartlett pear, cored and thinly sliced
1	cup edamame beans, blanched
	sweet potato chips for garnish
1	avocado, halved and thinly sliced
1	mango, diced, for garnish
1	baby English cucumber, diced
2	Tbsp (approx) black sesame seeds, for sprinkling

❯ Rinse the rice in cold water at least 3 times to remove the excess starch. Bring the water and rice to a boil in a large saucepan. Cook, uncovered, for 2 minutes. Reduce the heat and simmer, covered, for 10 to 15 minutes or until the water has been absorbed. Remove the saucepan from the heat; let stand for 5 minutes.

❯ Meanwhile, make the sushi vinegar. Combine the vinegar, sugar and salt in a bowl. Mix thoroughly and briskly until the sugar and salt have dissolved.

❯ Fold the sushi vinegar into the cooked rice with a rubber spatula. Cover with a clean dish towel and allow it to stand for another 5 minutes.

❯ Place the surimi in a bowl. Cut the lemon slices into quarters; stir into the surimi until it is well coated. You can squeeze a bit of lemon juice (about 1 tsp) from the other half of the lemon into the bowl as well.

❯ Make the dressing: Whisk together the soy sauce, vinegar and sesame oil in a small bowl. Set aside.

❯ Line a 2" springform pan or a large ramekin with plastic wrap. Press enough of the rice into it to fill to desired height (the exact amount will depend on what container you use). Turn it over onto your serving plate. Repeat several times until all of the rice is used or until you have enough for the number of people you are serving.

❯ Top the sushi rice with the the surimi and pears. Sprinkle the edamame beans over the fish. Drizzle the dressing over and garnish with the sweet potato chips.

❯ Place the avocado slices and cubed cucumber and mango all around the perimeter.

❯ If you are making it in a serving bowl, place the rice in the bowl and top with all the other ingredients. Place the chips and sesame seeds on top. Pour the dressing over the salad.

Makes 6 servings.

Whole-Wheat Pasta Salad with Tomatoes and Feta

This recipe brings back memories of a bright, hot sun on a shimmering lake.

I took a picture of this dish one day at the cottage. I had thrown it together, inspired by the sweet and crunchy tomatoes that we had picked up from the market. It was so pretty that I, of course, snapped a picture of it right in my favorite mixing bowl, before anyone was allowed to eat a morsel. Those are delicious memories.

I used some fresh basil leaves that we always have growing on the window sill, but if you want to use the cubes, you can add 2 to 3 defrosted cubes of basil during the last 5 minutes that the tomato sauce is cooking.

1	**Tbsp olive oil**
3	**small cloves garlic, minced**
3	**plum tomatoes, diced**
2	**cups yellow cherry tomatoes or grape tomatoes, halved (red tomatoes are fine, too)**
	Kosher salt and freshly ground black pepper
8	**fresh basil leaves**
1	**bag (1 lb) whole-wheat penne**
½	**cup crumbled feta cheese**

❯ Heat the olive oil in a heavy saucepan set over medium heat. Add the garlic and sauté for 1 minute. Add the plum and cherry tomatoes; cook for about 15 minutes or until the cherry tomatoes just start falling apart. Season with salt and pepper. Stir in the basil leaves when you are just about to remove the saucepan from the heat.

❯ Meanwhile, in a large pot of boiling, salted water, cook the pasta for 8 to 10 minutes or until *al dente*.

❯ Place the pasta in a bowl, top with the tomato sauce and feta cheese. Serve warm or at room temperature. Season with additional freshly ground black pepper, if desired.

Makes 6 to 8 servings.

Creamy Pasta Salad

This can be served as a main dish or a side dish and is delicious served both warm and at room temperature. While this salad can be made any time of year, the bright flavors just sing of spring.

¾	cup frozen peas
1	bag (1 lb) pasta, in any desired shape
2	Tbsp extra virgin olive oil
⅓	cup ricotta cheese
	zest of 1 lemon
1	Tbsp freshly squeezed lemon juice
1	clove garlic, minced
	Kosher salt and freshly ground black pepper, to taste

> In a large pot of boiling salted water, cook the pasta for 6 minutes. Add the peas. Cook for another 3 to 4 minutes or until the pasta is *al dente* and the peas are tender and a bright green color. Drain immediately. Transfer to a bowl; stir in the olive oil until the pasta is evenly coated. Add the ricotta cheese, lemon zest, lemon juice and garlic, mixing until well combined.

> Season to taste with salt and pepper.

> Serve and enjoy!

Males 6 to 8 servings.

Colorful Couscous Salad

Couscous is one of my favorite side dishes. It can easily be made on Yom Tov and throughout the year and creates almost no mess. Roast the beets up to three days ahead, and this salad becomes a beautiful, quick, throw together dish. Try to dice the vegetables into uniform pieces to create a nice effect.

2	Tbsp olive oil, plus some for rubbing beets
2	large beets (1 yellow and 1 red)
½	cup onion, finely chopped
¾	tsp ground cumin
1½	cups whole-wheat couscous
1½	tsp freshly ground black pepper
¾	tsp Kosher salt
1½	cups boiling water
3	Tbsp freshly squeezed lemon juice
1	cucumber (unpeeled), diced
¼	cup fresh mint, chopped
½	cup fresh flat-leaf parsley, chopped
2	cups (approx) baby spinach leaves

❯ Preheat the oven to 425°F.

❯ Rub olive oil over the beets; wrap each one separately in aluminum foil. Bake in the center of the preheated oven for 50 to 60 minutes (less for smaller beets) or until fork tender. Unwrap the beets. When the beets are cool enough to handle, rub off the skins, dice, and set aside.

❯ Heat 1 Tbsp of the olive oil in a large skillet set over medium heat. Add the onions and cumin; sauté until translucent. Stir in the couscous, pepper, and salt until the couscous is coated with the oil. Stir in the boiling water. Remove from heat, cover, and let stand for 15 minutes. Fluff with a fork; transfer to a large serving bowl.

❯ Add the reserved beets, lemon juice, cucumber, mint, parsley, and remaining 1 Tbsp of oil. When ready to serve, toss with the spinach leaves. Serve at room temperature.

Makes 4 to 6 servings.

COMMENTS

If you can find preserved lemons (a Sephardic or Moroccan delicacy) at your grocery store, add a few finely cut wedges for an additional, wonderful flavor, or see the recipe for them in the Preserved Lemon and Olive Roast Chicken recipe on page 224.

Endive and Orange Salad

This salad has a refreshing and exotic taste to it. The hazelnuts add a bit of crunch. It's a combination that works especially well during the winter months when oranges are at their best.

½   **cup hazelnuts**
4   **heads Belgian endive**
3   **oranges**
1   **Tbsp toasted sesame seeds**

Dressing:
3   **Tbsp extra virgin olive oil**
3   **Tbsp orange juice (reserved from oranges in salad)**
1   **tsp toasted sesame oil**
     Kosher salt and freshly ground black pepper, to taste

❯ Preheat the oven to 350°F. Spread the hazelnuts evenly on a rimmed baking sheet. Bake in the center of the preheated oven for 10 to 15 minutes or until the nuts are pale golden beneath the skin.

❯ Let the hazelnuts cool briefly, then transfer to a dish towel. Fold the towel to enclose the nuts and rub briskly to remove as much of the skin as possible.

❯ Coarsely chop the nuts and set aside. Chop the endive and place in a bowl.

❯ Using a sharp knife, cut away the peel from the oranges, including the pith. Holding each orange over a bowl to catch any juices, remove orange segments by cutting on either side of the segment, close to the membrane. Cut each segment in half if they are large and add them to endive.

❯ Dressing: Combine all of the ingredients for the dressing in a bowl, mixing well. Pour the dressing over the salad, tossing to evenly coat.

❯ Sprinkle with the hazelnuts, garnish with the sesame seeds and serve.

Makes 4 to 6 servings.

Asian Purple Cabbage Salad

The beautiful colors of this salad add visual appeal to any buffet or dinner. It is simple to prepare and has a delicious, crunchy texture. This recipe first appeared in "Kosher Inspired" and I know it was a real hit with the readers because I keep coming across it at other people's simchot or events.

1	**lb purple cabbage, shredded**
½	**cup frozen peas, thawed**
2	**scallions, chopped**
1	**can (6 oz) sliced water chestnuts, drained**
½	**cup toasted slivered almonds or cashews**

Dressing:

½	**cup extra virgin olive oil**
⅓	**cup vinegar**
¼	**cup honey**
1½	**tsp low-sodium soy sauce**

❯ Place the cabbage, peas, scallions and water chestnuts in a large mixing bowl.

❯ Dressing: Combine all of the ingredients for the dressing in a bowl, mixing well until combined. Thirty minutes before serving, toss the salad with the dressing. Add the nuts immediately before serving, tossing well.

Makes 8 servings.

Classic French Vinaigrette

❯ Whisk together **3 cloves garlic, minced, ½ tsp of both salt and pepper, 1 Tbsp grainy mustard and 2 Tbsp red wine vinegar** in a small bowl.

❯ Gradually whisk in ⅓ **cup of canola or vegetable oil** in a thin steady stream, pouring until emulsified.

Dressing can be refrigerated in airtight jar for up to 1 week.

To see a demo, go to **kosherscoop.com/video**

Asian-Style Chicken Salad

The many flavors in this recipe blend together to create a wonderful, wholesome salad that is a meal on its own.

Within 5 minutes of the photo shoot, this big bowl of salad was consumed by some hungry taste-testers. It is best to dress the salad close to serving time.

2	tsp soy sauce
½	tsp ground ginger
½	tsp garlic powder
3	boneless skinless chicken breasts, tenderized
1	Tbsp olive oil

Dressing:

½	cup freshly squeezed lime juice
¼	cup olive oil
4	tsp soy sauce
2	tsp light brown sugar or honey
2	tsp sesame oil
2	tsp finely chopped fresh ginger
2	tsp Dijon mustard
1	clove garlic, minced

Salad:

1	head baby romaine lettuce, cut into thin strips
2	scallions, chopped
1	mango (or 2 peaches), peeled and cubed
1	handful chow mein noodles
1	handful toasted slivered almonds or cashews, optional

> Combine the soy sauce and spices in a glass bowl. Add the chicken, tossing until well coated. Cover and marinate in the refrigerator for 1 hour or up to 24 hours.

> Heat the olive oil in a non-stick skillet set over medium-high heat. Remove the chicken breasts from the marinade; discard the marinade. Add the chicken to the skillet; sear on each side for 4 minutes or until cooked through and tender. Cool slightly. Cut into strips.

> Dressing: Combine all of the dressing ingredients in a jar and seal tightly; shake well. The dressing can be refrigerated for up to 1 week.

> Place the lettuce in a bowl. Add the mangoes and scallions. Stir in the chicken. Pour the dressing over, tossing gently until well combined. Sprinkle with the chow mein noodles and almonds, if using.

Makes 4 servings.

From strength to strength

HEALTHY LIVING

A large bowl of leafy greens, **segments of juicy oranges,** ***crusty, chewy bread,*** **OLIVE OIL.** Vitamins, minerals, protein, fiber. A handful of nuts, **a tall glass of milk,** source of nutrients, *pathway to health.* **Fish, meat, eggs: the foods that we need,** THE BOUNTY SURROUNDS US. **To run, to jump, to kick, to compete.** ***Full of energy,*** **vigor and strength.** *Small growing bodies,* **BIG STURDY BONES,** **good habits last a lifetime.** Fresh ingredients, *FABULOUS FOOD,* ***you deserve the best.*** The gift you give yourself.

fresh

FISH

Herb-Covered Sea Bass

Seriously simple and simply delicious.

3	cubes frozen minced garlic, defrosted
8	cubes frozen chopped dill, defrosted
1½	tsp extra virgin olive oil
4	sea bass fillets, skin on
	Kosher salt, for sprinkling

> Mash together the garlic, dill and ½ tsp of the olive oil in a small bowl until it forms a paste.

> In a heavy skillet, heat the remaining oil over medium heat. Wash the fish and pat dry with paper towels. Sprinkle with Kosher salt. Add to the pan. Cook, skin side down, for 5 minutes. Flip the fish over and cook for 4 to 5 minutes or until the fish is opaque and the top is slightly browned.

> Preheat the oven to broil.

> Smear the paste over the top of the fish. Broil for 1 to 2 minutes or until it begins to brown.

> Serve warm or at room temperature.

Makes 4 servings.

COMMENTS

Variation: Throw 1 cup of shelled pistachios into the bowl of a food processor fitted with the metal "S" blade along with garlic and dill. Purée. With the machine running, gradually add 2 Tbsp of oil.

White Fish With Herbed Tomato Sauce

This recipe works well with a variety of white fish. I used tilapia for this version, but sole, turbot and halibut are all excellent substitutions. I make it in an oven-to-tableware dish and serve it straight from the oven, still in the baking dish.

4	tilapia fillets
¾	cup tomato paste
½	cup mayonnaise (low-fat is fine)
1	Tbsp packed light brown sugar
1	Tbsp dried basil
2	tsp onion soup mix (no msg)
½	tsp freshly ground black pepper
¼	cup fresh flat-leaf parsley, chopped

› Preheat the oven to 400°F.

› Place the fish in a deep baking dish. Mix together all of the remaining ingredients, except for the parsley, to make a sauce. Spread over the fish.

› Bake in the center of the preheated oven for 35 to 40 minutes or until the fish flakes easily with a fork. Sprinkle with the fresh parsley. Serve warm.

Makes 4 servings.

Salt-Crusted Fish

I admit that this may be a bit different than your usual gefilte fish but it's certainly a fun fish to make. The first time I made it, it took me back to a Grade 7 science fair kind of feeling. Be creative with the aromatics, customizing them to your own taste.

I used a black sea bass, but trout, striped sea bass and salmon are all good options. Rinse the fish, pat it dry and rub the skin with a bit of oil to make it easier to remove the crust later. The salsa verde is compliments of Chef Sam Kanner.

1	whole fish, skin intact (2 lb total)
4½	cups Kosher salt
3	large egg whites
¼	cup water
	aromatics of your choice (garlic cloves, lemon wedges, bay leaves, shallots, sprigs of thyme and parsley)

Salsa Verde:

½	lemon
2	Tbsp celery, finely diced
2	Tbsp cucumber, finely diced
2	Tbsp fresh flat-leaf parsley, finely chopped
2	Tbsp extra virgin olive oil
1	Tbsp small capers, drained
1	Tbsp pitted brine-cured green olives (such as picholine), sliced

❯ Preheat the oven to 400°F.

❯ Mix the salt, egg whites and water together in a bowl to create a paste-like consistency. Using half of the paste, create a "bed" for the fish on a cookie sheet, spreading a layer about ¼" thick that is the approximate size of the fish. Lay the fish down on the "bed." Cover the fish completely with the remaining salt mixture, leaving the tail uncovered if the fish is too long for the tray. Try to ensure that the fish is sealed by the paste on all sides.

❯ Bake in the center of the preheated oven for about 25 minutes, adding 5 minutes for every additional pound.

❯ Salsa Verde: Using a small, sharp knife, remove the peel and white pith from the lemon. Working over a bowl, cut between the membranes to release the segments. Cut each segment into 3 pieces. Add the lemon pieces and the next 6 ingredients to a bowl.

❯ Remove fish from oven and allow to rest for 10 minutes. Remove the salt crust and skin. Serve immediately with salsa verde.

Makes 4 to 6 servings.

COMMENTS

Salsa Verde is great with chicken, too.

SALMON...
so good

Cedar Plank Salmon with Maple Glaze

Roasting on a cedar plank has three main advantages. First, the plank imparts a wonderful flavor to the fish. Second, the house smells of toasty cedar wood instead of cooked fish. And thirdly (and most importantly), it's a sure-fire way to impress your guests. Cedar planks are available at Home Depot and many major supermarkets.

¾	**cup pure maple syrup**
¼	**cup soy sauce**
2	**Tbsp honey**
2	**scallions, finely chopped**
5	**garlic cloves, minced**
1	**tsp freshly ground black pepper**
2½	**lb center-cut salmon fillet with skin**
	untreated cedar plank
	olive oil

❭ Soak cedar planks in water for 1 hour. When ready to use, remove from the water and proceed with recipe. (Do not pat dry.)

❭ Place the first 6 ingredients in a saucepan; bring to a slow boil. Remove from the heat and let cool slightly.

❭ Place the salmon in a shallow dish. Reserving about ¼ cup, pour the glaze over the salmon. Marinate at room temperature for 30 minutes.

❭ Preheat the oven to 400°F.

❭ Place the cedar plank directly on the middle rack in the oven and bake for 8 to 10 minutes or until the wood is lightly toasted. Remove the plank from the oven. While still hot, brush with a thin coating of olive oil.

❭ Remove the salmon from the marinade; discard the marinade. Place the salmon directly on the hot plank and then in a shallow roasting pan.

❭ Roast in the center of the preheated oven for 20 to 25 minutes, basting with the reserved ¼ cup during the last 10 minutes or until the fish flakes easily with a fork. Glaze the fish with the reserved sauce.

Makes 6 servings.

Walnut-Crusted Salmon

This recipe is a powerhouse of good-for-you nutrients. Just a handful of walnuts a day provides you with 2.5 grams of ALA, the plant-based source of omega-3 fatty acid, 4 grams of protein, 2 grams of fiber and 10% of your daily dosage of magnesium and phosphorus. Add this to the extra omega 3's found in the salmon and you've got a honey of a meal. P.S. It also tastes great.

¾	cup walnuts, finely chopped
3	Tbsp fresh breadcrumbs or panko
1	Tbsp lemon zest, grated
1	Tbsp fresh thyme, chopped
1	Tbsp olive oil
¼	tsp each Kosher salt and freshly ground black pepper
1	Tbsp Dijon mustard
4	salmon fillets, skin on (5 to 6 oz each)

> Preheat the oven to 400°F.

> Stir together the walnuts, breadcrumbs, lemon zest, thyme, oil, salt and pepper. The mixture should loosely hold together when pressed. Brush the mustard all over three sides of the salmon. Press the walnut mixture onto the fish. Place the salmon on an aluminum foil-lined baking sheet. Let stand at room temperature for 15 minutes

> Bake in the center of the preheated oven for 10 to 12 minutes or until the fish flakes easily with a fork.

Makes 4 servings.

Salmon with Herbed Breadcrumbs

I love this recipe. It is light and delicious and I often interchange the parsley with fresh dill. When making fresh breadcrumbs, it's best to use bread that is at least 1 day old as it's easier to grind when the bread is a bit drier. In fact, this recipe was inspired by some two-day-old multigrain rolls that needed to be taken care of!

6	slices multigrain bread, crusts removed
2	Tbsp fresh flat-leaf parsley, finely chopped
	zest of 1 lemon
1½	tsp extra virgin olive oil
¼	tsp Kosher salt
6	salmon fillets
6	Tbsp honey mustard

> Preheat the oven to 375°F.

> In the bowl of a food processor fitted with metal "S" blade, pulse the multigrain bread into coarse crumbs. Pour into a bowl. Add the parsley, lemon zest, oil and salt, mixing until well combined.

> Place the salmon on a parchment paper-lined baking sheet. Brush each fillet with 1 Tbsp of the honey mustard. Top with an even coating of the breadcrumbs.

> Bake in the center of the preheated oven for 15 minutes.

> Serve warm or at room temperature.

Makes 6 servings.

Pan-Seared Salmon with Creamy Cucumber Sauce

Pan searing is my absolute favorite way to cook salmon. A thin crust covers a moist, flavorful fish. This light sauce is the perfect accompaniment, and can double as a salad dressing.

4	salmon fillets
	Kosher salt and freshly ground black pepper, for seasoning
1–2	Tbsp oil, for frying

Creamy Cucumber Sauce:

1	piece English cucumber, about 5" long, unpeeled, chopped
¾	cup sour cream or plain yogurt
¾	cup mayonnaise (low-fat is fine)
2	anchovies (or 1 Tbsp anchovy paste)
2	scallions, chopped
1	clove garlic
2	Tbsp fresh flat-leaf parsley, chopped
2	Tbsp lemon juice
½	tsp dried tarragon
	Kosher salt and freshly ground black pepper, to taste

❯ Cucumber Sauce: Place all of the ingredients in the bowl of a food processor and blend until smooth. Season to taste with salt and pepper. Refrigerate until ready to use or for up to one week.

❯ Season the salmon lightly with salt and pepper. Heat the oil in a large, heavy skillet set over medium-high heat.

❯ Add the salmon, flesh side down, and sear for 3 minutes or until golden brown and crisp. Turn the salmon over and sear skin side down for about 3 minutes or until the salmon is just cooked through. (You may need to cook it a few minutes more over low heat if you want it well done.) Remove the salmon from the pan. Let cool for a few minutes and serve with the cucumber sauce.

Makes 4 servings.

Moroccan Fish Soup

For those of Ashkenazi descent, do not be scared off by the name! This dish has an amazing blend of flavors. I eliminated the broth-making step by wrapping the fish heads and tails loosely in cheesecloth, cooking them with the soup and then discarding them without any mess. Cooking the soup with the fish heads intensifies the flavor and imparts a light gelatinous texture, which you may very well find an interesting change. The mock crab puffs up as it cooks, creating the illusion of pasta, making it ideal for a one-pot dinner.

⅓	cup extra virgin olive oil
4	large leeks, white and light green parts only, sliced
4	stalks celery, peeled and cut in thirds
4	large cloves garlic, peeled
1	bunch flat-leaf parsley
1	red pepper, seeded and cut into chunks
1	head and tail of a large salmon, sea bass or other big fish, quartered and loosely, but securely, wrapped in cheesecloth
4	cups canned crushed tomatoes
2	large potatoes (or 1 medium celery root), cut in ½" cubes, peeled
1	cup dry white wine
1	Tbsp paprika
½–1	tsp cayenne
	generous pinch ground cloves
3	bay leaves
2	good pinches of saffron
	Kosher salt, to taste
10	cups water
2	Tbsp anisette or arack, optional
3	lb boneless, skinless fish (such as salmon or snapper), cut into 1" cubes
1	lb frozen mock crab, thawed and flaked (or more of the fish you are already using)
	freshly ground black pepper, to taste

> Heat the oil in a wide, heavy pot set over medium-high heat.

> Coarsely grind the leeks, celery, garlic, parsley and red pepper in the bowl of a food processor fitted with the metal "S" blade. Add the mixture to the pot. Sauté for 6 to 8 minutes or until the liquid has evaporated

> Add the cheesecloth-wrapped fish, tomatoes, potatoes, wine, paprika, cayenne, cloves, bay leaves, saffron, salt and water. Bring to a boil.

> Reduce the heat to medium and cook, covered, for 45 minutes.

> Add the anisette or arack, if using, fish, mock crab and pepper. Cook for another few minutes, just until the fish is cooked through.

> Squeeze the cheesecloth-wrapped fish against the side of the pot to release as much liquid as you can before discarding it. Discard the bay leaves. Season to taste with salt and pepper.

Makes 10 servings.

Oven-Fried Fish

Aside from the fat, nothing is missing from these oven-fried fish fillets. Panko crumbs are thicker than regular bread crumbs and can be bought in herbed flavors for a nice change. If you cannot find panko crumbs, homemade breadcrumbs are an excellent substitute.

4	turbot fillets (or sole or halibut)
1	tsp garlic powder
1	tsp salt
½	tsp freshly ground black pepper
2	Tbsp mayonnaise
1	large egg, lightly beaten
½	cup panko crumbs
	olive oil

> Preheat the oven to 450°F.

> Season the fish with the garlic powder, salt and pepper. Coat the fish lightly with the mayonnaise. Dip each fillet into the beaten egg and coat in panko crumbs.

> Pour a thin layer of olive oil onto a cookie sheet. Place the tray into the oven for 2 minutes to heat the oil. Carefully remove from the oven and place the breaded fillets onto the pan. Bake in the center of the preheated oven for about 10 minutes, until the breadcrumbs have browned.

Makes 4 servings.

COMMENTS

Quick tartar sauce: Mix together **¼ cup of mayonnaise** *with* **3 chopped pickles** *and* **½ tsp of pickle juice** *in a bowl.*

Smoked White Fish Pâté Packets

This simple combination results in a creamy and tasty pâté. I often serve it in a small, baked shell, but my favorite way to serve it is in a smoked salmon "packet".

12	oz smoked white fish
5	Tbsp mayonnaise
1	Tbsp freshly squeezed lemon juice
½	tsp granulated sugar
	pinch Kosher salt
12	rectangular slices of lox or smoked salmon (try to find ones that have been cut in even, rectangular pieces)

❯ Prepare the pâté: Combine all of the ingredients, except the 12 slices of lox, in the bowl of a food processor fitted with the metal "S" blade. Process until smooth.

❯ Prepare the packets: Line 6 medium-size ramekins with plastic wrap, making sure that the plastic wrap overhangs the sides of each ramekins by about 2". Take 2 of the lox slices and place one across the top, pressing it down into the center so that it lines the ramekin. Lay the other piece of lox perpendicular to the first one and also press it in to create a "bowl" for the pate. Repeat with remaining ramekins.

❯ Spoon the pâté into the ramekins, filling them about 3/4 of the way up. Close the packet by folding the plastic wrap over the pate.

❯ Invert the ramekin onto a plate. Repeat with remaining ramekins. Refrigerate for at least 1 hour or for up to 7 days. Remove ramekin; remove plastic wrap.

Makes 6 servings.

Simple Sesame Glazed Fish

There is a fish called Arctic Char that has become popular in our household. I'm always trying new ways to serve it, and here is my most recent concoction that was really good! The sauce also goes really well with salmon.

1	side Arctic char
¼	cup teriyaki sauce
3–4	Tbsp sesame seeds
2	Tbsp honey
1	Tbsp toasted sesame oil

❯ Preheat the oven to 350°F.

❯ Wash the fish and pat dry with paper towels. Lay on a parchment paper-lined baking sheet, skin side down. Mix the remaining ingredients together in a bowl; pour evenly over the fish. Let stand at room temperature for 20 minutes.

❯ Bake in the center of the preheated oven for 20 to 25 minutes or until the fish flakes easily with a fork.

Makes 4 servings.

Arctic Char with Toasted Coriander Crust

When I told my friend about this recipe, she made a face, and exclaimed, "That means I gotta go buy coriander seeds?" Well, the short answer is yes, but it's worth it! With almost no added fat and tons of added flavor, she agreed that the errand paid off. I use Arctic Char here, a fish my family likes, but you can use salmon trout as well.

2	arctic char fillets
¼	cup coriander seeds
1½	tsp Kosher salt
2	Tbsp oil

❯ Preheat the oven to 400°F.

❯ Toast the coriander seeds in a dry, heavy skillet over medium heat, swirling the pan to avoid any browning, just until fragrant. Cool slightly. Place the seeds in a Ziploc™ bag; roll a rolling pin over the bag until the seeds are lightly crushed. Add the salt and pepper. Rub the seeds onto the top surface of the fish and drizzle with the oil.

❯ Bake in the center of the preheated oven for about 18 minutes or until the thickest part of the fish is cooked through. Remove from the oven and let cool.

Makes 6 servings.

COMMENTS

The seeds of the coriander plant interestingly bear no resemblance to the flavor of fresh coriander leaves. The seeds are mildly fragrant with an aromatic, citrusy flavor that also has hints of caraway and sage. The seeds are actually the dried ripe fruit of the plant, which is indigenous to Asia and Mediterranean regions.

HOLIDAYS

Round raisin challah, ruby-red pomegranate seeds, **songs of triumph,** a nation prevails. A white Yom Kippur, *solemnity and prayer,* **SAVORING TRADITION.** Colorful decorations sway in the breeze, PIPING HOT CIDER, *crisp white tablecloths.* Neat rows of glowing candles, *dry red wine,* **deep-fried doughnuts in white powdered sugar,** *bowls of steaming soup.* Host, hostess, guests, and children, **CONVERSATION FLOWS LATE INTO THE NIGHT.** THIN CRISP MATZAH, Mom's famous torte, *crowded tables,* **family feast.** Creamy, fluffy cheesecakes, *blintzes with blueberry sauce,* **THE FORGING OF A PEOPLE.** *Mournful silence, sadness and triumph intertwined.* Joined in holiday spirit.

the main
COURSE

Slow-Cooked English Ribs or Spare Ribs

Don't let the short ingredient list fool you. Although few in number, these ingredients add up to a lip-smacking, delicious meat dish, tender and full of flavor.

3	**Tbsp oil**
1	**Spanish onion, finely chopped**
6	**English ribs or spare ribs (or use any other meat on the bone)**

Sauce:

¾	**cup packed light brown sugar**
¼	**cup ketchup**
3	**Tbsp red wine vinegar**
2	**Tbsp black peppercorns**
2	**Tbsp soy sauce**
1	**Tbsp mustard**

❯ Heat 2 Tbsp of the oil in a skillet set over medium heat. Sauté the onion until soft; set aside in a bowl.

❯ Meanwhile, preheat a large slow cooker to high.

❯ Add the remaining Tbsp of oil to the skillet. In batches, sear the meat, turning once, for 3 minutes per side. Transfer the meat with the pan juices to the slow cooker.

❯ Stir all of the sauce ingredients into the reserved onions, mixing well. Pour the sauce over the meat, coating the meat well.

❯ Cover and bake on high for 3 hours, then reduce the heat to low and cook for 6 to 8 hours or until very tender.

Makes 6 servings.

Horseradish Cream *Enough for 6 to 8 servings.*

This creamy condiment with its subtle kick of heat is perfect to serve with simmered ribs.

Whip ⅓ **cup oil-based, non-dairy whip topping** to soft peaks.

Drain ½ **cup bottled horseradish**; fold the cream into the horseradish.

Serve with meat.

Grilled Chicken Breasts with Chimmichuri Sauce

Grilled chicken is always delicious (when cooked correctly, that is!!!). Add this zesty sauce with its fresh flavors and bright colors for a special treat. Try making this dish when it's cold and dreary outside. Close your eyes and chew...it will feel incredibly just like summer!!

Chimichurri Sauce:

1	cup fresh flat-leaf parsley
3	cloves garlic, peeled
½	cup extra virgin olive oil
¼	cup red wine vinegar
2	Tbsp water
1	tsp Kosher salt
¼	tsp red pepper flakes

6	boneless skinless chicken breasts

Marinade:

¼	cup extra virgin olive oil
1	Tbsp soy sauce
1	tsp balsamic vinegar
3	cloves garlic, minced (or 3 cubes frozen garlic)
	freshly ground black pepper

> Chimichurri Sauce: Place all of the ingredients into the bowl of a food processor fitted with the metal "S" blade; process until smooth. Set aside or cover and refrigerate for up to 1 week.

> Marinade: Stir together all of the marinade ingredients in a small bowl. Place the chicken in a Ziploc™ bag. Pour in the marinade. Remove any excess air and close the bag securely. "Massage" the chicken until the marinade is evenly dispersed. Marinate in the refrigerator for 30 minutes or for up to 24 hours.

> Preheat the grill to medium.

> Remove the chicken from the marinade; discard the marinade. Grill on the preheated grill, covered, for 5 minutes. Flip the chicken over; cook for about 10 minutes or until juices run clear when pierced.

> Pour the chimichurri sauce over the grilled chicken.

Makes 6 servings.

COMMENTS

The mariande can be made up to 3 days ahead.

Sweet and Sour Chicken Wings

I like to split the chicken wings in half for a more gourmet look. Simply bend the connecting knuckle backwards, pulling the bones away from each other to separate them easily.

16-20	chicken wings, cut in half and patted dry	Sauce:		
		1	can (20 oz) pineapple (crushed or in chunks), drained
½	Tbsp light soy sauce	⅓	cup granulated sugar
1	tsp garlic powder	¼	cup soy sauce
½	tsp salt	¼	cup vinegar
	pinch freshly ground	2	Tbsp cornstarch
	black pepper	2	Tbsp sweet paprika

> Place the wings in a large bowl and add the soy sauce, garlic powder, salt and pepper. Cover with plastic wrap and let marinate in the refrigerator for 1 hour.

> Preheat the oven to broil.

> Lay the chicken in a single layer on a parchment paper-lined baking sheet and broil for 15 minutes. Remove from the oven; pour off the juices and discard.

> Lower the oven to 350°F.

> Meanwhile, place all of the ingredients for the sauce into a large sauce pan set over medium-low heat. Cook, stirring often, for 5 to 7 minutes or until thickened. Immediately pour over the chicken. Bake in the center of the preheated oven for 15 minutes.

Makes 10 servings.

Sweet Corn Flake Chicken

As I was editing this book and came across this recipe, a wave of nostalgia washed over me. At one point a few years ago, this was my go-to dinner recipe. I'm not sure when that stopped being true, but I certainly plan on making it again, and I am so glad I can now share it with your family as well.

8	chicken drumsticks
2½	cups Corn Flake crumbs
	Pinch Kosher salt

Marinade:

1	cup apricot preserves
1½	Tbsp apple cider vinegar
1½	Tbsp yellow mustard
1	Tbsp honey
¼	tsp dried thyme leaves
⅛	tsp paprika

❯ Marinade: Combine all of the ingredients in a bowl, stirring until almost smooth.

❯ Wash the drumsticks and pat dry with a paper towel. Place the chicken in a Ziploc™ bag. Pour in the marinade. Remove any excess air and close the bag securely. "Massage" the chicken until the marinade is evenly dispersed. Marinate in the refrigerator for at least 1 hour, up to 24 hours.

❯ Preheat the oven to 350°F.

❯ Mix together the corn flake crumbs and salt in a shallow bowl. Remove the drumsticks from the marinade; discard the marinade. Roll each drumstick evenly in the crumbs until well coated. Transfer to a parchment paper-lined baking sheet.

❯ Cover and bake in the center of the preheated oven for 40 minutes. Uncover; bake for 20 minutes.

Makes 8 servings.

Braised Lemon Chicken with Herbs

This is a special-occasion chicken dish. The many herbs included give it a gourmet flair. This dish was inspired by a delicious chicken dish I ate in a restaurant. I wrote down the list of aromatics on a napkin, and then recreated it at home a few days later. Very successfully, I might add!!

6	chicken leg quarters
¾	cup all-purpose flour
6	tsp oil
1	Spanish onion, finely chopped
3	cloves garlic, minced
1½	tsp dried thyme, crushed
1	tsp dried basil, crushed
1	tsp ground coriander
½	tsp dried rosemary, crushed
¼	tsp each Kosher salt and freshly ground black pepper
1	cup white wine (semi-sweet or sweet)
1¼	cups chicken broth
2	Tbsp balsamic vinegar
	juice of 1 lemon
1	Tbsp honey

❯ Preheat the oven to 350°F.

❯ Place the flour in a shallow bowl. Coat the chicken legs with the flour.

❯ Heat all but 1 tsp of the oil in a large, oven-proof pan or shallow pot set over medium-high heat. In batches, if necessary, add the chicken in a single layer and sear on both sides, about 10 minutes total. Remove the chicken and set aside.

❯ Add the remaining tsp of oil to the pan. Add the onion, garlic, thyme, basil, coriander, rosemary, salt and pepper and sauté until soft. Pour in the wine; cook until reduced by half. Add the remaining ingredients and cook for about 5 minutes or until flavors have melded. Return the chicken to the pan, spooning the sauce over to cover. Cover the pan; bring to a boil.

❯ Bake in the center of the preheated oven for 1½ hours. Serve with the sauce.

Makes 6 servings.

Cumin-Spiced Brisket with Leeks and Dried Apricots

Every year, as Holiday season nears, a little culinary tug of war starts to occur in my kitchen. Do I follow a long-standing tradition and serve the brisket that I know my family and friends adore, accompanied by their favorite holiday chicken? Or do I dare to wade into innovative territory and attempt to introduce some new flavors at my Seder table? The answer, of course, is that I can actually do both: honor my family's preferences and their longing for tradition and yet satisfy my need for creativity. Roasts, be they beef, lamb, veal or chicken, are quintessentially festive and regal. They're easy to prepare and generally require less fuss in the kitchen than individual cuts of meat or quartered chickens. You just need to dress them up and leave them be in the oven to magically transform themselves into the divine and delicious. How you dress them up is key, however. The wardrobe possibilities are endless and that's what makes choosing a roast so exciting. Brisket, especially, takes well to any number of flavor combinations, be they a sweet cranberry-and-onion combination, a sweet potato-and-prune duo or a pomegranate sauce laced with rosemary. Here, this sublime recipe takes its inspiration from Northern Africa with the heady spice medley of cumin, coriander, ginger and cinnamon, tickled with the sweetness of honey and dried apricots.

For a hint of vibrant color, reserve half of the apricots to put in the roasting pan as the meat slices are rewarming. The bright orange will contrast beautifully with the darkness of the sauce and the lush green of the fresh coriander.

Rub:

2	Tbsp each olive oil and honey
2	tsp salt
1	tsp each ground cumin and coriander
1	tsp each ground ginger, cinnamon and pepper
¼	tsp cayenne pepper, optional
1	double brisket, about 4½ lb
2	large leeks, white and pale green parts only, sliced
1	onion, chopped
24	dried apricots
12	cloves garlic, peeled
2	tsp dried thyme
½	tsp each Kosher salt and freshly ground black pepper
2	cups red wine
1	cup beef stock
¼	cup fresh coriander, chopped

〉 Stir together the olive oil, honey, salt, cumin, coriander, ginger, cinnamon, pepper and cayenne pepper, if using, in a bowl. Rub on both sides of the brisket. Transfer the brisket to a large roasting pan; cover and refrigerate overnight.

〉 Preheat the oven to 325°F.

〉 Toss the leeks, onion, apricots, and garlic with the thyme, salt and pepper in a separate bowl. Arrange the vegetables around the brisket in the roasting pan. Pour in the wine and beef stock. Cover the pan tightly; roast in the center of the preheated oven for 2½ to 3 hours or until very tender. Let sit at room temperature for 30 minutes. Refrigerate, covered, overnight.

❯ Transfer the meat to a cutting board. Slicing across the grain, slice the meat as thinly as possible. Remove as much of the fat as possible from the pan. Set the apricots aside. Pour the remaining juices, leeks and garlic into the bowl of a food processor; purée until smooth. Stir the coriander into the sauce. Pour the sauce back into the roasting pan. Add the apricots and sliced meat back into the roasting pan. Rewarm for 30 to 45 minutes in a 300°F oven.

Makes 8 to 10 servings.

Slow Roasted Lamb with Herbs and Mushrooms

For extra flavor, feel free to substitute fresh fennel for the celery. Its anise-like flavor will complement the thyme and rosemary. The lamb should be served the day it is made. Unlike other braising cuts such as brisket, which fares better made a day or two ahead, the lamb may lose its succulence.

1	boneless lamb shoulder roast (about 4½ lb)
3	Tbsp olive oil
1	Tbsp dried oregano
2	tsp dried thyme
1	tsp dried rosemary, crumbled
¾	tsp each Kosher salt and freshly ground black pepper
1	onion, chopped
2	each, carrots (peeled) and celery stalks, chopped
4	cloves garlic, chopped
4	cups button mushrooms, stemmed and sliced
1	can (13.5 oz) tomatoes (or 1½ cups)
1	bottle (25 oz) dry white wine
2	bay leaves
1	Tbsp cornstarch
3	Tbsp water

❯ Preheat the oven to 300°F.

❯ Pat the lamb dry. Brush all over with 1 Tbsp of the oil. In a small bowl, combine the oregano, thyme, rosemary, salt and pepper; rub all over the roast.

❯ Heat the remaining oil in a large, ovenproof Dutch oven or casserole set over medium-high heat. Brown the roast all over. Transfer the roast to a plate. Add the onion, carrots, celery, garlic and mushrooms to the pot. Cook, stirring, for 10 minutes or until softened and any excess liquid released from the mushrooms has evaporated. Pour in the tomatoes, wine and bay leaves; bring to a boil. Return the meat to the pot.

❯ Bake in the center of the preheated oven for 2½ to 3 hours or until the meat is extremely tender.

❯ Transfer the meat to a cutting board. Tent with foil. Skim off as much fat from the reserved juices as possible. Remove the bay leaves. Set over medium-high heat. Bring to a boil, boil for 15 minutes. Dissolve the cornstarch in 3 Tbsp of water. Whisk into the sauce. Boil gently for 5 minutes or until thickened.

❯ Slice the lamb. Serve topped with the sauce.

Makes 8 servings.

Lamb with Lemon-Mint Sauce

People often tell me they don't "go" for lamb. Well, then they haven't tasted this lamb recipe. It's moist and the flavors create a perfect harmony. Okay, I may be getting a little carried away, but at least tell me you'll try it!!

4	lamb chops
1½	Tbsp extra virgin olive oil
½	tsp Kosher salt
½	tsp freshly ground black pepper

Sauce:

1–2	cloves garlic, minced
4–5	mint leaves, very finely chopped
	zest of 1 lemon
¼	tsp ground cumin
¼	tsp Kosher salt
½	tsp extra virgin olive oil

❯ Coat the lamb with the oil. Sprinkle with the salt and pepper. Let marinate for 30 minutes at room temperature.

❯ Meanwhile, stir together all of the ingredients for the sauce, mixing until well combined and a thick paste is formed. Set aside.

❯ Preheat the barbecue to medium-high or preheat the broiler. Place the lamb on the barbecue; grill for 4 minutes. Turn over and brush with ½ tsp (or more) of the sauce. Let cook for a few minutes more or until the desired tenderness is reached. Serve with the remaining sauce.

Makes 4 servings.

Capons with Vegetable Stuffing

At Kosher butcher shops, capons are chicken thighs and legs that have been deboned. Leaving the skin intact while baking helps retain moisture and creates an even juicier chicken. We make this recipe all year round but especially enjoy it on Passover. It's one of those recipes I think my children will make or eat when they're older and think of mom's home-cooking.

8	chicken capons, skin on or deboned chicken legs
1	onion, chopped
3	carrots, peeled and chopped
2	stalks celery, chopped
2	zucchini, chopped
¼	lb white button mushrooms
2	Tbsp oil
	Kosher salt
	freshly ground black pepper
2½	Tbsp all-purpose flour or potato starch
1	Tbsp dried basil
1½	cups duck sauce

> Preheat the oven to 350°F.

> Finely grate all of the vegetables in the bowl of a food processor fitted with the metal "S" blade.

> Heat the oil in a high-sided or deep skillet set over medium-low heat. Add the grated vegetables; cook, stirring, for 30 minutes or until very soft. Stir in the salt, pepper and basil. Add in the flour and stir for 1 minute.

> Spread the capons out flat, skin side down. Place about 2 Tbsp of the filling on top. Roll up each capon. Place seam side down on baking sheet. Pour the duck sauce over the capons and smear gently until evenly coated.

> Bake, covered, in the center of the preheated oven for 1½ hours. Uncover; bake for 30 minutes.

Makes 8 servings.

COMMENTS

Appetizer Variation: Each chicken capon is a dinner-size portion, so for appetizers I cut each one in half and create a smaller portion. Pack tightly in a pan and follow the baking directions as above. Serve with roasted mini potatoes and a sprig of rosemary or thyme.

Standing Rib Roast with Fig and Wine Sauce

It doesn't get any more special than this. Carve this glorious roast at the table for maximum effect. Make sure you let the roast stand for 15 minutes before slicing it to allow the juices to recede back into the center of the roast. And don't forget that the roast will continue to cook for about 5 minutes after you take it out of the oven, so gauge your temperature accordingly.

1	beef standing rib roast (about 6 lbs)
¼	cup grainy Dijon mustard (or duck sauce)
2	Tbsp horseradish
1	Tbsp cracked black pepper
2	Tbsp olive oil
3	cloves garlic, minced
2	tsp dried thyme
¾	tsp Kosher salt

Sauce:

3	cloves garlic, minced
2	Tbsp potato starch (or all-purpose flour)
½	cup red wine
1 ¼	cups beef stock
¾	cup dried figs, chopped

> Place the roast, bone side down, on a greased rack in a roasting pan. Mix together the mustard, horseradish, oil, black pepper, garlic, thyme and salt; spread over the top and sides of the roast. Let stand at room temperature for 1 hour.

> Preheat the oven to 325°F.

> Roast the meat in the center of the preheated oven for 2 to 2½ hours or until a meat thermometer registers 140°F for rare or 150°F for medium-rare. Transfer the meat to a cutting board; tent with foil. Let stand for 15 minutes. Reserve the juices.

> Place the roasting pan over medium-high heat. Stir in the garlic, mixing for 30 seconds. Sprinkle the potato starch over the fat in the pan. Cook, stirring, for 1 minute. Pour in the wine; bring to a boil, scraping up any brown bits from the bottom of the pan. Pour in the stock and figs. Reduce the heat and simmer for 3 to 5 minutes or until the sauce is thickened and the figs are softened.

> Slice the meat; serve with the red wine gravy.

Makes 8 servings.

Mexican-Style Chicken Wraps

I think I almost cried the other night at dinnertime. I made these wraps and sort of mentally cringed from the anticipation of the protests of my finely honed food testers. The problem is that they seem to have an aversion to chicken, at least the ones younger than 9 years old. I courageously grilled the chicken, set up the wraps and handed each child a plate...and held my breath. There was no complaining, no whining, and just the sweet sound of....chewing. I slowly let myself relax... and even began to hope. Could it be true? They were tears of joy.

6	**boneless chicken thighs (use boneless chicken breasts for a lower-fat alternative)**
2	**tsp soy sauce**
2	**tsp olive oil**
1	**clove garlic, crushed (or 2 cubes frozen garlic)**
6	**flour tortilla wraps**
2	**ripe avocados**
½	**lime**
1	**cup cherry tomatoes, sliced in half**
½	**red onion, peeled**
1	**cup canned corn, drained**
½	**cup pareve sour cream**
¼	**cup fresh cilantro, chopped**

❯ Stir together the chicken, soy sauce, oil and garlic in a bowl. Marinate for at least 30 minutes or cover and refrigerate overnight.

❯ Preheat a grill or grill pan to high. Place the chicken on the grill; grill the meat, turning once, for about 8 minutes or until it is no longer pink inside. Remove from the heat and let rest for 10 minutes.

❯ Meanwhile, cut the avocado into large cubes. Squeeze the halved lime over the avocado to prevent it from browning. Set aside. Use a peeler to peel the onion into very thin slices.

❯ Assembly: Place one piece of chicken on each tortilla; top with avocado, cherry tomatoes, onions, corn, a dollop of pareve sour cream and cilantro. Roll up into wrap. Serve immediately.

Makes 6 servings.

COMMENTS

This can easily be served buffet-style for a quick and delicious meal.

Seder Celery Root Chicken

My grandmother grew up in Pressburg, but her great-grandmother originally came from a small town in Hungary called Deberecen. "It was a small city where people were more into cooking than fashion," she relates. My grandmother remembers that they used to go shopping in a marketplace, where all the local farmers would bring their livestock to sell. She still remembers how the prospective customers would blow into the chickens before they bought them to judge whether the birds were skinny or fat.

My grandmother still makes a chicken dish with celery root that she originally learned from her mother. Celery root, you might fairly say, is the ugly duckling of root vegetables; the gnarled brown bulbs are rather a challenge to peel. However, the homely exterior conceals a white jewel of a vegetable inside. Cut into julienne strips and tossed with dressing (lemon juice, olive oil and garlic work well for Pesach), celery root makes crunchy, fresh-tasting salads; cut into chunks or grated, it lends an aromatic heft to stews.

"In Hungary, they didn't have kosher l'Pesach oil," my grandmother says. So her mother would make this recipe with rendered goose shmaltz. Surely the goose shmaltz added a unique flavor (not to mention a unique form of bad cholesterol), but since you can't really find it on the shelves these days anyway, we substituted oil for goose fat.

My grandmother and her sister both make this recipe. The chicken comes out soft, and the gravy gives it a wonderfully mellow flavor. There are so few ingredients, but so much great taste!

6	chicken bottoms
½	tsp each freshly ground black pepper, Kosher salt and sweet paprika
1	Tbsp oil
1	onion, thinly sliced
6-8	cloves garlic, crushed
½	cup water
1	celery root, peeled and finely grated

› Sprinkle the chicken with the pepper, salt and paprika. Line the bottom of a wide, shallow pot with oil. Add the onion and garlic. Arrange the chicken on top. Pour in about ½ cup of water to prevent the vegetables from sticking to the bottom of the pot during cooking.

› Cook over high heat for 10 minutes. Reduce the heat to low and cook for 30 minutes. Cover the chicken with the celery root. Cook for another 30 to 45 minutes or until the chicken is cooked through.

Makes 6 servings.

Sweet 'n Sour Tongue

I prefer pickled tongue for this recipe, but regular tongue works as well. My mother made this recipe for years, both as an appetizer and as a main course. The sweetness, melded with the saltiness of the pickling spices, makes it appealing to youths and adults alike.

1	**pickled tongue (approximately 3 lb)**
2	**Tbsp oil**
1	**Spanish onion, finely chopped**
⅓	**cup apricot jam**
2	**Tbsp packed light brown sugar**
1½	**Tbsp freshly squeezed lemon juice**
½	**cup raisins, optional**
½	**cup toasted slivered almonds, optional**

❯ Bring a large pot of water to a boil. Add the tongue. Reduce the heat and cook for about 1½ hours or until cooked through. Drain the water. While the tongue is still hot, peel off the outer skin completely and discard. Cool the tongue; transfer to an airtight Ziploc™ bag and refrigerate until thoroughly chilled. Slice thinly and arrange in overlapping slices in a large ovenproof serving dish.

❯ Sauce: Heat the oil in a skillet set over medium heat. Add the onion; cook, stirring occasionally, until soft and brown. Stir in the jam, brown sugar, lemon juice, raisins and nuts, if using. Cook, stirring occasionally, until the mixture has liquefied. Pour the sauce over the tongue slices. Reheat for about 30 minutes in a 250°F oven.

Makes 8 to 10 servings.

COMMENTS

Appetizer Variation: Cut the tongue into cubes and serve over a scoop of cooked basmati rice.

Sharp Mustard Sauce

This sharp, tangy dressing is the perfect accompaniment to any pickled meat. Serve sauce at room temperature alongside the meat.

Mix **1 Tbsp prepared yellow mustard, 1 Tbsp honey mustard or Dijon mustard, 1 Tbsp oil, 1 Tbsp water, 1 Tbsp mayonnaise, 1 Tbsp prepared white horseradish, 1 tsp yellow mustard seeds, 1 tsp honey** together in a bowl. Use a whisk to blend vigorously until the sauce is smooth and creamy. Refrigerate up to one week.

Maple Roast

When my friend Rachelli came by with this roast after I had my son Chaim, I was positive that she had put chocolate in it. Chocolate is always on my mind and the roast is sweet scent with rich tones of flavor all but convinced me. (Did I mention I was a chocoholic?)

Alas, I blamed my inability to detect the inclusion of maple syrup and soy sauce on my post-partum status, but based on the success of this recipe, I would have to guess this was one of the best baby gifts I ever received. A great recipe is the kind of present you use over and over again.

1	brisket or brick roast (about 3-4 lb)
3	Tbsp Dijon mustard
2	onions, sliced
2	sweet potatoes, cut into large chunks
1	cup red baby potatoes, cut in half
	Kosher salt and freshly ground black pepper, to taste
½	cup maple syrup
⅓	cup soy sauce

> Preheat the oven to 350°F.

> Spread the Dijon mustard over the sides and top of the roast.

> Arrange the onions in the bottom of a Dutch oven. Top with the sweet and baby potatoes. Place the meat on top of the potatoes.

> Sprinkle the salt and pepper evenly over the meat and potatoes. Stir together the maple syrup and soy sauce in a small bowl. Pour over the meat. Cover the Dutch oven and bake for 2½ hours. Let cool. Chill overnight. Slice the meat, return to the pot with the vegetables. Reheat in a 250°F oven until warmed through.

Makes 12 servings.

To see a demo, go to **kosherscoop.com/video**

Spanish Chicken with Herbs and Peppers

The colorful peppers make this a very pretty dish. It's lovely served over couscous or rice.

6	chicken thighs, bone-in
1½	tsp Kosher salt
½	tsp freshly ground black pepper
2	Tbsp olive oil
1	red pepper, sliced
1	yellow pepper, sliced
1	jalapeño pepper, diced
2	cloves garlic, chopped
2	Tbsp tomato paste
1	can (19 oz) diced tomatoes
½	cup white wine
3	Tbsp granulated sugar
¼	cup fresh flat-leaf parsley, chopped
1	Tbsp fresh thyme leaves, chopped
1	tsp fresh oregano leaves, chopped
2	Tbsp capers or olives, drained, optional
½	cup chicken stock

❯ Season the chicken with the salt and pepper. Heat the oil in a large, heavy skillet set over medium heat. Sear the chicken on both sides until browned. Remove from the pan and set aside.

❯ Reduce the heat to low. Add the peppers and cook for 3 minutes. Add the garlic; cook for 1 minute. Add the tomato paste; cook for 2 minutes. Stir in the tomatoes, wine, sugar, parsley, thyme, oregano and capers or olives, if using, scraping up any browned bits from the bottom of the pot. Return the chicken to the pan along with the stock; bring the mixture to a boil. Reduce the heat and simmer, covered, until the chicken is cooked through, about 1 hour.

Makes 6 servings.

Citrus Cornish Hens

The subtle taste of beer, with the undertones of citrus, gives a flavorful twist to my favorite kind of poultry. The sauce is excellent on chicken as well. This recipe has become my go-to dish for holiday dinners, especially Succot.

1	large orange, sliced into rounds
4	Cornish hens, butterflied*

Citrus Sauce:

2	Tbsp oil
2	Vidalia onions, finely chopped
2	Tbsp granulated sugar
1	cup beer
1	Tbsp cornstarch
1	cup orange juice
1	Tbsp honey
1	Tbsp soy sauce
⅛	tsp ground ginger
	zest of 1 lemon, optional

❯ Sauce: Heat the oil in a skillet set over medium-high heat. Add the onions. Reduce the heat to medium and cook for 3 minutes. Add the sugar; reduce the heat to medium-low. Cook for about 10 minutes or until the onions are light brown. Pour in the beer; cook until the liquid is reduced by half. Dissolve the cornstarch in the orange juice. Stir into the pan. Cook until the mixture is thickened.

❯ Stir in all of the remaining sauce ingredients until well combined. Remove from heat. Cool and refrigerate until ready to use or for up to 4 days.

❯ Preheat the oven to 350°F.

❯ Arrange the orange slices in a large roasting pan; place the Cornish hens on top, skin side up. Brush the hens with the sauce. Cover the pan tightly.

❯ Bake in the center of the preheated oven for 45 minutes. Uncover, baste with the sauce, and bake for 20 minutes more.

Makes 8 servings.

COMMENTS

*To butterfly a Cornish hen, use a pair of kitchen shears. Cut the hen down one side of the backbone and through the ribs. Make an identical cut on the opposite side to remove the backbone completely; discard (or reserve for stock). Place the bird cut-side down (skin side up) and flatten with the heel of your hand; use both hands if you need to apply extra pressure.

This sauce is a wonderful accompaniment to Miami or spare ribs. Brush onto the ribs; bake for about 2 hours, basting every 30 minutes.

back to the grind

To see a demo, go to **kosherscoop.com/video**

Best Burgers Ever

Try to ensure your beef is as fresh as possible. The mushrooms add great texture and taste. Sorry, but there ain't no comparing homemade to frozen burgers. These are in a league of their own.

2	portobello mushrooms, cleaned		1	tsp ground parsley flakes
1	onion		½	tsp garlic powder
2½	lb good quality lean ground beef		½	tsp freshly ground black pepper
2	large egg whites		¼	tsp salt
1	Tbsp ketchup			

> Pulse the mushrooms and onion in the bowl of a food processor fitted with the metal "S" blade until finely chopped. Place all of the remaining ingredients into a large bowl. Add the mushroom mixture. Mix together gently and then gently shape into 6 to 8 patties.

> Preheat the grill to high. Place the burgers on the grill; cook for about 4 minutes per side for medium. Don't overcook them or they will dry out. Let sit for 6 to 8 minutes before serving.

Makes 6 to 8 servings.

COMMENTS

Do not move the burgers on the grill until they are ready to be flipped. It's best to leave them in one place to cook evenly.

Lamb Burgers

Chef David Blum of Hartmans meat store in Toronto demonstrated how to make these awesome burgers during a cooking class series organized by Kosher Scoop. All the attendees had a great time and the delicious burgers were a big hit. Visit kosherscoop.com to watch Chef David demonstrate.

3	lb ground lamb meat*		2	tsp garlic, minced
2	Tbsp fresh cilantro, chopped			Kosher salt and freshly
2	tsp fresh rosemary, chopped			ground black pepper, to taste
2	tsp onion powder			

> Mix all of the ingredients together just until combined. Form loose 3" patties, taking care not to press/squash them too much.

> Preheat a barbecue to medium-high. Place the patties on the grill; cook without moving or jiggling the patties around the grill for 5 minutes, with the lid open. Flip the patties over. Reduce the heat to medium and close the lid. Cook for 4 to 5 minutes or until the patties are no longer pink inside. Closing the grill top after you flip the burgers allows the resulting steam to cook the inside of the burger.

> Serve on a lightly toasted bun with your favorite condiments and sliced grilled vegetables.

Makes 12 servings.

COMMENTS

*The recipe calls for lamb meat but we used 80% lean ground beef and 20% lamb fat for the same great burger. Ask your butcher for some lamb fat since you probably won't find it on the shelves. If you are using pure beef or lamb, make sure it's not too lean or the burger will be dry and crumbly.

Hickory Hamburgers

The secret to these delicious burgers is smoked paprika, which gives them a wonderful hickory flavor.

3	slices bread
1	large egg
½	small onion, finely grated
3	Tbsp ketchup
1	tsp smoked paprika

1	heaping tsp dried parsley
	Kosher salt and freshly ground black pepper
1	lb ground chicken
1	lb ground beef

› Preheat the grill to medium-high heat.

› Remove the crusts from the bread and let the bread soak in a bowl of water for 5 minutes. Strain the water out and squeeze the bread to release any extra water.

› Place the bread in a large bowl along with the egg, grated onion, ketchup, herbs and spices, mixing until well combined. Mix in the ground meats until just combined.

› Shape into loose 3" patties. Grill on the preheated grill, turning once, for about 8 minutes or until the patties are no longer pink inside.

Makes 8 servings.

COMMENTS

I love experimenting with spices and herbs. This recipe is the perfect example of how one small teaspoon of a particular spice can alter the whole flavor of a recipe. Spices and herbs are the perfect way to add creativity to your cooking. A bit of dried thyme in your soup, some basil in your roasted vegetables and rosemary in your potatoes...a little bit goes a long way.

New Meatloaf

Meatloaf is an old classic where you basically can't go wrong. There is actually nothing "new" about this meatloaf. It's just how I dubbed it for my files, to differentiate it from my old one. I made it this "new way" once and my kids told me they liked it better. Okay, out with the old, in with the new. A new classic.

1	shallot
3	springs fresh dill
1	clove garlic
3	slices pastrami
1	lb ground beef
½	cup panko crumbs
2	large eggs
1	tsp Kosher salt
½	tsp freshly ground black pepper
4–5	large onions, sliced
1	cup sweet 'n sour duck sauce

❯ Preheat the oven to 350°F.

❯ Finely chop the shallot, dill, garlic and pastrami in the bowl of a food processor fitted with the metal "S" blade. Transfer the mixture to a bowl; add the ground beef. Stir in the panko crumbs, eggs, salt, and pepper.

❯ Place the sliced onions in the bottom of a 13" x 9" glass baking dish.

❯ Shape the meat into a loaf. Arrange on top of the sliced onions. Cover tightly with aluminum foil.

❯ Bake in the center of the preheated oven for 1 hour. Uncover; brush with the duck sauce. Bake, uncovered, for 35 to 40 minutes or until cooked through.

❯ Slice and serve with the onions.

Makes 6 to 8 servings.

Classic Beef Lasagna

In this classic meat lasagna, ground beef joins forces with ground veal for a spectacular taste sensation. The celery seed in the tomato sauce perks it up while the addition of cooked spinach lightens the entire dish. If you like, you can substitute puréed squash for the spinach. Simply boil or roast 4 cups cubed squash. When tender, purée in the food processor. Season to taste with salt and pepper before adding to lasagna.

2	Tbsp olive oil
12	oz ground beef
8	oz ground veal
1	each onion, carrot (peeled) and celery stalk, chopped
4	cloves garlic, minced
2	tsp each dried oregano and dried basil
1	tsp Kosher salt
¼	tsp celery seed
	pinch each freshly ground black pepper and hot pepper flakes
1	Tbsp granulated sugar
1	can (28 oz) tomatoes, chopped
1	can (14 oz) tomato sauce
12	lasagna noodles
2	bunches (10 oz each) baby spinach, trimmed and washed

> In a large saucepan or Dutch oven, heat the oil over medium-high heat. Add the beef and veal; cook, stirring often, for about 10 minutes or until the beef and veal are no longer pink inside. Transfer to a plate. Spoon off all but 2 Tbsp of oil. Add the onion, carrot, celery and garlic; cook, stirring, for 3 minutes. Stir in the oregano, basil, salt, celery seed, pepper and hot pepper flakes. Stir in the sugar. Return the beef to the pot, adding the tomatoes and tomato sauce. Bring to a boil. Reduce the heat and simmer gently for 30 minutes or until thickened.

> Meanwhile, in a very large pot of boiling salted water, cook the lasagna noodles for 8 to 10 minutes or until tender but firm. Drain; chill under cold running water. Arrange in a single layer on a damp tea towel.

> With the water still clinging to the leaves, cook the spinach in a skillet set over medium-high heat for 3 minutes or until wilted. Drain well, squeezing out any excess water.

> Preheat the oven to 350°F.

> Spread 1½ cups of the meat sauce onto the bottom of a 13" x 9" baking dish. Layer with 3 of the lasagna noodles. Spread 2 cups of the meat sauce evenly over the noodles. Layer again with 3 noodles. Spread the spinach evenly over the noodles. Layer again with three noodles. Cover with 2 cups of the meat sauce. Repeat the noodle and meat sauce layers one more time. Cover the top with the remaining 1½ cups of sauce.

> Bake in the center of the preheated oven for 35 to 40 minutes or until bubbling and heated through. Let the lasagna rest for 10 minutes before cutting into servings.

Makes 8 servings.

Spicy Meat Sauce for a Crowd

This recipe takes a few minutes to throw together in the morning. Cook up your favorite pasta at dinnertime and serve. You will need a 5-quart slow cooker to fit all the ingredients, but you can halve it successfully, if you prefer. I make the full recipe and freeze it in batches for up to 3 months for future dinners. I also like to use canned tomato sauces which are seasoned with herbs, to add an extra kick of flavor.

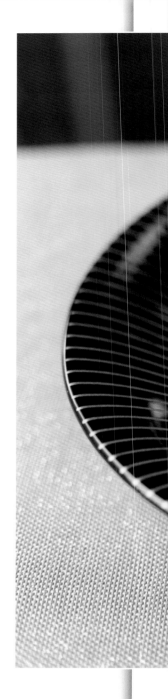

1	Tbsp oil
1	large onion, finely chopped
4	cloves garlic, minced
1	green pepper, seeded and diced, optional
3	large, spicy sausages or hot dogs, diced into very small pieces
2	lb ground beef
2	cans (28 oz each) diced tomatoes
2	cans (5½ oz each) tomato paste
2	cans (20 oz each) tomato sauce
½	cup chicken soup or broth
½	cup dry red wine
1	Tbsp packed light brown sugar
2	tsp dried basil
1	tsp dried oregano
2	bay leaves
1	tsp Kosher salt, or to taste
1	tsp freshly ground black pepper, or to taste

❯ Heat the oil in a large skillet set over medium heat. Add the onion, garlic and green pepper, if using, and sauté until just lightly browned.

❯ Add the sausage and ground beef. Cook, breaking up any lumps with a potato masher, for about 10 minutes or until the meat is browned.

❯ Preheat the slow cooker to medium. Transfer the meat mixture to the slow cooker. Stir in the remaining ingredients, mixing until well combined. Cook for 6 to 8 hours or until tender. Remove the bay leaves before serving.

❯ Serve with your favorite pasta and top with freshly chopped basil or parsley leaves.

Makes 12 to 14 servings.

COMMENTS

I like to serve this sauce with fettuccine ricci, a great pasta I found at my supermarket that looks like a very narrow version of lasagna noodles.

This recipe can easily be made in a large pot on the stove top. After browning the meat, add the remaining ingredients and cook, covered and stirring occasionally, for 30 minutes. Remove the bay leaves before serving.

Eye of London Broil with Red Onion Marmalade

This juicy pan-fried steak, topped with a sweet and tangy red onion mixture, is an easy and delicious dish. You can serve this "marmalade" with any grilled steak or even burgers for a gourmet touch.

3	Tbsp oil
3	red onions (about 1 lb), thinly sliced
1	Tbsp vinegar
1	Tbsp dry red wine
3	Tbsp light brown sugar
1	tsp salt
1	eye of London Broil (1½ lb)
¼	tsp coarsely ground pepper

❯ Heat 2 Tbsp of the oil in a large, non-stick skillet set over medium heat. Add the onions and cook, stirring occasionally, for 15 to 20 minutes or until tender. Stir in the vinegar, wine, brown sugar and ½ teaspoon of the salt. Reduce the heat and simmer for 5 minutes. Spoon the red onion marmalade into a small bowl; keep warm. (Marmalade can be refrigerated for up to 3 days.)

❯ Wash the skillet and wipe dry. Sprinkle the meat with the remaining ½ teaspoon of salt and the pepper. Heat the remaining 1 Tbsp of oil in the skillet set over medium-high heat. Add the steak and cook 6 to 8 minutes per side for medium-rare or until desired doneness.

❯ Slice steak and serve with red onion marmalade.

Makes 4 to 6 servings.

Fruity Moroccan Chicken

You may have to dig into the back of your spice cabinet for this recipe, or do some updates, but it's totally worth it! I bought these skewers pre-made at my local butcher shop, and I was determined to find a way to make them myself. They're great for a Yom Tov day meal, as they can be assembled easily and take almost no time to cook. They are absolutely delicious served over quinoa, couscous or rice.

½	cup prunes
½	cup dried apricots
3	boneless, skinless chicken breasts or 6 pieces boneless chicken legs
	oil, for brushing
	Kosher salt, for sprinkling

Spice Mixture:

2	tsp ground ginger
2	tsp ground cumin
2	tsp sweet paprika
1	tsp cinnamon
1	tsp turmeric
1	tsp ground coriander
½	tsp crushed red pepper flakes
3	Tbsp extra virgin olive oil
	juice of ½ lemon
3	Tbsp (approx) water

❯ Soak the prunes and dried apricots in a small bowl of hot water.

❯ Meanwhile, cut the chicken into bite-size pieces. Combine all of the ingredients for the spice mixture in a mixing bowl, adding a bit more water if it's too thick; it should be easy to brush onto the chicken.

❯ Preheat the grill to high. Drain the dried fruit. Alternating fruit and chicken, thread onto skewers. Brush the kabobs lightly with oil and sprinkle with salt.

❯ Grill the skewers on the preheated grill for 4 minutes. Turn over and brush with the spice glaze. Cook for about 5 minutes—brushing again a minute or two before it's done for an even stronger flavor-until the chicken is no longer pink inside.

Makes 4 servings.

COMMENTS

These can be done on an outside grill, but for holidays or during the winter months I do it on my grill pan. If you are using wooden skewers, soak them in water for about 20 minutes before assembly to prevent burning.

Estee's Favorite Brisket

This recipe is the culmination of many brisket trials over many years. I tried so many different versions and somehow, always come back to this one, which works every time.

4	**Tbsp oil**
1	**double brisket (about 4 lb)**
6–8	**large onions, sliced**
6	**cloves garlic, coarsely chopped**
4	**Tbsp blending flour, divided**
2	**cups dry or semi-sweet red wine**
2–3	**bay leaves**
1–2	**Tbsp packed light brown sugar, depending on the sweetness of the wine**
1	**Tbsp dry mustard**
	freshly ground black pepper, to taste
	Kosher salt, to taste

〉 Preheat the oven to 325°F.

〉 Heat 2 Tbsp of the oil in a large Dutch oven set over medium-high heat. Add the brisket and brown on both sides for 3 to 4 minutes per side. Remove the meat and set aside.

〉 Remove the Dutch oven from the heat. Arrange the onions and garlic on the bottom of the pot. Mix in 3 Tbsp of the blending flour until the onion mixture is well coated. Add the wine, bay leaves and brown sugar.

〉 Combine the mustard and remaining 1 Tbsp flour in a small bowl. Rub the top and sides of the meat with the flour mixture. Cover with the remaining 2 Tbsp oil, smearing it onto the meat to create a paste. Sprinkle generously with freshly ground black pepper and season generously with Kosher salt.

〉 Cover and bake in the center of the preheated oven for about 1½ hours or until very soft. Remove the bay leaves. Let the meat cool to room temperature. Refrigerate overnight or until thoroughly cooled.

〉 Skim off the fat, if desired. Transfer the meat to a cutting board. Cutting against the grain, slice the meat to desired thickness. Return the meat to the pan, covering it with gravy. Reheat in a 300°F oven for at least 1 hour or for up to 2 hours.

Makes 10 to 12 servings.

To see a demo, go to **kosherscoop.com/video**

Saucy Savory Ribs

I don't know about the rest of the world, but in my hometown, English-cut ribs are very popular. It's basically flanken cut in the wrong direction, so like flanken the ribs become soft and tender.

1	bottle (750 mL) red wine
2	Tbsp oil
6	English-cut or short ribs, trimmed
	Kosher salt, for sprinkling
1	tsp freshly ground black pepper
10	cloves garlic, peeled
8	large shallots, peeled, trimmed, rinsed, and halved
2	carrots, peeled, cut into 1" lengths
2	stalks celery, cut into 1" lengths
2	Tbsp grated fresh horseradish, optional (but recommended)
1	leek, white and light green parts only, coarsely chopped
6	sprigs fresh flat-leaf parsley
2	sprigs fresh thyme
2	bay leaves
	freshly ground white pepper, to taste
2	Tbsp tomato paste
8	cups chicken or beef broth

> Pour the wine into a saucepan set over medium-high heat. Bring to a boil; boil gently until reduced by half. Remove from the heat.

> Preheat the oven to 350°F.

> Heat the oil in a Dutch oven or a roasting pan large enough to hold 6 ribs, set over medium-high heat. Season the ribs all over with salt and the black pepper. Add the ribs to the pot, in batches if necessary, and sear for 4 to 5 minutes on each side or until well browned.

> Transfer the browned ribs to a plate. Remove all but 1 Tbsp of fat from the pot; lower the heat to medium. Add the vegetables, herbs and white pepper to taste. Cook, stirring, for 5 to 7 minutes or until lightly browned. Stir in the tomato paste and cook for 1 minute to blend.

> Add the reduced wine, browned ribs and broth to the pot. Bring to a boil.

> Bake in the center of the preheated oven, tightly covered, for about 2½ hours or until the ribs are tender enough to be easily pierced with a fork. Every 30 minutes or so, lift the lid and skim and discard any fat that has bubbled up to the surface.

> Carefully transfer the meat to a serving platter with a lip and keep warm. Boil the pan juices until they thicken and are reduced to approximately 4 cups. Season with salt and pepper and pass through a fine mesh strainer; discard any remaining solids.

> Pour the sauce over the meat, serve and enjoy.

Makes 6 servings.

Roast Duck with Orange-Cherry Sauce

I don't make duck often and I always feel like it needs something more than just a plain old bake in the oven. When I mentioned my hesitations to my sister-in-law, she insisted that I call her cousin who makes duck "like nobody else."

There's nothing like calling your sister-in-law's cousin for a random recipe, but I did it, and I'm glad I did. The sauce can be used for chicken, white fish, or turkey (and it goes really well with vanilla ice cream, too — I tried it!).

1	whole duck
1	Cortland or Granny Smith apple, peeled
1	orange, peeled
	Kosher salt and freshly ground black pepper, for sprinkling
1	clove garlic, crushed
2	Tbsp apricot jam
1	cup orange juice
1	cup sweet white or pink wine
½	cup apple juice

Cherry Sauce:

1	can (15 oz) sour cherries
½	cup orange juice
⅓	cup apricot jam
2	Tbsp fruit liqueur
2	tsp freshly squeezed lemon juice
¼	cup granulated sugar
2	Tbsp potato starch or cornstarch, dissolved in ¼ cup cold water

❯ Preheat the oven to 400°F.

❯ Wash the duck and pat dry with paper towels. Place in a 13" x 9" roasting pan and place the apple and orange into the cavity. Sprinkle the skin with salt and pepper and rub the entire surface with the garlic. Spread the jam evenly over the skin. Cover well and bake in the center of the preheated oven for 1 hour.

❯ Remove the pan from the oven. Pour out all of the liquid. Add the orange juice, wine and apple juice. Cover well. Lower the oven temperature to 325°F and bake for 1½ hours. Uncover and bake for 20 more minutes.

❯ Meanwhile, make the sauce. Combine all of the sauce ingredients in a pot. Bring to a simmer, stirring occasionally, and cook until thickened. You may want to break the cherries up while stirring.

❯ Serve the sauce alongside the duck.

Makes 4 to 6 servings.

For every matter there is an appointed time and season [KOHELET 3:1]

SEASONS

Fingers curled around a large, warm mug, **HOT STEAM,** *white frost.* SMOOTH BUTTERNUT SQUASH, *slow-cooked ribs,* **THICK, CREAMY TOMATO SOUP.** Neat rows of proud tulips, **rhubarb compote,** *glistening berries,* **the smell of rain.** SOLDIER-STRAIGHT GREEN ASPARAGUS, fresh, sweet peas with lemon zest and cream. *HOMEMADE STRAWBERRY SHORTCAKES.* Sizzling hot grills, **ice-cold lemonade,** JUICY, DRIPPING PEACHES. **Fiery-red sunsets, sprinkles atop a cone of vanilla ice cream.** *MAPLE SYRUP,* yellow, orange, crimson. Apples, leaves, pumpkin pie. Nutmeg, **FLORIDA ORANGES,** *onion soup with mounds of melted cheese,* **woolen mittens.** Time flies.

on the
SIDE

Pumpkin Bowls with Wild Rice

A fun way to use the best of the season's bounty! When I saw these adorable little pumpkins sitting in bushels, I just couldn't leave them there. I baked one to see if it was even edible and it turned out to be delicious and so easy to scoop out the flesh. They make fantastic bowls for any grain you favor.

12	**baby pumpkins, approximately fist-sized**

Rice Medley:

½	**cup dried cherries**
1	**cup boiling water**
4	**tsp oil**
1	**Vidalia onion, finely chopped**
2	**cups rice blend (I like Lundberg Wild Blend)**
	Kosher salt and freshly ground black pepper, to taste
1	**scallion, finely chopped**
	zest of 1 lemon

> Preheat the oven to 350°F.

> Place the pumpkins on a cookie sheet. Bake in the center of the preheated oven for 20 minutes. Remove from the oven and let cool. Cut off the tops and scoop out the seeds, creating a bowl for the rice mixture.

> Rice medley: Soak the cherries in the boiling water. Meanwhile, heat the oil in a large saucepan set over medium heat. Add the onion; cook until softened. Add the rice, stirring until coated with the oil. Add as much water as directed on the package. Season with salt and pepper. Bring to a boil. Lower the heat and simmer, covered, for 40 minutes or until the rice is almost finished cooking. Add the soaked cherries with about ¼ cup of the water they were soaking in. Cook until the rice is completely tender. Stir in the scallions and lemon zest.

> Fill the pumpkin cavities with the rice mixture. Rewarm all together on a cookie sheet, or serve at room temperature.

Makes 12 servings.

Fingerling Potatoes

For this recipe I like to use an old-fashioned mustard, one that has whole mustard seeds in it. If you cannot find it, just use Dijon mustard and add 1 Tbsp of mustard seeds.

2	lb fingerling potatoes
1	bulb fennel

Dressing:

¼	cup old-fashioned Dijon mustard
¼	cup extra virgin olive oil
1	clove garlic, minced
2½	Tbsp white wine (preferably sweet)
1	Tbsp vinegar
1	Tbsp ground white horseradish
½	tsp Kosher salt
½	tsp freshly ground black pepper

❯ In a large pot of boiling, salted water, cook the potatoes for about 20 minutes or until cooked through but not too soft. Drain and cool

❯ Dressing: Whisk together all of the dressing ingredients until well combined; set aside.

❯ Shave the fennel crosswise with a peeler to create very thin strips.

❯ Gently toss the potatoes and fennel with the dressing until the vegetables are well coated.

Makes 6 to 8 servings.

Have you ever taken a stroll down the condiment aisle in a large supermarket? The variety of mustards is staggering. This recipe was inspired by good, old-fashioned grainy mustard which I just couldn't leave sitting all by its lonesome self on the shelf. Other favorites are sweet chili or "sweet heat" Russian and horseradish mustard. Let the flavors inspire you on your next trip to the grocery store.

Crunchy Sweet Potato Fries

This is a side dish that goes with any kind of meal. It's an anytime-dish that was very well received around here.

1	bag (1.65 lb) sweet potato fries		1	tsp paprika
	or 3 sweet potatoes cut into strips		½	tsp dried rosemary
	(resembling french fries)		1	tsp Kosher salt
½	cup panko crumbs		1	large egg white
1	tsp ground cumin		1	Tbsp oil

> Preheat the oven to 425°F. Lightly grease a large baking sheet.

> Combine the panko crumbs, cumin, paprika, rosemary and salt in a bowl, mixing until well combined.

> In a large bowl, beat the egg white vigorously with a fork until frothy. Whisk in the oil. Stir in the sweet potato fries. Sprinkle with the crumb mixture, tossing until the potatoes are well coated.

> Transfer the potatoes to the prepared baking sheet. Sprinkle with any remaining crumbs. Bake in the center of the preheated oven for about 15 minutes or until the edges of the fries begin to brown. Serve warm or at room temperature.

Makes about 6 servings.

Spicy BBQ Corn

Before we went to the cottage last year, my sister bought a large container of Montreal steak spice from Costco. We were sprinkling it on everything the whole summer, but it was especially tasty on fresh, sweet corn on the cob. Follow the cooking method below for a delicious treat.

8–10	ears of sweet corn
2	Tbsp light olive oil
1	Tbsp Montreal steak spice
1	tsp honey

> Peel off all but 1 or 2 layers of the corn husks. Pull the remaining husks down but not off each ear of corn. Remove as many of the silk strands as you can (the rest will come off easily after they char). Pull up the husks; tie with a strip of husk if you like.

> Preheat the grill to high. Grill the corn, covered and turning often, for about 8 minutes or until completely tender.

> Meanwhile, whisk together the oil, Montreal steak spice and honey in a small bowl.

> Just before serving, peel off the husks and brush with the Montreal steak spice mixture. Return to the grill for 1 minute, just to give it an extra toasting. Serve immediately.

Makes about 6 servings.

Medley of Mushrooms

Mushrooms are a delicious side dish any time of year. They go with just about anything, and the wine in this dish complements both fish and poultry exceptionally well. The thyme gives it that gourmet flair.

2	Tbsp olive oil
1	lb mixed mushrooms (shiitakes, cremini and white button mushrooms), chopped
2	cloves garlic, minced
3	Tbsp shallots, finely chopped
	Kosher salt and freshly ground black pepper
	splash balsamic vinegar
¼	cup dry sherry or white wine
1	Tbsp each fresh thyme and fresh flat-leaf parsley, chopped

❯ Heat the oil in a sauté pan set over medium-high heat. Add the mushrooms, garlic and shallots. The mushrooms will absorb all of the oil. Sprinkle with salt and pepper. Cook, stirring gently with a wooden spoon, for 2 to 3 minutes or until the mushrooms start to release their moisture and begin to shrink. Cook for 5 minutes, stirring infrequently, until the mushrooms start to brown.

❯ Add the wine; cook until evaporated. Stir in the thyme and parsley; cook for 30 seconds.

❯ Garnish with additional fresh thyme and parsley right before serving

Makes 6 to 8 servings.

If necessary, use 1 tsp of dried thyme in place of fresh.

Fried Couscous Cakes

Daphna wrote this original and tasty recipe for a Hanukkah story. A reader sent in an enthusiastic email, commenting that if I ever write another book, I should be sure to include this recipe. Michelle, this is for you.

A wonderful, grainy alternative to potato latkes, these take virtually minutes to put together since couscous itself takes only five minutes to steam.

1	Tbsp vegetable oil
6	scallions, chopped
1⅓	cups chicken stock
1¼	cups couscous
¼	cup fresh flat-leaf parsley, chopped
¼	tsp each salt and pepper
2	large eggs, lightly beaten
	vegetable oil

❯ Heat the oil in a saucepan set over medium heat. Add the scallions; cook, stirring, for 3 minutes. Pour in the chicken stock. Bring to a boil. Stir in the couscous. Cover and remove from the heat. Let stand for 5 minutes. Fluff with a fork. Stir in the parsley, salt and pepper and then the eggs.

❯ Heat about ¼" of oil in a large, non-stick skillet set over medium-high heat. Using a ¼ cup measure, scoop out the couscous, patting it into the measuring cup. Add it to the pan, flattening slightly into a cake-like shape. Fry for 3 to 5 minutes per side or until golden brown. Transfer to paper towel-lined racks to drain slightly. Serve warm.

Makes 4 servings.

Grilled Vegetable Skewers

Cut a variety of your favorite vegetables into bite-size chunks. Thread onto skewers, alternating colors and variety. In a bowl, whisk together ¼ cup olive oil, 1 Tbsp balsamic vinegar, 1 tsp each of dried basil and oregano and 2 cloves garlic, minced. Season to taste with salt and pepper. Grill the skewers over medium heat, turning often and basting with the balsamic dressing, for about 6 minutes or until charred and softened.

Of course, choose the vegetables you and your family prefer, but don't forget about more seldom used ones such as pearl onions (which will need to be blanched), eggplant, fennel, radishes, zucchini, peppers and cherry tomatoes.

Honey Balsamic Rice

I love this for a Yom Tov meal, when you prepare all the parts in advance and then put them together right before warming up the dish. Your best bet, of course, is to put up a fresh pot of rice.

1	onion, sliced
2	stalks celery, sliced
1	lb button mushrooms, sliced

Dressing:

2	Tbsp honey
4	tsp balsamic vinegar
1	tsp salt
1	cube frozen garlic, thawed
	Pinch pepper
2	cups raw rice, cooked according to package directions

⟩ Sauté the onion in a large, non-stick skillet set over medium-high heat for about 5 minutes or until slightly golden. Add the celery and mushrooms and sauté another 5 to 7 minutes or until vegetables are softened. Remove from the heat and set aside.

⟩ Mix together the dressing ingredients in a large serving bowl. Stir in the warmed vegetables and rice, tossing gently until rice is well coated.

Makes 12 servings.

Roasted Asparagus with Creamy Lemon Dressing

Preheat the oven to 400°F. Peel **asparagus stalks**; cut off and discard the hard woody base and tips. (If using white asparagus, leave whole.) Arrange on a parchment paper-lined cookie sheet. Drizzle with **extra virgin olive oil** and sprinkle with **Kosher salt** and **freshly ground black pepper**. Roast for 8 to 10 minutes or just until the stalks begin to soften. Meanwhile, combine ½ cup low-fat mayonnaise, the zest of 1 lemon, 1 tsp lemon juice, 1 tsp of granulated sugar and 1 tsp of water as well as ½ tsp vinegar in a bowl, mixing until well combined. Drizzle over the warm asparagus.

Herbed Couscous in Tomatoes

This simple recipe is a great combination of summery flavors. You can serve the couscous in the tomato as shown, or just make the salad recipe and serve with any meal.

6　tomatoes
　　extra virgin olive oil, to coat

Couscous salad:

1	cup couscous	8–10	fresh chives, chopped
1⅛	cups boiling water	½	lemon, juiced
2½	tsp extra virgin olive oil	1	clove garlic, minced
½	tsp Kosher salt		(or 1 cube frozen garlic)
¼	cup fresh flat-leaf parsley leaves, chopped		Kosher salt and freshly ground
¼	cup fresh basil leaves, chopped		black pepper, to taste

〉 Preheat the grill to medium heat.

〉 Slice the tops off of the tomatoes. Cut away the inside of each tomato, scooping out the inner flesh and seeds. Rub the tomatoes with the oil.

〉 Grill on the preheated grill, turning once, just until softened. Set aside.

〉 Stir together the couscous, boiling water, oil and salt in a large bowl. Cover and let sit for 10 minutes. Fluff with a fork. Stir in all of the remaining ingredients, mixing until well combined.

〉 Spoon the salad into the tomato "bowls" and serve warm or at room temperature.

Makes 12 servings.

NOODLE KUGLES...
tradition with a twist

Cabbage & Noodle Kugel

One day, as I was making cabbage and noodles (nothing like the good ol' classics), I thought to myself that I haven't ever seen a recipe for a cabbage and noodle kugel. Well, here it is...ladies and gentlemen, once again, a new twist on an old, beloved classic...I don't think it ever took me this many tries to perfect a kugel recipe. I hope you really like it.

5	Tbsp oil
1	lb shredded green cabbage
3	leeks, white and light green part only
	or 2 Vidalia onions, finely chopped
1	tsp granulated sugar
1	package (12 oz) egg noodles, fine or medium width
4	large eggs
1	large egg yolk
⅔	cup granulated sugar
⅔	cup oil
¼	cup fresh breadcrumbs
1	tsp Kosher salt
¼	tsp freshly ground white pepper

❯ Heat 4 Tbsp of the oil in a very large shallow pot set over low heat. Add the cabbage and leeks; cook, stirring, for 20 minutes. Stir in the 1 tsp of sugar. Cook, stirring occasionally, for about 25 minutes or until the vegetables are tender and caramelized.

❯ Preheat the oven to 450°F.

❯ In a large pot of boiling salted water, cook the egg noodles for 5 minutes. Drain and rinse under cold running water. Transfer to a bowl; toss with 1 Tbsp of the oil to prevent the noodles from sticking together.

❯ Stir together the eggs, yolk, ⅔ cup of the sugar, ⅔ cup oil, breadcrumbs, salt and white pepper in a bowl. Stir in the noodle and cabbage mixture. Grease 2 9"-round pans or 1 12-cup muffin or cupcake tin (you may need more). Pour in the noodle mixture.

❯ Bake in the center of the preheated oven for 15 minutes. Reduce the oven heat to 350°F. Bake 30 minutes more for muffins, or 45 minutes more for 9"-rounds.

Makes 12 servings.

Maple Noodle Kugel

The truth is that I wasn't going to include this recipe in the book because we already had the cabbage and the onion kugels, both of which are knockouts. My friend Dassi insisted, saying, "It's a simple one that everyone will love." The sweet mellow flavor of maple syrup gives this classic noodle (lokshen) kugel a subtle new taste.

1	package (12 oz) fine egg noodles
4	large eggs
½	cup oil
½	cup granulated sugar
¼	cup fresh bread crumbs
¼	cup maple syrup, plus extra for brushing
2	tsp vanilla sugar
1	tsp Kosher salt
½	tsp cinnamon, plus more for sprinkling
¼	tsp freshly ground white pepper

❯ Preheat the oven to 350°F.

❯ In a large pot of boiling salted water, cook the noodles for 5 to 6 minutes or until *al dente*. Drain and rinse. Cool slightly.

❯ Place all of the remaining ingredients into a bowl and mix well.

❯ Add the noodles to the egg mixture, mixing well.

❯ Transfer the noodle-egg mixture to a 9"-round pan and sprinkle the top lightly with cinnamon.

❯ Bake in the center of the preheated oven for 50 minutes.

❯ If you like an additional maple syrup taste, as we do, brush the top of the kugel generously with maple syrup while it is still hot. The maple syrup seeps through the kugel giving it a wonderful flavor. Serve warm.

Makes 8 servings.

Three creative classics

Onion-Noodle Kugel

In my quest for creativity I turned my sweet and peppery noodle kugel into a delicious onion-noodle kugel. The addition of the fried onions really brought this dish up a notch to serve up some wonderful flavor and was still in keeping with the traditional Shabbat noodle kugel.

¼	cup oil
1	large sweet onion, diced
4½	cups water
1	cup granulated sugar
¼	cup trans fat free margarine (½ stick)
2	tsp salt

½	tsp freshly ground black pepper, or to taste
1	bag (12 oz) thin noodles
2	large eggs
3	Tbsp light brown sugar
3	Tbsp oil

> Preheat the oven to 350°F. Grease 2 standard loaf pans or a Bundt pan.

> Heat the ¼ cup of oil in a large skillet set over medium heat. Add the onion and cook for 20 minutes or until softened and just beginning to brown

> Meanwhile, bring the water, sugar, margarine, salt and pepper to a boil in a saucepan. Remove from heat; add the noodles. Let the noodles sit until softened and all of the water has been absorbed. Let cool slightly.

> Stir the eggs, brown sugar and 3 Tbsp of oil as well as the sautéed onion into the noodles. Mix well and pour into prepared loaf pans or Bundt pan. Bake in the center of the preheated oven for 1½ hours or until the top is golden brown.

Makes 10 to 12 servings.

This recipe was inspired by a great big pile of radishes that my mother had left over after a Passover seder. It is my family's custom to dip a radish into salt water during "karpas" and there were lots remaining this particular year. I had read something about roasting radishes and, while I wasn't hopeful, I reasoned it couldn't hurt to try. Wow!! What a transformation. The radishes completely lost their sharpness turning into a mellow, earthy, not to mention gorgeous side dish. Now we buy extra radishes on purpose...all year long.

Roasted radishes can be a great addition to any leafy salad or stir fry. Don't hesitate to serve them as delicious side dish on their own.

Roasted Radishes

1	bunch radishes, about 12
1	Tbsp olive oil
1	tsp dried thyme
	Kosher salt and freshly ground black pepper, to taste
¼	lemon
1	Tbsp fresh flat-leaf parsley, finely chopped

> Preheat the oven 400°F.

> Wash and cut the radishes into quarters, removing any unwanted stems.

> Place the radishes on a parchment paper-lined baking sheet. Drizzle with the olive oil, thyme, salt and pepper.

> Roast in the center of the preheated oven for about 20 minutes or until the edges are starting to brown. Remove from the oven and squeeze the lemon over the radishes. Transfer the radishes to a bowl. Add the parsley and serve warm or at room temperature.

Makes 4 servings.

Also known as yucca or tapioca, the cassava is a root vegetable with a wonderful, nutty flavor that is similar in taste and texture to chestnuts. It is a fantastic alternative to potatoes.

Cassava Cubes

2	large cassava roots, peeled and sliced into long chunks or strips
	olive oil
	Kosher salt, to taste
	freshly ground black pepper, to taste
1	Tbsp dried rosemary, or to taste

> Bring a large pot of salted water to a boil. Add the cassava pieces and cook, uncovered, for about 5 minutes or until the cassava has softened slightly. Drain and let cool. When the cassava is cool enough to handle, cut into bite-size chunks.

> Heat a thick layer of oil in a large skillet set over medium-high heat. Add the cassava chunks; sprinkle generously with salt, pepper and rosemary. Cook, stirring occasionally, for 8 to 10 minutes or until slightly browned. Serve warm.

Makes 6 to 8 servings.

Caramelized Ginger Carrots

This dish boasts a wonderful combination of flavors that is sure to enhance any chicken or meat entrée. The carrots are sweet and sticky while the ginger adds just a bit of heat.

4–5	large carrots, peeled
3	pears, peeled, pitted and cut into small wedges
½	cup olive oil
½	cup + 2 Tbsp granulated sugar
¼	cup orange juice
2	tsp minced fresh ginger
½	tsp Kosher salt

> Preheat the oven to 400°F.

> Using the slicing blade of a food processor or a mandoline, evenly slice the carrots.

> Place the carrots and remaining ingredients in a large Ziploc™ bag and shake well to thoroughly combine. Grease a baking sheet and empty the contents of the bag onto it, in a shallow, even layer.

> Bake in the center of the preheated oven for 35 minutes. Remove the carrots from the oven, stir them around and bake for 5 to 10 more minutes. Serve warm or at room temperature.

Makes 4 to 6 servings.

Okra with Chunky Tomatoes

Be careful not to overcook the okra, as it is best served vibrant green and slightly crunchy. Serve this dish warm as a side, or at room temperature as a salad.

2	Tbsp oil
1	yellow onion, finely diced
1	can (14.5 oz) diced tomatoes
1	Tbsp granulated sugar
1	Tbsp dried basil
½	tsp freshly ground black pepper
1	lb fresh okra, washed and trimmed

> Heat half of the oil in a large skillet set over medium heat. Add the onion; cook, stirring, for about 3 minutes or until softened. Add the tomatoes, sugar, basil and pepper. Reduce heat to medium-low; cook, stirring, for 10 to 15 minutes or until most of the juices evaporate. You will have a chunky tomato sauce.

> Meanwhile, heat the remaining oil in a wok or large skillet set over medium-high heat. Add the okra and stir-fry for 2 to 3 minutes or until the green color brightens. Immediately stir the okra into the chunky tomatoes. Serve warm.

Makes 6 to 8 servings.

Roasted Mini Peppers with Basil-Walnut Pesto

If you cannot find those adorable mini peppers, simply cut large ones into bite-size cubes. You can also add 2 or 3 zucchini (sliced) for even more variety. Mrs W. wrote, "Thank you for this outstanding recipe. When I made it last Passover, my son asked me to make it more often. He said, 'Mom, this was worth coming home for.'"

1	lb assorted mini colorful peppers
½	cup pearl onions, peeled
2	Tbsp oil
	Kosher salt and freshly ground black pepper, to taste

Basil-Walnut Pesto:

1	cup fresh basil leaves
½	cup shelled whole walnuts
¼	cup flat-leaf parsley, lightly packed
1	small clove garlic, optional
	Kosher salt and freshly ground black pepper, to taste
¼	cup olive oil

> Basil-Walnut Pesto: Place all of the pesto ingredients except for the oil in the bowl of a food processor fitted with the metal "S" blade and pulse until the ingredients are combined. With the machine running, slowly pour in the oil and process until a paste forms.

> Preheat the oven to 425ºF.

> Place the peppers and pearl onions on a well-greased baking sheet. Toss with the oil. Sprinkle with salt and pepper. Roast in the center of the preheated oven for 12 to 15 minutes or until the peppers' skins start to blacken.

> Cool the peppers slightly. Transfer to a serving bowl; stir in the desired amount of pesto. Serve warm or at room temperature.

Makes 6 servings.

Stuffed Mushrooms

I love recipes like this one. It has a gourmet feel without being complicated at all. The combination of walnuts, mushrooms and red wine is divine.

17	large crimini mushrooms, approx
2	Tbsp olive oil
1	cup whole walnuts, shelled
3	Tbsp Passover crumbs or Panko crumbs
2	Tbsp fresh flat-leaf parsley, chopped
½	tsp Kosher salt
½	tsp freshly ground black pepper
1	Tbsp red wine (dry or sweet)
	oil, for drizzling

> Preheat the oven to 425°F.

> Remove the stems from the mushrooms by gently pulling them out. In the bowl of a food processor fitted with the metal "S" blade, pulse the stems and 5 mushrooms until they are the size of large crumbs. Transfer to a bowl.

> Heat 1 Tbsp of the oil in a large sauté pan set over medium-high heat. Add the remaining whole mushrooms and cook for about 5 minute or until just softened.

> Meanwhile, pulse the walnuts and Pesach crumbs in the bowl of the food processor until they are the size of crumbs. Transfer to the bowl with the mushroom mixture, mixing in the parsley, salt, pepper and red wine.

> Spoon about 1 Tbsp of the mixture into the cavity of each of the remaining whole mushrooms. Place on a well-greased baking dish, stuffing side up. Drizzle the remaining oil over the mushrooms and bake in the center of the preheated oven for 15 minutes.

Makes 12 servings.

Inspired Sides

Similar ingredients, a creative addition and twist in flavoring: two magnificent side dishes.

Parsnip and carrots combine to create a beautiful side dish that is both tasty and sweet. I love roasting vegetables, which highlights and then intensifies their natural flavors while simultaneously accentuating their inherent sweetness. The addition of fennel seed adds an extra dimension of unexpected flavor.

4	carrots, peeled
4	small parsnips, peeled
1	Tbsp vegetable oil
1	Tbsp fennel seed
	sea salt and freshly ground black pepper
¼	cup fresh flat-leaf parsley, chopped

> Preheat the oven to 400°F.

> Slice the carrots and parsnips into thin coins that are thick enough to not furl or fold easily. Transfer to a bowl.

> Toss the carrots and parsnips with the olive oil. Stir in the fennel seed, salt and pepper.

> Arrange in a single layer on a parchment paper-lined cookie sheet. Roast in the center of the preheated oven for about 35 minutes, stirring once halfway through, or until the edges begin to brown.

> Cool for 5 minutes. Toss the parsley into the mixture. Serve warm or at room temperature.

Makes 4 to 6 servings.

I added fennel to my ultimate, favorite side dish, along with some balsamic vinegar and honey...and voila, a new favorite was born!!

1	large fennel bulb, halved and sliced
1	lb carrots, peeled and cut into 2" lengths
1	lb parsnips, peeled and cut into 2" lengths
2½	cloves garlic, minced
2½	Tbsp olive oil
2½	Tbsp balsamic vinegar or freshly squeezed lemon juice
2½	Tbsp maple syrup
1	sprig fresh thyme (or ½ tsp dried)
	Kosher salt and freshly ground black pepper

> Preheat the oven to 400°F.

> Arrange the fennel, carrots, parsnips and garlic in a single layer on a parchment paper-lined cookie sheet. Drizzle with the olive oil, vinegar and maple syrup. Sprinkle with salt and pepper to taste. Tuck the thyme into the vegetables.

> Roast, uncovered, in the center of the preheated oven, stirring for about 45 minutes or until edges the begin to brown. Stir once to redistribute,

Makes 6 servings.

COUNTER CAKES

INSPIRED BY

The small things that make a big difference.

Blueberry Poppy Bundt Cake

This cake will be dairy if you use milk. For a pareve version, substitute the milk with soy milk or lite coconut milk. If using frozen blueberries (only during the winter months please!), place them in a colander and run them under cold water for a few seconds, in order to remove any excess juice. Lay them out on a paper towel for a few minutes to absorb the moisture. Then, make sure you fold in the blueberries with a light hand. This will be helpful in preventing the batter from turning purple.

3	cups all-purpose flour
2½	cups granulated sugar
1½	tsp baking powder
	pinch salt
1⅓	cups oil, plus more for brushing
¾	cup orange juice
¾	cup whole milk or soy milk (see above)
3	large eggs
1½	Tbsp poppy seeds
1½	tsp lemon extract
1½	tsp vanilla
1¼	cups blueberries, fresh or frozen

❯ Preheat the oven to 350°F. Grease a 10- or 12-cup Bundt cake pan with baking spray.

❯ Whisk together the flour, sugar, baking powder and salt in a large bowl.

❯ Combine the oil, orange juice, milk, eggs, poppy seeds, and lemon and vanilla extracts in the bowl of an electric mixer fitted with the paddle attachment; beat on medium speed until combined. Gradually beat in the flour mixture until well combined. Fold the blueberries into the batter with a rubber spatula.

❯ Pour the batter into the prepared Bundt pan and bake in the center of the preheated oven for 60 to 70 minutes or until golden on top and a toothpick inserted in the center comes out clean. Remove to a rack to cool completely. Once cooled, unmold.

Makes 12 servings.

Chocolate Chip Butter Pound Cake

This cake has a wonderful buttery flavor, with a touch of chocolate. Sometimes I wonder why I even bother making any other recipes, because there ain't nothing like butter!

1	**cup unsalted butter, at room temperature (2 sticks)**
1½	**cups granulated sugar**
3	**large eggs**
2	**cups all-purpose flour**
2	**tsp baking powder**
½	**cup milk**
2	**tsp vanilla**
1	**cup mini chocolate chips**

❯ Preheat the oven to 350°F. Grease a 10- or 12-cup Bundt cake pan with baking spray.

❯ Cream together the butter and sugar in the bowl of an electric mixer fitted with the paddle attachment until light and fluffy.

❯ Add the eggs, one at a time, beating well after each addition.

❯ Mix together the flour and baking powder. Reduce the speed of the mixer to low. Alternating between the flour mixture and the wet ingredients, beat in the remaining ingredients, mixing until just combined. Mix in the chocolate chips until just combined.

❯ Pour the batter into the prepared pan. Bake in the center of the preheated oven for 1 hour or until a toothpick inserted in the center comes out clean. Remove to a rack to cool completely. Once cooled, unmold.

Makes 12 servings.

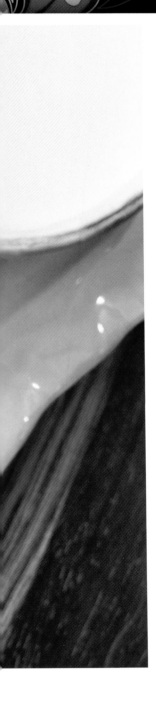

Deborah's Chocolate Cake

This cake gets better with age, though up to a limit, of course. The truth is, I really wouldn't know since the cake never lasts longer than two days in my home. This is one of those recipes that travelled from neighbor to friend and back to another neighbor and I was very happy when it landed, in the form of a cake, on my doorstep, a present from my cousin, Deborah.

1¾	**cups all-purpose flour**
2	**cups granulated sugar**
¾	**cup unsweetened cocoa powder, sifted**
1½	**tsp baking powder**
1½	**tsp baking soda**
¼	**tsp salt**
2	**large eggs**
1	**cup soy milk or any unflavored pareve milk substitute**
½	**cup oil**
2	**tsp vanilla**
1	**Tbsp coffee granules, dissolved in 1 cup boiling water**

Icing:

1	**cup confectioners' sugar**
3	**Tbsp hot water**
3	**Tbsp unsweetened cocoa powder, sifted**
3	**Tbsp oil**

❯ Preheat the oven to 350°F. Grease a 10- or 12-cup Bundt cake pan with baking spray.

❯ Place all of the ingredients, in the order in which they are listed, in the bowl of an electric mixer fitted with the paddle attachment. Mix until combined.

❯ Pour the batter into the prepared Bundt pan. Bake in the center of the preheated oven for 50 minutes or until a toothpick inserted in the center comes out clean. Remove to a rack to cool for 5 minutes. Invert the cake onto a plate. Remove the pan. Let cool completely.

❯ Whisk together all of the icing ingredients together in a bowl. Pour the icing over the cooled cake, letting any excess drizzle down the sides.

Makes 12 servings.

Coconut Bundt Cake

There is story to this cake as well. I was shopping in an upscale food shop (I always love to see what unique products I will find there) when I chanced upon a piña colada syrup. I love the flavor of piña colada, and I haven't been able to find a syrup with kosher certification for some time now. Well, of course I brought it home, and this cake was born a few weeks later. I know coconut-flavored sweets can be a topic of hot debate with very strong opinions about either loving or hating the flavor of coconut. I have to say I am a very strong pro-coconut advocate, so this cake is one of my favorites.

2½	cups all-purpose flour, plus more for dusting
2	tsp baking powder
½	tsp Kosher salt
½	cup unsalted butter or trans fat free margarine, at room temperature (1 stick)
1¾	cups granulated sugar
¾	cup oil
6	large eggs
1	tsp vanilla
1	tsp coconut extract
1	cup orange juice
½	cup flaked sweetened coconut

Tropical Glaze:

2	cups confectioners' sugar
3	Tbsp piña colada syrup (or pineapple juice)
1	tsp very hot water

❯ Preheat the oven to 350°F. Grease a 10- or 12-cup Bundt cake pan with baking spray.

❯ Whisk together the flour, baking powder and salt in a small bowl.

❯ Cream together the butter and sugar in the bowl of an electric mixer fitted with the whisk attachment or electric beaters. Add the oil and beat for 5 minutes or until the color lightens.

❯ Beat in the eggs, one at a time, beating well after each addition. Beat in the vanilla and coconut extracts. Beat in the orange juice until combined. Slowly beat in the dry ingredients until the mixture is smooth. Add the coconut flakes and mix just until combined.

❯ Pour the batter into the prepared pan. Bake in the center of the preheated oven for 60 to 70 minutes or until a toothpick inserted in the center comes out clean. Remove to a rack to cool for 5 minutes. Then invert the cake onto a separate rack; remove the pan. Let cool completely.

❯ Tropical Glaze: Whisk together the sugar, syrup and hot water in a bowl, just until smooth.

❯ Once the cake has cooled, ladle the glaze over the cake. Top with additional flaked coconut, if desired. Let the glaze set before serving.

Makes 12 servings.

Vanilla Nectarine Cake

The nectarines on my counter were begging to be used. I love nectarines and I did a little jig in the fruit store when they finally made their appearance this spring. I think I may have been a tad over-enthusiastic, as I had a bunch leftover that were getting a bit soft. This cake was born as a result and, I must say, it's scrumptious. It just sings of summer. I use a product called ground vanilla beans to get the lovely vanilla flavor and scent into the cake. You can actually see the small black flecks in the picture. You can also scrape the inside of a fresh vanilla bean for the same effect, or, if all else fails, use vanilla extract. I buy the vanilla bean powder online from Bakto flavorings. I highly recommend it.

4	small nectarines
	juice of 1 lemon
¼	cup granulated sugar

Cake:

½	cup trans fat free margarine or unsalted butter, at room temperature (1 stick)
¼	cup oil
1⅓	cup granulated sugar
1½	cups all-purpose flour
1	tsp baking powder
½	tsp salt
¾	tsp ground vanilla bean or 1 tsp vanilla (see above)
4	large eggs

❭ Peel the nectarines (they don't have to be perfect!). Cut each one in half and then into thin slices. Combine them with the lemon juice and sugar in a bowl. Macerate for 30 minutes or for up to 3 hours.

❭ Preheat the oven to 350°F. Place an oven rack in the lower third of the oven. Butter and flour a 9" x 5" x 3" non-stick loaf pan.

❭ Beat together the margarine, oil and sugar on high in the bowl of an electric mixer fitted with the whisk attachment until the mixture becomes fluffy and turns a pale-yellow color.

❭ Meanwhile, combine the flour, baking powder and salt in a bowl. Add to the beaten margarine, along with the ground vanilla beans or extract. Add the eggs, one at a time, beating well after each addition, until just incorporated.

❭ Pour half of the mixture into the prepared pan. Drain the nectarines if any juices have accumulated. Arrange the nectarines in a single layer on top of the batter. Pour the remaining batter over the fruit.

❭ Bake in the center of the preheated oven for about 1 hour or until a cake tester inserted into the center of the cake comes out clean. Cool in the pan on a wire rack for 20 minutes. Remove the cake from the pan and cool completely on a wire rack.

Makes 12 servings.

Marble Pound Cake

The coffee in this recipe adds a rich intensity to the chocolate flavor. This cake is so simple to throw together and is always a family favorite! In fact, it's so easy to make, I think it will become your favorite as well. There are many versions of this cake out there but I couldn't, in all "food consciousness," write a section on counter cakes and leave this one out.

2	**cups granulated sugar**
2	**cups all-purpose flour**
1	**cup oil**
2	**tsp baking powder**
	pinch Kosher salt
1	**tsp vanilla**
6	**large eggs**
2	**tsp coffee granules**
2	**Tbsp boiling water**
¼	**cup unsweetened cocoa powder, sifted**
¼	**cup chocolate syrup**

❯ Preheat the oven to 350°F. Grease a 12-cup Bundt pan with baking spray.

❯ Place the first 7 ingredients in the bowl of an electric mixer fitted with the paddle attachment. Mix until all the ingredients are well combined.

❯ Dissolve the coffee granules in the boiling water in a separate bowl. Stir in the cocoa powder and the chocolate syrup. Stir 1 cup of the batter into the chocolate mixture, mixing until well combined.

❯ Pour the remaining white batter into the prepared pan. Drop chocolate batter over white batter and swirl gently with a knife to combine, about 5 to 6 strokes. Bake in the center of the preheated oven for 1 hour. Remove to rack to cool for 5 minutes. Invert the pan onto a plate and remove the pan. Let cool completely.

Makes 12 servings.

Moist Banana Cake

Do you always have soft, brown bananas at home? It certainly seems like we do because I make this cake so often. Whenever I don't want to bake, I stick the overripe bananas in the freezer. When I need them, I simply defrost them in a bowl for 1 hour and peel them, they are ideal for baking.

1½	cups granulated sugar
1	cup oil
4	large eggs
2	Tbsp orange juice
2	tsp vanilla
1½	cups mashed banana (or 2 very large bananas)
1½	cups all-purpose flour
1½	cups whole-wheat pastry flour
2	tsp baking powder
½	tsp baking soda
½	tsp cinnamon
¼	tsp ground cardamom
½	tsp Kosher salt
1	cup semi-sweet chocolate chips or half chocolate and half caramel chips
½	cup walnuts, finely chopped, optional

Lemon Glaze:

¾	cup confectioners' sugar
2	Tbsp freshly squeezed lemon juice
½	tsp vanilla

Chocolate Glaze

½	cup confectioners' sugar
3	Tbsp unsweetened cocoa powder, sifted
1½–2	Tbsp brewed coffee or water as needed

❯ Preheat the oven to 350°F. Grease a 10- or 12-cup Bundt cake pan with baking spray.

❯ Whisk together the sugar, oil, eggs, orange juice and vanilla in a large bowl, until smooth. Stir in the mashed bananas. In a separate bowl, mix together the flours, baking powder, baking soda, cinnamon, cardamom, salt, chocolate chips and walnuts, if using. Fold the dry ingredients into the batter and blend well.

❯ Pour the batter into the prepared pan and bake in the center of the preheated oven for 55 to 70 minutes (depending on the pan you have used), or until the cake springs back when gently pressed. Remove to a rack and cool for 10 minutes. Invert onto serving plate; remove the pan. Let cool completely.

❯ Lemon or Chocolate Glaze: In a bowl, stir together the confectioners' sugar with the other ingredients, adding water as required to achieve a thick but pourable glaze. Spoon or drizzle the glaze onto the cooled cake.

Makes 12 servings.

Jubilant Jelly Doughnut (Sufganiyot) Bundt

On kosherscoop.com, we have been running a series of contests where our readers can submit their best-ever recipes in a chosen category. Our team of judges reviews the submissions and selects a winner. This cake was the Best-Ever Bundt Cake Winner. Although not typically a counter cake, it's so wonderful and unique that I couldn't leave it out.

This delectable cake is perfect for Chanukah, during which foods are fried in oil to commemorate the miracle that happened thousands of years ago. Donuts ("sufganiyot" in Hebrew) are a traditional, fried food but this cake takes the tradition one step further by layering small, filled donuts that bake gloriously into a single cake.

1	cup milk, warmed	¼	cup unsalted butter, melted
1	pkg (¼ oz) rapid rise yeast	3	Tbsp orange juice
1	cup + 3 Tbsp granulated sugar, divided	1	Tbsp orange liqueur (such as Sabra™)
3	cups bread flour		
1	tsp Kosher salt	1	tsp cinnamon
¼	cup oil		confectioners' sugar
¼	cup seedless red raspberry preserves	½	tsp vanilla

⟩ Grease a 12-cup Bundt pan with baking spray.

⟩ Pour the warm milk into the bowl of an electric mixer fitted with the dough hook*. Sprinkle with the yeast and the 3 Tbsp of sugar. Stir to combine. Let the mixture sit for 5 minutes.

⟩ Add the flour, salt and oil. Beat on low speed until a ball of dough forms. Knead on low speed for 5 minutes, until the dough is smooth and elastic. Let rest for 10 minutes.

⟩ Divide the dough in half. Roll each half into a 2"-thick log. Cut each log into 10 to 12 pieces. Flatten each piece of the dough with your fingers; place ½ tsp of the preserves into the center of each dough round and fold the dough over the preserves to form a ball. Pinch the dough together to seal.

⟩ Meanwhile, combine the melted butter, orange juice, liqueur and vanilla in a small bowl. In another small bowl, combine the remaining 1 cup of sugar and cinnamon. Dip each ball of filled dough first in the butter mixture and then in the cinnamon-sugar, rolling to coat. Place in the prepared Bundt pan, creating two layers of balls. The second layer of balls should rest above the empty spaces between the balls of the first layer. Cover with plastic wrap and let rest at room temperature for 45 minutes.

⟩ Preheat the oven to 350°F.

⟩ Uncover the Bundt pan. Bake in the center of the preheated oven for 30 to 35 minutes or until the dough appears golden. Remove to a rack to cool for 15 minutes. Run a rubber spatula around the edges and center of the pan. Invert the cake onto a serving plate. Sprinkle with confectioners' sugar.

⟩ This cake is best served warm from the oven. If not serving immediately, wrap tightly in foil and heat in a 300°F oven for 5 to 10 minutes or until warm.

Makes 12 servings.

*This may also be done by hand. Stir together the ingredients in a large mixing bowl until dough is formed. Turn out onto a lightly- floured surface and knead for 5 to 10 minutes until dough is smooth and elastic. Proceed as above.

Vanilla Bean Apple Bundt Cake

I recently came across a vanilla cane sugar with actual vanilla bean seeds in it. It is so far superior to artificially flavored vanilla sugar that I decided to use it as the main flavoring in this recipe. If you cannot find this sugar, take a vanilla bean, cut a slit on one side, and use a sharp knife to scrape out the seeds inside. Combine the seeds with 1½ cups of granulated sugar, mixing together well. Submerge the opened vanilla pod in the sugar as well. It's heavenly. Let the mixture sit for 24 hours. You cannot compare the taste of this sugar to that of fake vanilla sugar.

6	McIntosh apples, peeled, cored and quartered
¼	cup vanilla sugar (see above)
1½	Tbsp freshly squeezed lemon juice
½	tsp cinnamon

Cake:

1	cup + 2 tbsp oil
2	cups granulated sugar
5	large eggs
2	Tbsp pure apple or orange juice
3	cups all-purpose flour
3½	tsp baking powder
½	tsp salt

❯ Preheat the oven to 325°F. Grease a 10- or 12-cup Bundt cake pan with baking spray.

❯ Slice the apples very thinly, using the slicing attachment of a food processor. Place them in a bowl. And the vanilla sugar, lemon juice and cinnamon. Let sit for 20 minutes

❯ Cake: Mix together the oil and sugar in the bowl of a standing mixer fitted with the whisk attachment. Add the remaining ingredients and mix until well combined.

❯ Place 1 cup of the batter in the bottom of the prepared Bundt cake pan. Layer about ⅓ of the apple mixture on top of the batter. Pour on another thin layer of batter, add another layer of apples. Layer the batter and apples one more time, but make sure there is at least a thin layer of batter covering the top layer of apples.

❯ Bake in the center of the preheated oven for 1 hour. Remove the cake to a wire rack. Let the cake sit in the pan for about 5 minutes and then turn it upside down onto a plate, removing the Bundt pan. Let cool completely.

Makes 12 servings.

Pecan Crunch Cake

This recipe went through many a metamorphosis from its original version to what it is now. The truth is, it's always delicious, but the addition of rum, coconut and ginger make it just that little bit more interesting.

Pecan Crunch:

½	cup packed light brown sugar
2	Tbsp all-purpose flour
1½	tsp cinnamon
1	tsp ground ginger
5	Tbsp oil
⅓	cup pecans, chopped
¼	cup shredded sweetened coconut

Cake:

3	large eggs
1¼	cups granulated sugar
¾	cup oil
½	tsp vanilla
2½	cups all-purpose flour
1½	Tbsp baking powder
½	tsp salt
¾	cup orange juice
1	tsp rum extract

〉 Preheat the oven to 350°F. Grease a 10- or 12-cup Bundt cake pan with baking spray.

〉 Pecan Crunch: Mix all of the ingredients together in a bowl; set aside.

〉 Place all of the cake ingredients, in the order in which they are listed, in the bowl of an electric mixer fitted with the paddle attachment. Mix until combined.

〉 Pour one third of the batter into the bottom of the prepared Bundt pan. Cover with half of the pecan crunch. Repeat the layers once, ending with the batter.

〉 Bake in the center of the preheated oven for 55 minutes or until a toothpick inserted in the center comes out clean. Remove to a rack to cool for 5 minutes. Invert the cake onto a serving plate; remove the pan. Let cool completely.

Makes 12 servings.
Variation: Omit the ginger and replace the rum extract with vanilla extract.

SPECIAL OCCASIONS

Milestones to celebrate, **pride of accomplishment,** **A TOAST!** Flying confetti, colorful streamers, party hats. BLOW OUT THE CANDLES, songs of cheer and laughter, **MEANINGFUL WORDS.** *Years fly by,* **building together.** DAD'S FAVORITE STEAK, beer in buckets of ice, *tiny hors d'oeuvres to savor.* Caramel popcorn, chocolate cake with pink flowers, bunches of balloons in crazy colors. A moment of reflection, FRIENDS GATHERED CLOSE, **happy wishes to all.** Make a wish.

the grand
FINALE

DESSERTS

Tropical Fruit Fritters

I made these one year for the shul Chanukah party and have been making them ever since upon request. Something tells me I won't be getting off too easily this year either.

Batter:

2	cups all-purpose flour
3	Tbsp granulated sugar
2	tsp baking powder
1	tsp cinnamon
½	tsp salt
2	large eggs
1	cup coconut milk
1	cup water
1½	Tbsp oil
	canola oil for frying
1	pineapple, cut into bite-size chunks
3	bananas, cut into bite-size pieces

> Combine all of the dry ingredients in a large bowl. Whisk in the eggs, coconut milk, water and oil, mixing until there are no lumps.

> Fill a deep fryer or a wok with 5" of oil. Heat the oil to 350°F.

> Using a wooden skewer, spear 2 to 3 pieces of the pineapple or banana. Dip into the batter, making sure each piece is well coated. Using a second skewer to help slide the fruit off the first skewer, drop the fruit into the hot oil. Cook, turning over halfway through, for about 3 minutes or until all sides are golden brown.

> With a slotted spoon, remove to paper towels to drain. Repeat with the remaining fruit.

> Dust with confectioners' sugar and cinnamon, if desired.

Makes 25 to 30 fritters.

COMMENTS

As with most fried foods, fritters are best served fresh.

A few days before this year's Chanukah party, I received an email from one of the shul members requesting the "pineapple fried things" I had served the year before. I went out and bought a large deep fryer. This was getting serious! ☺

Baked Apples with Maple Sauce and Walnut Crunch

These baked apples are worthwhile just for the smell they produce. This is a great Friday night or cold winter evening dessert.

6	**Granny Smith apples**
½	**cup raisins, dried cranberries or dried currants**
⅓	**cup packed light brown sugar**
1	**tsp cinnamon**
½	**cup maple syrup**
¾	**cup apple cider**
1	**cinnamon stick**

Walnut Crunch:

⅓	**cup packed light brown sugar**
⅓	**cup old-fashioned rolled oats**
1	**Tbsp all-purpose flour**
¼	**tsp cinnamon**
	pinch salt
2	**Tbsp butter or margarine, melted**
2	**Tbsp walnuts or pecans, chopped**

❯ Peel the top third of each apple. Core halfway down the center. Mix the raisins, cranberries or dried currants, 2 Tbsp of the brown sugar and the cinnamon in a small bowl and fill each cavity with the mix.

❯ Place the apples in a slow cooker. Pour the maple syrup over the apples. In another bowl, dissolve the remaining brown sugar in the cider. Pour into the slow cooker as well. Place the cinnamon stick in the liquid.

❯ Cover and cook on low for about 3 hours or until the apples are soft. Keep warm until ready to serve. Top with some sauce and a spoonful of walnut crunch.

❯ Walnut Crunch: Preheat the oven to 325°F. Mix together all of the ingredients and spread out on cookie sheet. Bake in the center of the preheated oven for 20 minutes, stirring once.

Makes 6 servings.

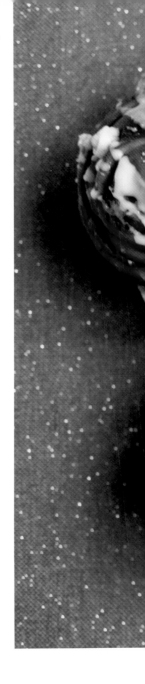

Chocolate Babke

My roots are Hungarian. Most of them anyway. It's a crazy thing, but I can't write a cookbook without including a great babke recipe. It just wouldn't feel complete. In my previous books, I included chocolate, cinnamon and cheese babkes all delicious, very popular recipes. This babke is a result of some improvements made to my previous recipes, with a whole new filling. It's a creamy, rich filling that spreads beautifully. I added a hazelnut-chocolate spread to add yet another dimension of flavor. A good quality chocolate spread can work, too. One thing I do know – babkes are not just for those of Hungarian descent. They are a favorite with everyone.

Dough:

3	cups water
2	cups granulated sugar
4	Tbsp active dry yeast
5	lb all-purpose flour
2	cups light grape juice
1	cup oil
½	cup trans fat free margarine at room temperature (1 stick)
2	large eggs
6	large yolks
	pinch salt
1	tsp oil + more for brushing

Filling:

1	cup oil
½	cup trans fat free margarine, softened (1 stick)
1¼	cups unsweetened cocoa powder, sifted
3½	oz semi-sweet chocolate, coarsely chopped
2½	cups confectioners' sugar
1½	cups hazelnut-chocolate spread or nut free chocolate spread
1	large egg

Egg Wash:

1	egg
1	Tbsp warm water

❯ Dough: Place the water, sugar and yeast in the bowl of an electric mixer that is large and strong enough to handle 5 lb of flour, fitted with the dough hook. Let the yeast proof for 10 minutes or until frothy.

❯ Add all of the remaining ingredients, (excluding the tsp of oil) leaving the salt for last. Knead for 8 to 10 minutes on medium-high speed.

❯ Place about 1 tsp of oil in the center of a large bowl. Transfer the dough to the bowl and flip it to completely coat with the oil. Cover with plastic wrap and let rise in a warm, draft-free area for 1 hour.

❯ Meanwhile, make the filling: Place the oil, margarine, cocoa powder. and chocolate in the bowl of a food processor fitted with the metal "S" blade. One at a time, add the remaining ingredients, blending well after each addition. Blend until smooth; set aside.

❯ Preheat the oven to 350°F. Grease eight 8"-round cake pans or disposable round fluted pans, or 8 loaf pans.

❯ Transfer the dough to a work surface. Divide the dough into 8 equal-size pieces. On a floured surface, roll out each piece as thinly as possible into a large rectangle; brush surface liberally with oil. Spread generously with one-eighth of the filling. Roll up very tightly into a log. Bring both ends of

each roll together and twist several times to form a babke.

> Transfer the babkes to the prepared pans. Let rise in a warm, draft-free area for 1 hour.
> Stir together the egg and water for an egg wash; brush over the risen babkes.
> Bake in the center of the preheated oven for 45 minutes.

Makes 8 babkes.

COMMENTS

Have fun and be creative with your babkes. To make babke flowers, slice the log into 2½" pieces. Place the pieces on their sides in parchment paper cups. Let rise as directed in the recipe. Bake for 35 minutes.

Jazzed-Up Bread Pudding

I am so excited about this recipe. There is something so rustic and enticing about bread pudding (especially when there is a whole challah left over from Shabbat to use). I incorporate unusual flavors, like orange and cardamom, and even the most conservative of my guests loved the combination.

1	**medium challah**
5	**large eggs**
1	**cup + 3 Tbsp granulated sugar**
½	**cup oil**
1	**pkg (3.3 oz) instant vanilla pudding**
4	**Granny smith/Gala apples, peeled, cored and thinly sliced**
1	**Tbsp cinnamon**
¾	**tsp ground cardamom**
2	**tsp grated orange zest**
½	**cup raisins or dried cherries**

❯ Peel or cut away the crust from the challah. Tear the challah into large pieces and soak in a large bowl of water for 30 minutes. Discard the water. Squeeze out any remaining water by pushing the wet challah against a colander.

❯ Preheat the oven to 350°F. Grease a 13" x 9" baking pan (or grease 16 4-oz ramekins).

❯ Transfer the challah to a large bowl. Add the eggs, 1 cup of the sugar, oil and pudding mix, mixing well.

❯ Stir in the apples, spices, orange zest and raisins.

❯ Transfer the mixture to the prepared pan or ramekins. Sprinkle with the remaining 3 Tbsp of sugar.

❯ Bake in the center of the preheated oven for 1 hour or until golden.

❯ Serve with warm pancake or maple syrup.

Makes 16 servings.

COMMENTS

I often serve this dish Friday night. I keep maple or pancake syrup in a double boiler on a hot plate and it keeps warm. Spoon the syrup over warm, fragrant cakes. Fantastic!

Doughnut Holes

As usual, I had left the annual shul Chanukah party preparations to the last minute. Well, really the last day. It was a busy time of year, with the kids off from school and my cousin's wedding taking place that week. So, with the party the next day, it was time to finalize the menu. I realized that I hadn't really thought about dessert, as it was to be the usual, highly requested pineapple fritters (see page 289) but today, the day before the chaos, the creative cook in me was a bit unhappy with serving the same dessert for three years running. I looked over my list and realized that store-bought doughnuts were included. The creative cook within me fought with my voice of reason—and won. I am happy to report that making doughnut holes for dessert, drizzling them with hot chocolate sauce and serving them with caramel ice cream and fresh blueberries, pomegranate arils and physalis was not only easier than I thought, it was also so incredibly GOOD that the adventure was a true triumph. Even my rational, organized and sane side had to reluctantly admit that it was a success. I made the dough the night before, covered it with plastic wrap and let it rise overnight in the fridge. About two hours before the party, I took the dough out of the fridge to reach room temperature. The deep fryer that I use exclusively at this time of year made frying the holes a real cinch. The kids shaped the balls and when we were ready for them, we threw them into the fryer and they cooked in only a few minutes. A quick assembly line got 40 portions out within a few minutes. I would do it again anytime, but just in case you are too sane or realistic to fry at your own party, I don't blame you for thinking that way...but you're invited over any time! ☺

This recipe came from my great aunt-Ada, who "has the best doughnut recipe ever." These doughnuts are light and airy, and the secret is the alcohol in the dough. Her mother told her that it prevents the oil from being overly absorbed. Thank you, Aunt Ada, for sharing your mother's recipe with me, and I hope you all enjoy these as much as the guests at our party did.

¼	cup warm water
1	pkg active dry yeast, or 1 oz
2	tsp granulated sugar
½	cup trans fat free margarine (1 stick)
6	cups all-purpose flour
¾	cup granulated sugar
1	large egg
1¾	cups boiling water
1	tsp vanilla sugar
	zest of ½ a lemon
	pinch salt
1½–2⅓	Tbsp whiskey
	oil, for frying

Topping:

1	cup confectioners' sugar, sifted
⅛	tsp ground nutmeg

❭ Place the water, yeast and 2 tsp sugar into the bowl of an electric mixer fitted with the dough hook and let stand for 10 minutes. Meanwhile, pour the boiling water over the margarine in a bowl, stirring until the margarine is melted. (If it doesn't fully melt, microwave on high for 20 seconds.) Let cool slightly.

❭ Add the melted margarine mixture and all of the remaining ingredients to the yeast mixture, mixing until a dough forms. Cover the bowl with plastic wrap. Let rise in a warm, draft-free area for 1 hour.

> Transfer the dough to a work surface. Shape the dough into small balls, about the size of a walnut. Transfer the balls to a greased cookie sheet. Cover with a damp cloth and let rise for 30 minutes.

> Meanwhile, preheat oil to 365°F. The key to good doughnuts is keeping the oil at a consistent temperature, so a deep-fry thermometer is highly recommended. The temperature of the oil can vary from 360°F to 375°F.

> In batches, add the doughnut holes to the oil; fry each doughnut hole for about 3 minutes, turning once, halfway through, or until golden. Remove with a slotted spoon to paper towels to cool slightly.

> Combine the confectioners' sugar with the nutmeg. While still warm, roll the doughnut holes in the sugar. Serve immediately.

Makes 36 doughnut holes.

Sweet Squash Muffins

Pumpkin pie spice is a blend of nutmeg, cinnamon, cloves, and allspice, which gives this muffin a warm, spicy undertone. I discovered sweet potato squash (also known as delicata squash) this winter while writing my monthly "Cooking Quest" column and I was hooked. It's great as a side dish on its own but pairs beautifully with sweet desserts as well.

2	sweet potato squash or 1 acorn squash

Topping:

¼	cup pecans, chopped
1	Tbsp dark brown sugar
1	tsp cinnamon

Muffin Batter:

¾	cup whole-wheat flour
¾	cup all-purpose flour
1	tsp baking powder
½	tsp baking soda
½	tsp salt
1	tsp pumpkin pie spice
2	large eggs
⅓	cup oil
1	cup packed dark brown sugar
1	generous cup cooked squash (from above-listed squash)

〉 Preheat the oven to 350°F. Slice the squash in half lengthwise and place, cut side down, on a parchment paper-lined baking sheet. Bake in the center of the preheated oven for 45 minutes.

〉 Remove from the oven. Scrape out the seeds and discard. Scrape out the flesh and place into a bowl. Set aside to cool.

〉 Line a muffin tin with paper cups.

〉 Topping: Combine all of the topping ingredients in a bowl. Set aside.

〉 Muffin batter: Combine all of the batter ingredients in a large bowl in the order in which they appear. Mix well to combine.

〉 Spoon the batter into the prepared muffin cups. Sprinkle evenly with the topping. Bake in the center of the preheated oven for 20 minutes or until golden.

Makes 12 servings.

COMMENTS

To prepare as a side dish, cut squash in half, brush the cut sides with some oil, and place cut side down on a parchment paper-lined baking sheet. Bake in a preheated 375°F for about 30 minutes or until tender. Scoop out the interior flesh, transfer to a serving bowl and enjoy in as an alternative to mashed potatoes. Try jazzing it up with a sprinkling of pumpkin pie spice on top.

Chocolate Maple Treats

These muffins (or petit fours) are legendary in Toronto, thanks to my friend who so graciously submitted this recipe. It was one of our most popular reader-generated recipes, and when you taste it, you'll know why. I like to garnish these treats with a crunch, easily purchased at most major supermarkets.

2	cups granulated sugar
1¾	cups all-purpose flour
¾	cup unsweetened cocoa powder, sifted
1½	tsp baking powder
1½	tsp baking soda
1	tsp salt
2	large eggs
1	cup milk (or non-dairy creamer)
½	cup oil
2	tsp vanilla
1	cup boiling water

Topping:

¾	cup confectioners' sugar
2	Tbsp oil
1	Tbsp water
⅛	tsp maple extract
	pinch salt

〉 Preheat the oven to 350°F. Lightly grease 12 muffin tins or line with paper cups.

〉 Combine all of the dry ingredients in a mixing bowl. Add all of the wet ingredients, except for the water, mixing well. Stir in the boiling water until thoroughly incorporated.

〉 Spoon the mixture evenly into the prepared muffin tins.

〉 Bake in the center of the preheated oven for 22 to 25 minutes or until the tops of the cakes spring back when lightly pressed. Remove the muffin tins to a rack to cool completely.

〉 Topping: Combine all of the ingredients in a bowl and stir until smooth. Pour over the cooled muffins.

Makes 12 muffins.

Better
with
BERRIES

Healthy Blueberry Pie

There's nothing like a pie made with fresh summer fruit. While frozen berries may be good as a stand-in, try to use fresh when possible. This is also a perfect recipe for health-conscience people who enjoy good food. I've replaced the usual crumb topping with a healthier granola option and call for an oil-based crust, rather than one using saturated fat.

Pie Crust:

2	**cups all-purpose flour**
½	**cup oil**
¼	**cup orange juice**
1	**large egg**
½	**cup granulated sugar**
¼	**tsp salt**

Blueberry Filling:

5	**cups blueberries**
½	**cup granulated sugar**
¼	**cup cornstarch**
¼	**cup water**

Topping:

1½	**cups Maple Granola (see page 70) or granola of your choice, preferably with pecans**

> Preheat the oven to 375°F.

> Place all of the ingredients for the pie crust in the bowl of a food processor fitted with the metal "S" blade; pulse just until a dough comes together. Remove and knead with your hands a few times until a smooth dough is formed. Cover in plastic wrap until ready to use.

> Roll out the dough very carefully between 2 pieces of parchment paper into a 12" circle. Transfer to a 10" pie dish, gently applying pressure along the sides of the dish and closing all the gaps. (If you have too much dough, discard the rest or save for another recipe.) Pierce the bottom with the prongs of a fork. Bake in the center of the preheated oven for 20 minutes or until the edges begin to brown.

> Meanwhile, place the blueberries in a deep saucepan set over low heat. Add the sugar and cornstarch and mix until the blueberries are well coated. Pour in the water and cook for about 10 minutes or until the blueberries are just starting to soften. Remove from heat.

> Pour the filling into the baked pie shell and sprinkle with granola. Lower the oven temperature to 350°F. Bake for 15 minutes. Serve at room temperature or warm with a scoop of vanilla ice cream.

Makes 8 servings.

Summer Strawberry Shortcake

We enjoy this lemon pound cake recipe all year long. The addition of strawberries and cream gives it that perfect summer touch. I often use this recipe to make cupcakes as well. See note below.

4	large eggs
1½	cups granulated sugar
2½	cups all-purpose flour
1	Tbsp baking powder
1	lemon, zested
1	cup oil
¾	cup orange juice
2	tsp lemon extract

Cream:

1	lb frozen strawberries
2	tubs (each 8 oz) dessert whip
½	cup confectioners' sugar
1	Tbsp vanilla sugar

❯ Preheat the oven to 325°F. Grease an 8"-high-sided sprinGForm pan

❯ Beat the eggs with the sugar in the bowl of an electric mixer fitted with the whisk attachment until light in color. Add all of the remaining ingredients and mix until a smooth batter forms. Pour the batter into the prepared pan.

❯ Bake in the center of the preheated oven for about 1 hour or until a toothpick inserted into the center comes out clean. Remove the pan to a rack to cool for 5 minutes. Run a sharp knife around the circumference of the cake and open the ring to let the cake cool completely.

❯ Cream: Thaw the strawberries slightly in a fine mesh sieve, letting most of the juices drip out. Meanwhile, beat the whip into stiff peaks, adding the confectioners' sugar and vanilla sugar as it stiffens. Fold in the strained strawberries. Cover with plastic wrap and refrigerate until ready to serve or for up to 24 hours.

❯ Cut the cake in half horizontally using a long, serrated bread knife. Place the bottom half on a serving plate. Top with a thin layer of the cream, spreading it to the edges. Top with the second half of the cake. Spoon dollops of cream all over the top of the cake and top with fresh blueberries, if desired. Chill until 30 minutes before serving.

Makes one-8" cake.

COMMENTS

These are really pretty as cupcakes as well. Divide the batter evenly into cupcake-holder-lined muffin tins. Bake for 30 minutes in a preheated 325°F oven, or until the tops spring back when lightly pressed. Cool and use a teaspoon to carve out a hole at the top of each cupcake, creating a "bowl" for the cream. Top with a generous dollop of the strawberry cream.

Summer Fruit Cobbler

Just reading this recipe conjures up images of a lake with a sandy beach and long summer afternoons. It's the ultimate summer dessert, in my opinion. This is the recipe my children will hopefully remember when they look back at summers spent with cousins, sprinklers and baseball.

Topping:

1 ¼	cups all-purpose flour
½	cup granulated sugar
1	tsp baking powder
½	tsp salt
½	cup unsalted butter or trans fat free margarine, melted (1 stick)
2	Tbsp oil
1	large egg
¼	cup milk or soy milk
1	lemon, zested

Filling:

8	small plums, pitted and cut into pieces
5	peaches, pitted and cut into pieces
2	cups blueberries
⅔	cup granulated sugar (or less, depending on how sweet the fruit is)
1	Tbsp freshly squeezed lemon juice
3	Tbsp cornstarch (generous)
1	tsp cinnamon
1	lemon, zested

❯ Preheat the oven to 350°F.

❯ Combine all of the ingredients for the topping in a mixing bowl in the order in which they appear, and mix just until it comes together. Let the mixture rest on the counter for 30 minutes.

❯ Combine the plums, peaches and blueberries in a 9"-square baking dish (a 13" x 9" baking dish is also fine). Add the sugar, lemon juice, cornstarch and cinnamon, mixing until well combined. Sprinkle the lemon zest over the top.

❯ Cover the pan tightly with aluminum foil. Bake in the center of the preheated oven for 15 minutes. Remove from the oven and uncover. Drop the topping by spoonfuls on top of the fruit. This dish has a rustic look, so don't worry about making it even.

❯ Bake for 45 minutes or until the top turns golden and the fruit filling is bubbling and lightly thickened.

Makes 12 servings.

Strawberry Mousse Crunch

I made this mousse four times in four different flavors. They all worked well, but the strawberry flavor won the popular taste test, though I personally liked the mango as well. I recommend making the almond crunch with some pecan pieces for the strawberry variation.

They were all delicious and pretty. This recipe was originally written with Passover in mind, but you can simply switch up the potato starch for regular, all-purpose flour if you want to make it at any other time of year.

Mousse:

3	large egg whites
¾	cup + 1 Tbsp granulated sugar
1½	Tbsp orange juice
1	Tbsp freshly squeezed lemon juice
⅛	tsp salt
1	lb frozen strawberries, or approximately 1 lb of any other fruit of your choice, partially thawed

Crunch:

¼	cup trans fat free margarine, at room temperature
1	cup potato starch or all-purpose flour
1	cup ground walnuts or almonds
1	cup packed light brown (or white) sugar
3–4	Tbsp oil
½	cup slivered almonds or pecan pieces, optional

> Preheat the oven to 350°F.

> Crunch: Place the margarine, potato starch or flour, brown sugar and walnuts in a bowl and crumble between your fingers to create a crumbly, sand-like consistency. Add the oil, 1 Tbsp at a time, mixing between your fingers until small clumps form. Lay the crunch evenly on a parchment paper-lined baking sheet. You can add the optional slivered pecans or almonds at this point.

> Bake in the center of the preheated oven for 18 minutes or until the edges just begin to brown. Remove from the oven and fluff with a fork to create crumbs. Let cool completely.

> Mousse: Beat the egg whites in a large mixing bowl fitted with the whisk attachment. Add the sugar in a slow stream. Add all of the remaining ingredients in the order they appear and beat for a full 10 minutes.

> Spread half of the mousse into a 13" x 9" dish. Sprinkle with a little less than half of the crumb mixture. Add the remaining mousse and top with the remaining crumbs. Freeze for at last two hours or until set. Scoop into cups before serving. (It's so soft that it scoops easily, even when frozen.)

> You may want to create small parfait-glass serving, layering the mousse, then crumbs, then mousse, and topping with crumbs. Let individual parfaits stand at room temperature for 15 to 20 minutes before serving.

Makes 8 servings.

Better with **BERRIES**

Italian-Inspired Fruit Dessert

This dessert has a few steps, but my Shabbat guests will attest that it was well worth it. Each step is simple and can be made in advance. I recently had the privilege of visiting Italy for a short while and I researched the cuisine before departing. I found a liqueur at my local wine store called lemoncello, which is a very popular Italian liqueur, as lemons grow there in abundance. It is an alcohol steeped with lemon peels and has a really lovely flavor when mixed with the cream below. (I have provided substitute suggestions, but this was my favorite.)

Meringue Topping (optional):
- 4   **large egg whites**
-     **pinch salt**
- 1   **cup granulated sugar**
- ½   **cup ground filberts**

Fruit Compote:
- ½   **cup orange juice**
- 1   **lemon, juiced**
- ½   **cup granulated sugar**
- 2   **bags (1 lb each) frozen blueberries, or 2 lb fresh**
- 2   **bags (1 lb each) frozen strawberries, or 2 lb fresh**
- 1   **Tbsp cornstarch, dissolved in 1 Tbsp cold water**

Cream:
- 1   **container (8 oz) pareve or dairy whip**
- 2   **Tbsp confectioners' sugar**
- 1   **Tbsp Lemoncello or any fruit-flavored liqueur of your choice (ameretto, cherry, orange, etc.)**

> If making the meringue, preheat the oven to 250°F. Beat the egg whites in the bowl of a beater fitted with the whisk attachment until the whites begin to solidify; add the salt. Add the sugar very slowly, about 2 Tbsp at a time, until stiff peaks form. Fold in the filberts. Spread the meringue evenly onto a parchment paper-lined baking sheet.

> Bake in the center of the preheated oven for 1 hour. Turn off the oven. Let the meringue sit in the turned-off oven for 6 hours or overnight.

> Fruit Compote: Place the orange juice, lemon juice, sugar and berries into a pot set over medium heat. Cook, stirring occasionally, for about 15 minutes or just until the berries have softened. Add the dissolved cornstarch and cook for 5 more minutes. Let cool and refrigerate until chilled, or for up to 3 days.

> Cream: Whip the dessert topping in the bowl of an electric fitted with the whisk attachment. As it thickens, add the confectioners' sugar and liqueur. Refrigerate until ready to use.

> Place some of the fruit compote on individual serving plates. Top with the cream. If using, break the meringue into pieces and serve it over the fruit and cream.

Makes 8 to 10 servings.

Berry Crisp with Whole-wheat Crumb Topping

The key to a fantastic crisp is a pre-baked topping, which won't get soggy or overcooked and stays crunchy. This is one of my favorite fruit combinations, but you can replace the apples with peaches in the summer.

Topping:

½	cup trans fat free margarine, at room temperature (1 stick)
¾	cup old-fashioned rolled oats
½	cup granulated sugar
½	cup packed light brown sugar
1	cup whole-wheat flour
1	tsp ground cinnamon
	pecans for garnshing

Filling:

2	cups fresh or frozen strawberries, hulled and sliced
2	cups fresh or frozen blueberries
1½	cups frozen cranberries, optional (no need to thaw first)
2 or 3	apples, peeled and thinly sliced
½	cup all-purpose flour
⅓	cup packed light brown sugar
1	tsp cinnamon

❯ Preheat the oven to 350°F.

❯ Topping: Place all of the ingredients for the topping in a large bowl and crumble between your fingers until a fine crumb forms and there are no large lumps of margarine. Spread on a parchment paper-lined cookie sheet. Bake for 15 minutes or until the crumb is cookie-like. Remove from the oven and use a fork to break up any big pieces.

❯ Meanwhile, combine all of the ingredients for the filling in a 13" x 9" Pyrex or serving dish, mixing gently. Cover well with foil and bake in the center of the preheated oven for 20 minutes. Lower the oven heat to 300°F. Remove the foil. Cover with the baked crumb mixture. Garnish with pecans. Bake for 20 minutes. Serve warm.

Makes 12 servings.

Plum Season Cake

We always make this cake when the small Hungarian or Italian plums are in season, usually from the beginning of September through October. This recipe yields 3 round cakes, and I usually make at least double the recipe! The cakes freeze beautifully, so there's no need to worry. I like to serve this cake either as a dessert or as a side dish. It's incredibly delicious served warm with some spiked whipped cream or ice cream.

2	lb Italian prune plums, halved and pitted
1	lemon, juiced
2½	cups granulated sugar
½	cup trans fat free margarine or unsalted butter, at room temperature (1 stick)
1	cup oil
3	cups all-purpose flour
1	Tbsp baking powder
6	large eggs
1	Tbsp orange juice
1½	tsp lemon extract
1	tsp ground coriander

❯ Preheat the oven to 350°F. Grease three 9"-round cake pans.

❯ Combine the pitted plums, lemon juice and ½ cup of the sugar in a bowl and let sit for 30 minutes.

❯ Meanwhile, beat together the margarine and remaining sugar in the bowl of an electric mixer fitted with the paddle attachment until it attains the texture of grainy sand. Add the oil and beat on high for 3 minutes, until pale and smooth. Lower the speed, add the flour, baking powder, eggs, orange juice and lemon extract. Beat for 4 minutes or until pale and smooth.

❯ Stir the coriander into the plum mixture and mix again to coat all the plums. Divide the cake batter evenly among the prepared cake pans. Press the plums, cut side down, into the batter, starting at the perimeter of the cake and working inwards. Place one plum half in the center. The plums should be close together, but not touching each other.

❯ Bake in the center of the preheated oven for 55 minutes.

Makes 3 9" cakes.

COMMENTS

It's the coriander that provides the unique flavor-twist that I love. You can substitute ground cinnamon if you prefer.

Filbert Cake

This cake has been a long-time family favorite, for both its good taste and because it's a no fail! Use a plain tube pan, not one with a non-stick coating. Although I originally developed this as a Passover cake, it's a real treat all year long.

7	large eggs, separated
½	cup granulated sugar
⅓	cup oil
3	tsp coffee granules dissolved in ⅓ cup boiling water
1	bag (12 oz) finely ground filberts
3	tsp unsweetened cocoa powder
½	tsp baking powder

Chocolate Cream:

¼	cup granulated sugar
¼	cup water
3½	oz bittersweet chocolate, coarsely chopped
3	Tbsp unsweetened cocoa powder, sifted
1	Tbsp vanilla sugar
4	large egg yolks
½	cup trans fat free margarine (1 stick)

〉 Chocolate Cream: Place the sugar and water in the top of a double boiler set over hot (not boiling) water; cook until the sugar dissolves. Add the chocolate, cocoa and vanilla sugar and cook until melted, mixing well. Stir the yolks into the mixture, mixing constantly until they are incorporated. Stir in the margarine until melted. Once the mixture is smooth, pour into a container and let it sit uncovered until it has completely cooled. Refrigerate or freeze.

〉 Preheat the oven to 350°F.

〉 Beat the egg whites in the bowl of an electric mixer fitted with the whisk attachment until soft peaks form. Add the sugar in a thin, slow stream and beat until stiff peaks form.

〉 In a second bowl, beat the yolks. Add the oil and the dissolved coffee. Mix the three remaining ingredients together in a third bowl. Alternating wet and dry ingredients, fold the yolk mixture and the flour mixture into the egg whites, mixing just until combined. Pour into a tube pan (not non-stick).

〉 Bake in the center of the preheated oven for 50 to 55 minutes, or until the surface of the cake springs back lightly when gently pressed. Remove from the oven; immediately turn upside down on the legs of the pan or on the neck of a glass bottle to cool completely. Freeze in the pan until solid, and then use a sharp knife to loosen the cake from the pan. Spread the chocolate cream over the cake while still frozen.

Makes 12 servings.

To see a demo, go to **kosherscoop.com/video**

COLD & CREAMY

Decadent Halva Ice Cream Cake

Brownie Layer:

½	cup unsalted butter or trans fat free margarine, melted
1	cup granulated sugar
2	large eggs
1	tsp vanilla
½	cup all-purpose flour
⅓	cup unsweetened cocoa powder, sifted
½	tsp salt
¼	tsp baking powder

Halva Ice Cream:

2	cups whip topping
3	large egg yolks
½	cup confectioners' sugar
½	cup soy milk or almond milk
6	Tbsp raw tahini
1	Tbsp vanilla sugar
5	oz vanilla flavored halva

Chocolate Topping:

1	bar (3.5 oz) 55% cacao chocolate, coarsely chopped
½	cup unsalted butter or trans fat free margarine
1	tsp light corn syrup

〉 Preheat the oven to 350°F. Line the bottom of a 9" sprinGForm pan with a round of parchment paper. Spray paper and pan with baking spray.

〉 Place the butter in a large bowl. Mix in the remaining ingredients until completely incorporated. Pour into the prepared sprinGForm pan. Bake in the center of the preheated oven for 20 minutes. Remove the pan to a rack to cool completely.

〉 Ice Cream: Whip the topping in the bowl of an electric mixer fitted with the whisk attachment, adding the yolks and sugar as it beats into peaks. Add the soy milk, tahini and vanilla sugar, combining well. With a sharp knife, shave the halva into thin pieces and fold into the ice cream mixture. Pour on top of the cooled brownie layer, spreading evenly. Cover with plastic wrap and freeze for about 8 hours or until set.

〉 Chocolate Topping: Place all of the ingredients in the top of a double boiler set over hot (not boiling) water. Cook, stirring, until melted and smooth. Remove from the heat; let cool for 5 minutes. Pour evenly over the ice cream layer. Cover with plastic wrap and return to the freezer.

〉 When ready to serve, run a sharp knife around the edges to release the cake from the sides of the pan. Open the sides of the pan; remove. Pull the parchment paper on the bottom of the cake to transfer it to your serving dish.

Makes 12 to 16 servings.

Nougat Semifreddo

Literally translated, semifreddo is a partially frozen Italian dessert, similar to ice cream. It has a soft consistency, which makes it a pleasure to scoop. The combination of dried cherries and dark chocolate is a personal favorite, but if you prefer another combination, give it a try. BUT only after you try this version first!!

2	large egg whites
½	cup granulated sugar
⅓	cup honey
¼	cup water
1½	cups whipping cream or non-dairy creamer
½	tsp almond extract
½	cup dried cherries or ¾ cup pomegranate arils
2	oz 72% dark chocolate, coarsely chopped
½	cup crushed, toasted nuts such as hazelnuts, almonds, or pistachios

〉 Beat the egg whites in the bowl of an electric mixer fitted with the whisk attachment until soft peaks form.

〉 Combine the sugar, honey and water in a small, heavy-bottomed saucepan set over low heat. Cook, stirring, until the sugar dissolves and the syrup is clear. Increase the heat and bring the mixture to a boil. Boil, without stirring, for 2 minutes. Remove from the heat.

〉 Carefully, in a slow, thin stream, beat the hot syrup into the egg whites. Continue beating for about 5 minutes or until the meringue has cooled.

〉 Beat the whipping cream with the almond extract in a separate bowl until it reaches the consistency of sour cream. Fold the cream and almonds into the meringue. Gently fold in the remaining ingredients. Transfer the mixture to a freezer-proof container. Cover and freeze overnight or for up to 3 months.

〉 To serve, scoop and enjoy!!

Makes 12 servings.

Pareve Chocolate Pudding

A few months ago, I set off on a mission...to my local supermarket. I went to buy tofu: silken (or soft), firm and extra firm. I was determined to uncover the truth about the wobbly white mass people were raving about. I came home armed with the whole range of available tofu products and began experimenting. I made stir fries and salads and then found a recipe for vegan chocolate pudding. I used the silken tofu and after a bit of tweaking, it evolved into this rich, creamy version that was an instant winner.

2	**Tbsp coffee granules**
¼	**cup boiling water**
⅔	**cup granulated sugar**
⅔	**cup unsweetened cocoa powder, sifted**
¼	**cup oil**
2	**bars (3.5 oz each) 72% cacao chocolate, coarsely chopped**
10.5	**oz silken tofu**
½	**cup coconut milk (or almond milk)**
⅛	**tsp Kosher salt**
	hazelnuts, toasted, for garnish

❯ Stir together the coffee granules and water in the top of a double boiler set over hot (not boiling) water. Add the sugar and cook until it has dissolved. Add the cocoa and oil; cook, stirring, until melted and smooth. Add the chocolate; cook, stirring, until completely melted. Remove from the heat; let cool for 5 minutes.

❯ Transfer the chocolate mixture, tofu and milk to the bowl of a food processor fitted with the metal "S" blade. Add the tofu and milk and pocess for about 30 seconds or until very smooth. Add the salt and process again for 30 seconds. Pour into cups, refrigerate for 3 hours or for up to 3 days. Garnish with toasted hazelnuts before serving.

Makes 12 servings.

Chocolate Chip Cookie-Dough Ice Cream

The cookie dough bakes into a soft sheet of deliciousness. When combined with vanilla ice cream for a cookie-dough ice cream, it's sure to be a hit with adults and kids alike! I serve it scooped into waffle cups and topped with chocolate syrup and chopped, toasted nuts and coconut. To all of you who don't want to use margarine in your cookies, here is your answer!

1	cup packed light brown sugar
½	cup granulated sugar
1	cup oil
2	large eggs
1	tsp vanilla
2½	cupsall-purpose flour
1	tsp baking soda
½	tsp salt
1	cup semisweet chocolate chips
2	tubs vanilla ice cream

❭ Preheat the oven to 350°F.

❭ Mix together the brown and granulated sugars and oil in the bowl of an electric mixer fitted with the paddle attachment, until smooth. One at a time, add the eggs. Add the vanilla.

❭ Mix together the flour, baking soda and salt in a separate bowl; add into the mixer bowl, mixing just until incorporated. Fold in the chocolate chips.

❭ Spread the mixture onto a parchment paper-lined baking sheet, covering the whole sheet with a thin layer of dough. Bake in the center of the preheated oven for 9 minutes. Remove from the oven and let cool on a rack.

❭ Meanwhile, partially defrost 2 tubs of ice cream. They should not be fully melted, just soft. Pour the ice cream into a large pan. Break the cookie into chunks; fold into the ice cream. Smooth with the back of a spoon. Freeze. Let stand for 5 minutes before serving.

Makes 12 servings.

COMMENTS

Drop the cookie dough by tablespoons onto parchment-lined baking sheets for soft and chewy cookies!

Creamy Coconut Fruit Salad Dip

Thread chunks of pineapple, persimmon, apricots or nectarines onto skewers. Brush with coconut milk and grill on a preheated grill pan or barbecue. Grill for about 5 minutes or until the sides begin to caramelize and brown. Serve with the fruit dip. This sauce is my mother's recipe and as a kid, I used to look forward to this dessert every Shabbat.

2	cups coconut milk
3	large egg yolks
	pinch salt
2 ¼	cups whipped cream (dessert topping)
¼	cup honey
3	Tbsp orange juice or 1 tsp rum extract

❯ Heat the coconut milk in a small pot until almost boiling. Pour into a bowl and add the egg yolks, one a time, and the salt, whisking vigorously and constantly until combined and foamy. Cover with plastic wrap, cool slightly and refrigerate for two hours. Stir in the whipped cream, honey, juice or rum extract, mixing well until smooth. Cover with plastic wrap and refrigerate immediately until chilled, or for up to 24 hours.

Makes 4 cups.

Rosemarie Mousse

The addition of hazelnut butter to my favorite chocolate mousse recipe takes this dessert to a whole new level. I made it for a charity function we hosted and I served it in mini chocolate cups. I got so many phone calls for the recipe afterward that I knew it had been a success. How bad can chocolate and hazelnuts be anyway, so I can't take the credit for that!

1	cup hazelnuts
1	Tbsp granulated sugar
1	Tbsp oil
7	oz dark chocolate (I use 1 bar of 55% cacao and 1 of 72%), coarsely chopped
7	large eggs, separated
1	Tbsp unsweetened cocoa powder, dissolved in 3 Tbsp boiling water
1	tsp Kosher salt
3	Tbsp confectioners' sugar

Topping:

3½	oz good quality dark chocolate, coarsely chopped
1	container (8 oz) pareve whipping cream
	candied hazelnuts and white chocolate shavings, for garnish, optional

❯ Preheat the oven to 350°F.

❯ Place the hazelnuts on a baking sheet and bake in the center of the preheated oven for 10 to 13 minutes or until golden. Remove the pan from the oven. Transfer the hazelnuts to a dish towel. Rub the nuts vigorously in the towel to remove the skins. Place the cooled hazelnuts in the bowl of a food processor fitted with the metal "S" blade. Add the sugar and oil; process for about 4 minutes or until smooth and fully combined.

❯ Melt the chocolate in the top of a double boiler set over hot (not boiling water) or in a bowl placed on top of a pot of simmering water. Once the chocolate is fully melted, add the egg yolks slowly, mixing constantly. Add the dissolved cocoa and then the hazelnut butter mixture, mixing until a smooth consistency is obtained.

❯ Meanwhile, beat the egg whites in the bowl of an electric mixer fitted with the whisk attachment. When almost stiff, add the confectioners' sugar and continue beating until stiff peaks form. Fold ⅓ of the egg whites into the chocolate mixture to lighten it. Fold the lightened chocolate mixture into the remaining egg whites just just incorporated.

❯ Spoon the mousse into individual glass cups or dessert bowls. Place in the refrigerator to set or freeze.

❯ Once the mousse is thoroughly chilled or frozen, make the topping: Melt the chocolate in the top of a double boiler set over hot (not boiling) water. Add the whipping cream, stirring until combined. Pour over the mousse and freeze again, if desired. Thaw or bring to room temperature before serving. Garnish with nuts and white chocolate.

Makes 8 servings.

Creative Cupcakes

This simple buttercream frosting is a fantastic way to dress up simple cupcakes. You'll be amazed at how easily you can create this wonderful treat.

1	**cup unsalted butter, at room temperature**
4	**cups confectioners' sugar**
3	**Tbsp milk**
1	**tsp extract of your choice**
	food colouring
8–10	**plain, un-iced cupcakes**

> Whip the butter with the sugar in the bowl of an electric mixer fitted with the beater attachment until well combined. Add the milk and extract. Beat until an even consistency is reached (you may add a bit more sugar if the mixture is too soft). Add just a bit of food colouring (see comment, below) and mix again until well blended.

> Place into a disposable or reusable piping bag fitted with a large star tip. Pipe around the circumference of each cupcake and continue the circular motion, getting small and smaller until a point is reached. You may refrigerate the cupcakes but be sure to serve them at room temperature.

> To make coloured sugar, simply add a dab of food coloring into coarse sugar and mix well. Sprinkle on top of iced cupcakes.

> For sugared flowers, mix an egg white with a few drops of water and paint onto edible flowers. Sprinkle the wet flowers with sugar and set aside to dry. Garnish as desired.

Makes enough to ice 8 to 10 cupcakes

COMMENTS

Only a tiny bit of food coloring is necessary when using the gel type. Use a toothpick to add very small amounts. You can always add, but you can't take away!

Chocolate Pecan Pie

I made 60 of these pies one year for Purim. Yes, I can recite this recipe in my sleep, just in case you are wondering.

3	large eggs
¾	cup corn syrup
¼	cup packed light brown sugar
1	tsp vanilla
2	Tbsp trans fat free margarine or unsalted butter, melted
1½	cups pecan halves
1	cup semi-sweet chocolate chips
2	Tbsp all-purpose flour
1	9" pie crust, frozen

❯ Preheat the oven to 350°F.

❯ Place the eggs, corn syrup, brown sugar and vanilla into a bowl and beat with a wooden spoon until fully combined. Mix in the margarine.

❯ Combine the pecans, chocolate chips and flour in a separate bowl. Transfer the pecan mixture into the frozen pie shell. Gently pour the liquid mixture over the pecan mixture. Place pie shell on a baking sheet.

❯ Bake in the center of the preheated oven for 50 to 55 minutes or until set.

❯ Serve gently warmed or at room temperature.

Makes 12 servings.

COMMENTS

I often make these in individual servings. A full recipe should yield 12 individual tarts.

Irresistible Cinnamon Buns

When we posted this recipe on Kosher Scoop, I knew it would be well-received, but it's popularity surpassed my expectations. It was the number-one-viewed recipe for 2 weeks! Everyone loves cinnamon buns!

Dough:

5¾	cups all-purpose flour
4½	tsp active dry yeast
½	cup granulated sugar
1½	tsp salt
1	cup soy milk
1	cup water
¼	cup trans fat free margarine or oil
2	large eggs

Filling:

2	cups packed dark brown sugar
¾	cup oil
3	Tbsp cinnamon
2	Tbsp vanilla sugar
¼	tsp Kosher salt

Coffee Glaze:

2	cups confectioners' sugar
3	Tbsp trans fat free margarine, melted
1	tsp maple syrup
¼	tsp coffee granules dissolved in 3–4 Tbsp hot water

Cream Cheese Frosting:

3	cups confectioners' sugar
¾	cup cream cheese, at room temperature
½	cup trans fat free margarine, at room temperature
1	tsp vanilla
¼	tsp salt

› Dough: Combine 2 cups of the flour, the yeast, sugar, and salt in the bowl of an electric mixer fitted with the dough hook.

› Heat the milk, water and margarine in a saucepan set over medium heat (or microwave) until warm. Add to the flour mixture. Add the eggs and the remaining flour and knead until smooth. Cover and let rise in a warm, draft-fee place for 1 hour.

› Filling: Combine all of the filling ingredients in a bowl.

› Punch down the dough and divide into 3 equal-size pieces. On a lightly floured work surface, roll out each piece into a 9" x 13" rectangle. Spread each rectangle with ⅓ of the filling. Starting with the 13" side, roll up tightly. Cut each roll into 9 slices. Divide buns among three 8"-square pans, placing 9 in each pan. Cover the buns and let rise another 30 minutes.

› Meanwhile, preheat the oven to 375°F.

› Bake the buns in the center of the preheated oven for 20 to 25 minutes or until golden brown.

› While the buns are baking, prepare the glaze or the frosting. Mix all of the ingredients for the glaze in a bowl. Drizzle over the warm buns. Alternatively, place all of the frosting ingredients in a mixing bowl. Beat until well combined. Spread over the warm buns before serving.

Makes 27 buns.

COMMENTS

This dough is quite sticky. It will become less sticky as it rises. If necessary, you can add more flour, but the less flour you add, the fluffier the cinnamon buns will be.

Caramelized Fruit Garnish

Even a simple brownie cut into a square and dusted with cocoa or icing sugar can become a masterpiece when a caramelized pear or star fruit is placed on top or beside it. Try dressing up a simple wedge of delicious cheesecake for a whole new look. You can use plain or blood oranges, slices of apple or pear, star fruit or banana rounds. Simply dip fruit pieces into granulated sugar until fully coated. Lay the fruit slices on a parchment paper-lined cookie sheet, arranging in a single layer. Bake the fruit in the center of a preheated 250°F oven for 1 hour, checking to see if the fruit is very watery and transferring to a clean parchment paper-lined baking sheet if necessary. Bake for an additional 35 to 45 minutes or until the fruit is completely dried out. The caramelized fruit can be easily stored for up to a month in a cool, dry area, stacked between sheets of parchment paper in an open container. Do not refrigerate.

Cherry Muffins

These pink-tinged muffins are a special treat for dessert or with a cup of tea. During the summer, when sour cherries are in season, we have a cherry pitting party with the kids and their friends. I make homemade cherry pie filling and it is fantastic in these low-fat muffins.

2	cups all-purpose flour
4	tsp baking powder
½	cup sliced or chopped almonds (sliced is preferable), divided
½	cup wheat germ
1	tsp salt
1–2	tsp orange rind, coarsely grated, or to taste
2	large eggs
¼	cup packed dark brown sugar
6	Tbsp soy milk
¼	cup oil
1	tsp almond extract
1	container (14 oz) cherry pie filling (or make your own – see below)

❯ Preheat the oven to 375°F. Lightly grease a 12-cup muffin tin.

❯ Combine the flour, baking powder, half of the almonds, wheat germ, salt and orange rind in a large bowl; mix thoroughly.

❯ Whisk the eggs, sugar, milk, oil and almond extract in a separate bowl, until well blended. Add the egg mixture to the flour mixture and stir just until combined. (If the mixture appears too dry or stiff, add a small amount of soy milk.) Add the cherries and blend together quickly.

❯ Spoon the batter into the prepared muffin tins. Sprinkle the remaining almonds on top of the muffins. Bake in the center of the preheated muffin for 22 to 25 minutes or until they just begin to brown on top. The muffins can be frozen in an airtight bag for up to 2 months.

Makes 12 servings.

COMMENTS

If you have sliced almonds, chop ¼ cup of them to use in the muffin batter and leave the remaining ¼ cup as is to sprinkle on top.

Tip: To make these muffins low-fat, use 2 Tbsp oil and 2 Tbsp applesauce in place of the oil. You can also substitute whole-wheat flour and a few spoons of ground flaxseed for part of the wheat germ.

Homemade Cherry Pie Filling

If you make your own cherry pie filling, you'll get a much more wholesome product with way more fruit in it and of course you can't compare the taste!

1	bag (1 lb) frozen pitted cherries or fresh pitted cherries
½–¾	cup granulated sugar or to taste
¼	cup + 2 Tbsp water
1–2	Tbsp lemon juice
2–3	Tbsp cornstarch
⅛	tsp almond extract, optional

❯ Place the cherries, sugar, ¼ cup of the water and lemon juice in a heavy-bottomed pot. Bring to a boil; lower the heat and simmer until the cherries are soft.

❯ Dissolve the cornstarch in 2 Tbsp of water and then add into hot cherry mixture. Bring the mixture back to a boil, stirring constantly, until thickened. Remove the pot from the heat. Add the almond extract, if using. Allow to cool.

❯ Cherry Filling can be stored in the refrigerator for up to 3 days or frozen for up to 2 months.

Makes 2 cups.

CHEESECAKES...
the ultimate in decadence

Lower Fat Cheesecake

Thanks goes to Peri for this Passover-friendly cheesecake recipe. It's a delightful alternative to full-fat cheesecakes.

Chocolate Base:

¼	cup unsalted butter, melted
½	cup oil
1¼	cups granulated sugar
2	Tbsp vanilla sugar
4	large eggs
⅔	cup unsweetened cocoa powder, sifted
½	cup all-purpose flour (or 1 cup potato starch)

Cheese Layer:

3	eggs, separated
¾	cup sugar, divided
2	tubs (1 lb) 1% cottage cheese, at room temperature
1	cup vanilla yogurt, at room temperature
1	Tbsp freshly squeezed lemon juice
2	Tbsp all-purpose flour (or 3 Tbsp potato starch)
2	Tbsp vanilla sugar

❭ Preheat the oven to 350°F. Grease a 10"-sprinGForm pan.

❭ Melt the butter in a small saucepan set over medium heat. Whisk in all of the remaining batter ingredients in the order they appear, beating with a whisk after each addition. The batter will be thick. Pour about half of the batter into the bottom of the prepared sprinGForm pan and reserve the other half. Bake for 20 minutes. Remove and cool.

❭ In the bowl of an electric mixer fitted with the whisk attachment, beat the egg whites until soft peaks form. Add ¼ cup of the sugar in a thin, slow stream and beat until stiff peaks form

❭ Cheese layer: Combine the yolks, cottage cheese, yogurt, lemon juice, remaining sugar, flour and vanilla sugar in a large bowl. Mix well. In thirds, gently fold in the egg whites. Gently pour the cheese mixture over the baked chocolate layer. Dollop the remaining chocolate batter over the cheese layer, swirling gently with a fork, without overmixing. There will be small chunks of chocolate.

❭ Bake in the center of the preheated oven for 45 to 55 minutes or until the center is firm when you shake the pan. Remove the pan to a rack to cool completely. The cake should be cooled for at least 5 to 6 hours before serving. It can also be refrigerated for up to 3 days.

Makes 12 to 16 servings.

COMMENTS

This cake also works great in a 13" x 9" pan.

No-Bake Blintz Cake

While this cake makes a beautiful and impressive appearance, it is actually quite simple to make. It is the star of every buffet table, and the perfect ending to a lavish meal. All the components can be made up to two days ahead, but it is best assembled the day it is served.

Crêpes/Blintzes:

7	large eggs
¾	cup (scant) all-purpose flour
½	cup orange juice
½	cup seltzer
½	cup milk
½	cup granulated sugar
1	Tbsp oil
2	tsp vanilla
	oil, for brushing pan

Filling:

2½	cups whipped cream cheese, at room temperature
2	cups ricotta cheese, at room temperature
1½	cups sour cream, at room temperature
1¼	cups confectioners' sugar
1	Tbsp vanilla sugar

Blueberry Sauce:

2	cups frozen blueberries
3	Tbsp granulated sugar
¼	cup water
1	Tbsp cornstarch, dissolved in ¼ cup of cold water

› Crêpes: Whisk together the eggs in a large bowl. Add the remaining ingredients and whisk vigorously until there are no lumps and the batter is smooth.

› Lightly brush some oil in a 9" non-stick skillet set over medium-high heat. Pour ⅓ cup of the batter into the center of the pan, swirling the pan to spread it evenly. Cook on one side until the edges begin to brown and bubbles appear on the surface. Loosen the crêpe from the side of the pan and flip over. Cook for 2 to 3 minutes, pressing down on the crêpe with a spatula to avoid burning. When done, flip onto a prepared plate. Repeat with the rest of the batter.

› Filling: Place all of the ingredients in a large mixing bowl and mix until combined.

› Blueberry Sauce: Bring the blueberries, sugar and water to a boil in a small saucepan. Add the dissolved cornstarch and bring to a boil again, stirring often. Remove from heat, stir and let cool to room temperature.

› Assembly: Place one crêpe on your serving dish, spread a layer of filling all over the crêpe, going all the way to the edges. Repeat with 10 more layers, ending with a crêpe.

› Pour the blueberry sauce over the top of the cake immediately before serving.

Makes 10 to 12 servings.

To see a demo, go to **kosherscoop.com/video**

Pareve Cheesecake Gems

I first saw these mini cakes at my friend Rina's party. She had them nicely lined up on hot-pink, Lucite™ trays. The effect was stunning and they tasted delicious as well. Hers were dairy but I think this pareve version is versatile and equally as delicious.

Crumb Mixture:

2½	cups cookie crumbs or see comment
½	cup unsalted butter, melted
1	cube frozen ginger or ½ tsp dried ginger

Cheese Filling:

2	containers (each 8 oz) pareve cream cheese (for a dairy version, use regular cream cheese), at room temperature
¾	cup granulated sugar
3	large eggs
1	Tbsp vanilla
1	Tbsp orange juice
1	can (16 oz) cherry pie filling

> Preheat the oven to 350°F.

> Crumb Mixture: Combine all of the ingredients for the crumb mixture in a bowl until thoroughly moistened. Press into 18 non-stick mini muffin tins.

> Bake in the center of the preheated oven for 10 minutes. Remove from the oven; cool to room temperature.

> Cheese Filling: Mix all of the ingredients, except for the pie filling, and spoon into the muffin tins. Bake for about 15 minutes or until set. Cool and remove from the pan, cutting around the edges if necessary.

> Meanwhile, spoon the cherry pie filling into a strainer. Use a spoon to gently discard as much of the "jelly" as possible, being careful not to break the cherries. Spoon about 2 to 3 cherries onto the center of each mini cheesecake.

> Refrigerate until completely chilled. Serve chilled.

Makes 18 servings..

COMMENTS

I recommend using Ostreicher lemon-flavored cookies. An 8-oz bag of cookies makes 2½ cups of crumbs. If unavailable, use graham crackers.

Light and Decadent Chocolate Chip Cheesecake

This recipe is both rich and light at once. Not possible? Try it for yourself and see! It refrigerates well for up to a week. Thanks again, Goldie.

Crust:

1	cup finely crushed chocolate sandwich cookies
¼	cup unsalted butter, melted
2	Tbsp granulated sugar

Filling:

3	containers (each 8 oz) whipped cream cheese, at room temperature
1¼	cups granulated sugar
3	Tbsp all-purpose flour
¼	tsp salt
4	large eggs, beaten slightly
¾	cup dairy or pareve whipping cream
1	tsp vanilla
1	cup mini chocolate chips

Topping (optional):

1	tsp unflavored granulated Kosher gelatin
1	Tbsp cold water
1	cup cold whipping cream
1	Tbsp granulated sugar
1	tsp vanilla extract (I like to use the clear vanilla extract for this)

› Preheat the oven to 300°F. Generously butter the bottom and sides of a 9" springform pan. An 8" pan will yield a taller cake but works just as well. Wrap the outside of the pan with aluminum foil, covering the bottom and extending all the way up the sides.

› Crust: Mix all of the crust ingredients together in a bowl until thoroughly moistened. Press into the bottom of the pan.

› Filling: Mix all the filling ingredients together in a bowl until combined. Pour gently over the crust. Place the springform pan into a second, larger pan. Pour 1 cup of water into the bottom of the larger pan. This creates a water bath for the cheesecake which yields a creamier consistency.

› Bake in the center of the preheated oven for 65 to 70 minutes or until completely set.

› Topping, if using: Place the gelatin in a heat-proof measuring cup. Stir in the cold water and let stand for about 1 minute or until thickened. Heat in the microwave for about 30 seconds or place in the top of a double boiler to heat and melt the gelatin. The mixture should be clear.

› Whip the cream in the bowl of an electric mixer fitted with whisk attachment until soft peaks just begin to form. With the mixer still running, add the sugar and beat until the cream stiffens into peaks (overmixing can cause the cream to curdle, so watch it carefully). Beat in the vanilla and add the melted gelatin in one shot, beating until fully incorporated.

› Cover and refrigerate for 30 minutes. Spread a thin layer on top of the cake.

› Slice with a hot knife for clean, even pieces, or use floss to cut nice wedges.

Makes 10 to 12 servings.

Cherry "Cheese" Strudel

No one will believe this strudel is pareve. It is the perfect finale to a barbecue or even Shabbat dinner.

6	oz firm or silken tofu, at room temperature
1	cup confectioners' sugar, plus more for dusting
3	oz pareve (tofu) cream cheese, at room temperature
3	Tbsp all-purpose flour
1	large egg yolk
	juice of ½ a lemon
1	tsp vanilla
7	sheets frozen phyllo dough, thawed
½	(approx) oil for brushing
½	cup graham cracker crumbs
1	can (16 oz) cherry pie filling
1	tsp cinnamon

❯ Preheat the oven to 375°F.

❯ Blend the tofu in the bowl of a food processor until smooth. Add the sugar, cream cheese, flour, yolk, lemon juice and vanilla and purée until combined.

❯ Stack the phyllo sheets on a flat work surface and cover with a slightly damp kitchen towel. Cut a piece of parchment paper so that it is slightly larger than the phyllo. Lay 1 sheet of the phyllo on the parchment paper with the long side facing you (keep the remaining phyllo covered). Brush lightly with oil, especially around the edges, and sprinkle with 1 Tbsp of the graham crumbs. Top with another sheet of phyllo, then brush again with oil and sprinkle with more crumbs. Repeat with the remaining phyllo sheets, topping each with oil and crumbs. Reserve the remaining oil and crumbs for the topping.

❯ Meanwhile, pour the cherry pie filling into a sieve and push the jelly through, leaving mostly the cherries.

❯ Spoon the tofu mixture across the length of the phyllo, leaving a 1" border at the long end closest to you, and a 2" border at the short ends. Place the cherries on top of the tofu mixture and sprinkle with the cinnamon. Starting with the long edge, use the parchment paper to roll the phyllo tightly over the filling to make a log. Tuck both ends underneath to close. Turn, seam-side, down onto the parchment paper. Brush with the remaining oil and sprinkle with the remaining crumbs. Transfer the parchment paper and strudel to a baking sheet.

❯ Bake in the center of the preheated oven for about 18 minutes or until golden, rotating the baking sheet halfway through. Slide the strudel onto a cutting board and let cool completely, about 1 hour. Dust with confectioners' sugar before serving.

Makes 8 servings.

Cranberry Pecan Biscotti

My wonderful neighbor sent these biscotti over when I had a baby. They were so pretty, much daintier looking than regular biscotti and they were seriously addictive. In fact, I finished the whole plate! Of course, I took the recipe and made them when my baby was only three days old!

1¾	cups regular or whole-wheat cake flour
½	tsp salt
½	tsp baking powder
½	cup oil, (scant)
1	tsp vanilla
1	cup granulated sugar
4	large eggs
2	cups pecans, chopped
1	cup dried cranberries

❯ Preheat the oven to 350°F.

❯ Mix all of the ingredients in the bowl of a mixer fitted with the dough hook until combined. Divide the dough in half; place into 2 small, unlined loaf pans.

❯ Bake in the center of the preheated oven for 45 minutes. Remove from the oven; place on a wire rack.

❯ Wet a paper towel or kitchen towel. Wring it out and cover the pans with it. Allow the cakes to cool this way for 40 minutes. Remove the the loaves from the pans and wrap each loaf in foil and freeze overnight (or until you need them). Defrost for 10 minutes and slice very thinly. Lay on a parchment paper-lined cookie sheet and bake in a preheated 350°F oven for 10 minutes on each side. Watch to make sure they don't burn.

Makes 36 biscotti.

COMMENTS

A very sharp knife will make it much easier to slice this biscotti thinly.

To look like a true "balabusta," my neighbor advised me to always have some of these half-baked loaves in the freezer, ready for slicing and baking at a moment's notice.

Lemon Rugelach

These are great for those who don't like cake that is too sweet. They have a delicious light and buttery flavor.

Dough:

½	cup unsalted butter or trans fat free margarine, at room temperature (1 stick)
1	cup oil
5	Tbsp granulated sugar
1	Tbsp vanilla sugar
6	cups all-purpose flour
2	oz active dry yeast
	pinch Kosher salt
3	large eggs
1	cup orange juice

Filling:

1	lb confectioners' sugar
3	Tbsp vanilla sugar
	juice and zest of 2 lemons
	oil, for smearing

Egg wash:

1	egg yolk
2	Tbsp water

> Dough: Place all of the ingredients, in the order listed above, in the bowl of an electric mixer fitted with the dough hook. Mix until an even dough forms. If the dough is a bit crumbly, add 1 to 2 Tbsp more oil to bring it together. Cover the bowl with plastic wrap and let rise for 1 hour (it's okay if the dough doesn't rise that much).

> Meanwhile, make the filling. Mix together the sugar, vanilla sugar and lemon zest in a large bowl.

> Preheat the oven to 350°F. Line 2 cookie sheets with parchment paper.

> Transfer the dough to a work surface. Cut the dough into 6 equal-sized pieces. Roll out one piece of the dough into a ¼" thick round circle. Smear generously with oil. Sprinkle with ⅙ of the sugar mixture. Squeeze some lemon juice (about half a lemon for each circle) all over the sugar.

> Cut the dough into 12 triangles, as you would a pizza. Roll each triangle up from the wider end, and place on the prepared cookie sheet. Combine the egg yolk and water for an egg wash; brush over the cookies. Repeat with the remaining pieces of dough.

> Bake in the preheated oven for 18 to 20 minutes or until golden.

Makes 6 dozen rugelach.

COMMENTS

The rugelach can be stored in an airtight container at room temperature for 3 days.

Pecan-Coconut Toffee Bar

These would probably be more appropriately named "everything-but-the-kitchen-sink" bars, but then you likely would have passed them by. It all started with an invitation to a kiddush and I wanted to contribute something homemade. I am quite renowned for sending the original toffee bars from Estee Kafra's "Cooking with Color," and I decided it was time for change. My husband came home, took a look and commented that they weren't especially pretty. My kids walked by; each grabbed one and turned right back for seconds. I quickly (yup, they're that quick and easy) whipped up a second batch and the kids were thrilled because there was now more for them! However, my poor friend did not receive any homemade goodies.

When you make these, prepare 2 batches because they won't last long! Have fun changing up the add-ins. I think I'm going to replace the marshmallows with peanut butter chips next time.

12	graham crackers
¾	cup unsalted butter or trans fat free margarine (1½ sticks)
¾	cup packed light brown sugar
1	tsp cinnamon
¼	tsp Kosher salt
2	cups mini marshmallows
1	cup coarsely shredded sweetened coconut
1	cup pecans, chopped (I used honey-glazed)

❯ Preheat the oven to 350°F. Line a cookie sheet with silver foil and then with parchment paper. Lay out the graham crackers in two rows of 6.

❯ Melt the butter with the brown sugar, cinnamon and salt in a small saucepan. Cook, stirring, until the mixture starts to thicken.

❯ Sprinkle the marshmallows over the crackers; pour the syrup over the crackers. Sprinkle the coconut and pecans evenly over the syrup.

❯ Bake in the center of the preheated oven for 13 minutes. Remove the pan to a rack to cool completely. Cut into triangles.

Makes 48 triangles.

Incredible (Passover) Nutty Bars

These are called Incredible (Passover) Nutty Bars because Paula originally wrote the recipe for Passover. Well, it was one of the most popular recipes on the site last Passover and I personally made it six times! I played with the ingredients a bit, substituting shelled pistachios for the walnuts and chopped dates at times. These bars are sooo good.

1	cup granulated sugar
½	cup oil, plus extra for greasing pan
1	large egg
1¾	cups ground almonds without skins (buy ground or grind in food processor)
3	Tbsp potato starch
¾	cup whole almonds, skin on, roughly chopped
⅔	cup walnut halves, chopped
¾	cup dried apricots, chopped into ½" pieces
¾	cup dried cranberries or raisins

❯ Preheat the oven to 350°F. Grease the bottom and sides of a 13" x 9" pan. Line with parchment paper, allowing for an overhang. Grease the top and sides of the parchment.

❯ Beat together the sugar, oil and egg in the bowl of an electric mixer fitted with the paddle attachment on medium speed until fully combined. Add the ground almonds and potato starch and mix well. Knead in the nuts and dried fruit until distributed throughout the dough.

❯ Press the mixture into the prepared pan as evenly as possible. Bake in the center of the preheated oven for 30 minutes or until the edges start to brown. Remove the pan to a rack to cool. Lift out of the pan and slice into rectangular or square bars.

Makes 27 bars.

COMMENTS

Store in an airtight container at room temperature for up to 5 days or freeze for up to 2 months.

Going nuts
for nuts

Butter Pecan Cookies

These are so simple, yet the butter flavor shines through and is a perfect complement to the earthy flavor of the pecans. These are my favorite cookies (this week ☺).

1	cup unsalted butter, at room temperature (2 sticks)
½	tsp fine sea salt
⅓	cup vanilla sugar
⅓	cup confectioners' sugar, sifted
1	large egg yolk
2	cups all-purpose flour
1	cup pecan pieces, divided in half

❯ Cream the butter in the bowl of an electric mixer fitted with the paddle attachment set on low speed or in a large bowl with a hand mixer, for about 1 minute or until the butter is smooth and creamy (not light and fluffy). Mix in the salt. Add the vanilla sugar and confectioners' sugar. Mix for 1 minute or until smooth, scraping down the sides of the bowl as necessary.

❯ Add the egg yolk and mix for 1 minute. Still on low speed, mix in the flour just until incorporated; the dough will be soft.

❯ Transfer the dough to a work surface and knead it gently a few times. Lay an 11" piece of plastic wrap on the counter. Spread ½ cup of the pecan pieces evenly over the plastic wrap. Divide the dough in half and shape each half into a 9" log. Press one log into the pecans, rolling it until completely coated with the nuts. Repeat with another piece of plastic wrap, the remaining pecans and the second piece of dough. Wrap the logs in the plastic wrap and refrigerate for at least 3 hours or until firm. (You can also freeze them for up to 2 months. Let sit at room temperature for about 10 minutes before cutting and baking; there's no need to fully defrost.)

❯ Preheat the oven to 350°F. Position the oven racks in the top and bottom third of the oven. Line two baking sheets with parchment paper or silicon baking liners.

❯ Cut the dough into ½" thick rounds using a sharp knife. Transfer to the prepared baking sheets, spacing about 2" apart.

❯ Bake the cookies, rotating and swapping the baking sheets' positions halfway through, for 18 to 22 minutes or until the cookies are brown around the edges and golden on the bottom. Remove the baking sheets to racks to cool for 5 minutes. Carefully transfer the cookies to a rack and let cool completely before serving. Cookies should not be eaten warm; they need to cool so that their texture will set properly.

Makes 40 cookies.

COMMENTS

Cookies can be stored in an airtight container at room temperature for up to 7 days or frozen for up to 2 months.

Peanut Butter Chocolate Chunk Cookies

The name is all you really need to describe this rich, decadent cookie. This recipe was submitted by Nanette Stoll, a self-proclaimed fan of Kosher Scoop.

½	**cup trans fat free margarine or unsalted butter, at room temperature (1 stick)**
1½	**cups packed dark brown sugar**
½	**cup granulated sugar**
⅔	**cup smooth peanut butter**
2	**large eggs**
1½	**tsp vanilla**
2½	**cups all-purpose flour**
2	**tsp baking soda**
½	**tsp Kosher salt**
2	**cups semi-sweet chocolate chips**
2	**cups honey-roasted peanuts, chopped**
	granulated sugar, for sprinkling

> Preheat the oven to 350°F. Line 3 cookie sheets with parchment paper.

> Cream together the margarine, brown and granulated sugars and peanut butter in the bowl of an electric mixer fitted with the paddle attachment, just until smooth. Beat in the eggs, one at a time, beating only until smooth after each addition. Beat in the vanilla.

> Mix together the flour, baking soda and salt in a separate small bowl; beat into the peanut butter mixture, scraping the bowl and beaters. Stir in the chocolate chips and peanuts.

> Scoop or spoon 2 Tbsp-size mounds of the dough onto the prepared pans. Dip the bottom of a glass into granulated sugar and flatten the cookies.

> Bake in the preheated oven for 10 minutes.

Makes 48 cookies.

Cookies can be stored in an airtight container at room temperature for up to 7 days or frozen for up to 2 months.

Nut Butter Cookies

I started to experiment with nut butters on Passover when we made a chocolate hazelnut spread for matzah. Nut butters are so simple to make and many varieties are becoming increasingly popular in stores across the United States, Canada and Israel, due to their health benefits. You can change up the kind of nut butter you use for this recipe, making it different each time. I love hazelnuts but I have tried both almond and cashew butters with great results.

1	cup old-fashioned oats
¼	cup + 2 Tbsp oil
½	cup trans fat free margarine, at room temperature (1 stick)
½	cup packed dark brown sugar
⅓	cup granulated sugar

1	large egg
1	cup + 2 Tbsp all-purpose flour
1	tsp baking soda
¼	tsp Kosher salt
½	cup hazelnut butter
½	cup pecans, chopped

> Preheat the oven to 350°F. Line two baking sheets with parchment paper.

> Mix the oats with 2 Tbsp of the oil in a bowl. Transfer to one of the prepared baking sheets. Toast in the center of the preheated oven for 10 minutes. Set aside to cool.

> Cream the margarine with the brown sugar and granulated sugar in the bowl of an electric mixer fitted with the paddle attachment, or in a large bowl with a hand mixer. Beat in the egg. Gently beat in the remaining ingredients as well as the toasted oats.

> Roll the dough into 1½" balls. Place the cookies 1" apart on the prepared baking sheets. Bake in the preheated oven for 12 to 15 minutes or until golden.

Makes 18 to 24 cookies.

Almond Toffee Squares

A new and updated version of my classic Toffee Bars from "Cooking with Color".

8	oz slivered almonds
12	graham crackers, cut in half
1	cup unsalted butter or trans fat free margarine
1	cup packed light brown sugar
1	tsp vanilla
2	Tbsp sesame seeds
2	oz semi-sweet chocolate, melted

> Preheat the oven to 375°F.

> Spread the almonds onto a parchment paper-lined cookie sheet. Toast in the center of the preheated oven for about 8 minutes, or until just starting to brown. Set aside.

> Place the graham crackers on a parchment paper-lined cookie sheet. They should be close, with no spaces between them.

> Melt the butter in a saucepan set over medium heat; add the brown sugar. Cook, stirring, until the sugar is dissolved. Bring to a boil; boil, stirring constantly, for 3 minutes. Remove from the heat and quickly stir in the vanilla and the toasted almonds. Pour the mixture over the graham crackers, spreading it quickly with the back of a spoon, trying to spread the almonds as evenly as possible.

> Place the pan in the center of the preheated oven. Immediately reduce the oven heat to 350°F. Bake for 10 to12 minutes or until lightly browned.

> Remove from the oven and run a sharp knife between the crackers to separate them. Let cool. Drizzle with the melted chocolate.

Makes 24 squares.

BEST BROWNIES

ever

Ellen's Brownies

My friend Dassi has been raving to me about Ellen's brownies for years. One day we finally decided that it was time to stop talking and start baking! Dassi took action and actually went to Ellen's house to witness the brownie-making process in person. She took meticulous notes and here we have it. I knew from the moment I tasted the batter that this one was an absolute keeper (and that she hadn't been exaggerating). To top it all off (literally), I had some chocolate cream in my fridge which I used as an icing. It was a match made in heaven. The cake is great on its own and the chocolate cream takes it to a new level.

1½	cups granulated sugar	4	large eggs
⅔	cup oil	1½	cups all-purpose flour
¼	cup water	½	tsp Kosher salt
2	cups good quality chocolate chips	½	tsp baking soda
2	tsp vanilla		

Chocolate Cream Frosting, optional:

¼	cup granulated sugar	1	Tbsp vanilla sugar
¼	cup water	4	large egg yolks
3½	oz bittersweet chocolate, coarsely chopped	½	cup trans fat free margarine (1 stick)
3	Tbsp unsweetened cocoa powder, sifted		

❯ Preheat the oven to 325°F. Grease a 13" x 9" foil pan.

❯ Combine the sugar, oil and water in a saucepan set over medium-high heat. Cook the mixture until it starts to boil. Remove from the heat. Add the chocolate chips and vanilla. Stir, using a wooden spoon, until the chocolate is fully melted and the mixture is smooth.

❯ Mix in the eggs, one at a time, until fully incorporated. Mix together the flour, baking soda and salt. Mix the dry ingredients, about a half cup at a time, into the chocolate mixture, mixing just until smooth.

❯ Pour the batter into the prepared pan. Bake in the center of the preheated oven for 35 to 40 minutes or until a toothpick inserted in the center comes out clean. Remove the pan to a rack to cool completely.

❯ Frosting: In the top of a double boiler set over hot (not boiling water) combine the sugar and water. Cook until the sugar dissolves. Add the chocolate, cocoa and vanilla sugar. Cook, mixing well, until the chocolate has melted. Add the yolks and cook, stirring constantly, until they are incorporated. Add the margarine, stirring until it has melted and the mixture is smooth.

❯ Pour the frosting into a container and let it sit, uncovered, until it has completely cooled. Refrigerate or freeze until spreadable.

❯ Spread the frosting over the cooled brownies, if desired.

Makes 12 to 16 brownies.

COMMENTS

Brownies can be stored, loosely covered, at room temperature, for up to 3 days or frozen for up to 2 months.

Inspired Brownies

I wrote this recipe for an article in "Mishpacha Magazine" and received wonderful feedback. Brownies are just one of those things everybody likes. Here you can custom-make your own brownie, or just bake it plain. Either way, you can't go wrong!

4	large eggs
3¾	cup oil
1	Tbsp vanilla
2	cups granulated sugar
1½	cups all-purpose flour
¾	cup unsweetened cocoa powder, sifted
2½	tsp baking powder

Add-ins:

1	cup mini marshmallows
1	cup chocolate chips or chocolate chunks
¾	cup walnut pieces
1	cup chocolate-covered mint patties, chopped
1	cup chocolate-covered coconut patties, chopped
½	cup sour cherries
1	cup chocolate lentils
1	cup pecan pieces
½	cup raspberry jam
2	Tbsp crystallized ginger, chopped
1	cup caramel chips
¾	cup rice crispies
½	cup peanut butter
1	Tbsp orange zest
1	cup jelly beans
½	cup shredded coconut

〉 Preheat the oven to 350°F. Lightly grease a 13" x 9" baking pan.

〉 Mix all of the basic ingredients together in a large mixing bowl. Add whatever you like from the add-ins, up to three.

〉 Pour the batter into the prepared pan. Bake in the center of the preheated oven for 30 to 35 minutes or until set.

Makes 16 brownies.

COMMENTS

The brownies can be stored in an airtight container at room temperature for up to 3 days or frozen for up to 2 months.

They'll-Never-Know Brownies

When my friend Karen told me about a chocolate cake in which chickpeas replace the flour, I was intrigued. The only reason I even would attempt to try that kind of thing is because I trust her. We did make it, and it was good, but we found it a bit dry. It took 3 batches of tweaking, but then we finally got it right. They are chocolatey and decadent, with a great texture. These brownies are gluten-free, but hey, they'll never know.

1½	cups semi-sweet chocolate chips
1	can (19 oz) garbanzo beans, drained and rinsed
4	large eggs
¾	cup granulated sugar
¼	cup oil
3	Tbsp Dutch-processed unsweetened cocoa powder, sifted
1	tsp vanilla
½	tsp baking powder
3	Tbsp walnut pieces
	confectioners' sugar, for dusting

> Preheat the oven to 350°F. Grease an 8"-square cake pan.

> Place the chocolate chips in a microwave-safe bowl. Microwave on high for about 2 minutes, stirring every 20 seconds after the first minute, until the chocolate is melted and smooth. If you have a powerful microwave, reduce the power to 50 percent.

> Combine the beans and eggs in the bowl of a food processor fitted with the metal "S" blade. Process until smooth. Add the sugar, oil, cocoa, vanilla and baking powder, and pulse to blend. Pour in the melted chocolate and blend until smooth, scraping down the corners to make sure the chocolate is completely mixed.

> Transfer the batter to the prepared cake pan. Sprinkle with walnuts, mixing gently to incorporate. Bake in the center of the preheated oven for 40 minutes or until a toothpick inserted in the center of the cake comes out clean. Remove the pan to a rack to cool for 10 to 15 minutes. Invert the pan onto a serving plate. Remove the pan. Dust with confectioners' sugar just before serving.

Makes 12 servings.

COMMENTS

The brownies can be stored in an airtight container at room temperature for up to 3 days or frozen for up to 2 months.

COMMENTS

If the lemon curd cools, it will harden and won't pour nicely. Try to make it right before the cake comes out of the oven or while the cake is still warm. If it does cool, reheat it gently to reliquify.

Note: These cheesecakes are a regular in our house during Passover. I use ground almonds in place of the vanilla wafer cookies or sometimes simply leave it crustless. The flour can be replaced with potato starch.

Luscious Lemon Cheesecake Squares

I always set aside about a cup of batter to bake separately for a cheesecake preview. I suggest you do the same, or your entire cake will be eaten before you know it. The cheesecake is delicious and its striking yellow top makes it both elegant and sophisticated.

Crust:

¼	cup melted unsalted butter
1½	cups vanilla wafer cookie crumbs (about ⅔ of the package)

Filling:

2	pkgs (8 oz each) cream cheese, at room temperature
2	tubs (8 oz each) whipped cream cheese, at room temperature
4	large eggs
1¼	cups granulated sugar
1	Tbsp vanilla sugar
2	Tbsp freshly squeezed lemon juice
2	Tbsp all-purpose flour
	zest of 1 lemon

Lemon Curd Topping:

½	cup freshly squeezed lemon juice (from 2 or 3 lemons)
½	cup granulated sugar
2	large eggs
2	Tbsp unsalted butter

> Preheat the oven to 325°F.

> Melt the butter in a small saucepan. Remove from the heat. Stir in the vanilla wafer cookie crumbs, stirring until thoroughly moistened. Press the mixture into the bottom of a 13" x 9" disposable baking pan; smooth the surface with the back of a spoon.

> Place a pan filled halfway with water on the lower shelf of the oven.

> Combine all of the ingredients for the filling in a large bowl and whisk until smooth. Pour the mixture over the prepared crust. Bake on the shelf directly above the pan of water for 40 minutes. Remove the pan to a rack to cool completely.

> Meanwhile, place a strainer over a medium-size bowl; set aside.

> Lemon Curd Topping: Whisk together the lemon juice, sugar and eggs in a separate bowl until thoroughly combined. Pour into a heavy-bottomed saucepan set over medium heat. Cook, stirring occasionally, for 4 to 7 minutes or until the mixture is steaming, but not boiling, and has thickened slightly. Remove from the heat; stir in the butter until melted. Pour the curd through the strainer into the bowl to remove any lumps. Pour the warm curd over the cheesecake. Let the cake cool completely. Refrigerate for at least 2 hours or for up to 8 hours until the topping is set and the cake is chilled through.

> For best results, run a sharp knife under hot water before cutting into bars.

Makes 16 bars.

Lemon Crinkle Cookies

The Baker's Daughter is a good friend of mine who wrote the "The Cookie of the Week" column for a whole year. She established quite a following and this was one of the most popular recipes.

½	cup trans fat free margarine, at room temperature (1 stick)
1	cup granulated sugar
1	large egg
½	tsp vanilla
1½	tsp lemon zest
1	Tbsp freshly squeezed lemon juice
1½	cups all-purpose flour
¼	tsp baking powder
¼	tsp Kosher salt
⅛	tsp baking soda
	confectioners' sugar, for rolling

> Preheat the oven to 350°F. Line a baking sheet with parchment paper.

> Cream together the margarine and sugar in the bowl of an electric mixer fitted with the paddle attachment until light and fluffy. Beat in the egg, vanilla and lemon zest and juice.

> Stir in all of the dry ingredients, except the confectioners' sugar, just until combined.

> Roll the dough into 1" balls. Place the confectioners' sugar in a bowl; roll balls of the dough in the sugar.

> Transfer the cookies to the prepared baking sheet, spacing about 1½" apart.

> Bake in the preheated oven for 11 minutes or until the bottoms are just slightly browned.

Makes 30 to 35 cookies.

Oatmeal Date Bars

These bars are so simple to throw together and are delicious!
They are a great breakfast-on-the-go treat.

1	**cup unsalted butter, at room temperature (2 sticks)**
¾	**cup packed light brown sugar**
½	**cup granulated sugar**
2	**Tbsp pure maple syrup**
2	**large eggs**
1	**tsp vanilla**
1½	**cups whole-wheat flour**
1	**tsp baking soda**
1	**tsp cinnamon**
3	**cups quick-cooking oats**
8	**oz chopped dates**
1	**cup pecan pieces**
¾	**cup semi-sweet chocolate chips, optional**

> Preheat the oven to 350°F. Grease a 13" x 9" baking pan well.

> Beat the butter, brown and granulated sugars and maple syrup in the bowl of an electric mixer fitted with the paddle attachment until creamy. Add the eggs, one at a time, beating the first one in thoroughly before adding the second. Beat in the vanilla.

> Combine the flour, baking soda and cinnamon in a bowl. Add to the butter mixture, mixing well. Beat in the oats, dates, pecans and chocolate chips, if using.

> Press the mixture into the prepared pan. Bake in the center of the preheated oven for 20 minutes. Remove the pan to a rack to cool completely before cutting into bars.

Makes 16 bars.

COMMENTS

The bars can be stored in an airtight container at room temperature for up to 1 week or frozen for up to 2 months.

Ginger-White Chocolate Biscotti

I love ginger and I adore biscotti, so when Nanette uploaded this recipe onto kosherscoop.com I made it that very same day. It was a hit, especially with my 8-month-old baby who used his biscotti as a teething soother (yes, we start them young!!).

3	large eggs
½	cup granulated sugar
½	cup packed light brown sugar
¼	cup oil
⅓	cup fancy molasses
1	tsp vanilla
2½	cups all-purpose flour
2	Tbsp ground ginger
1	tsp baking soda
1	tsp cinnamon
½	tsp Kosher salt
¼	tsp ground cloves
8	oz white chocolate, coarsely chopped (or white chocolate chips)

❯ Preheat the oven to 350°F. Line a cookie sheet with parchment paper.

❯ Beat the eggs with the granulated sugar in the bowl of an electric mixer fitted with the paddle attachment until light and fluffy. Beat in the brown sugar. Add the oil in a thin, steady stream, followed by the molasses and vanilla.

❯ Whisk together the flour, ginger, baking soda, cinnamon, salt and cloves in another bowl; add to the egg mixture, stirring just until combined. Stir in the chocolate. Refrigerate the dough for 1 hour or until firm.

❯ Divide the dough in half; form each half into 2 equal-sized rolls. Place about 4" apart on the prepared baking sheet. Flatten each roll until about 3" wide, leaving the tops slightly rounded.

❯ Bake in the center of the preheated oven for 30 minutes or until firm and the tops are golden. Let the pan cool on a rack for at least 1 hour. Transfer the logs to a cutting board. With a serrated knife, cut into ½" thick slices. Place the biscotti, cut side down, on the baking sheet.

❯ Reduce the oven heat to 300°F. Bake the cookies, turning once, for 8 minutes per side or until dry and crisp. Remove the pan to a rack to cool completely.

Makes 24 biscotti.

Cookies can be stored in an airtight container for up to 2 weeks or frozen for up to 2 months.

*I substitute the white chocolate chips with real dark chocolate chips or with slivered almonds–
or sometimes even both!!*

Estee Kafra

After completing photography classes in both Israel and Manhattan, Estee's interest in beautiful food photography led her to photograph some well-known kosher cookbooks. Estee later joined the team at Binah magazine, where she served as food editor for four years, publishing two best-selling cookbooks during her tenure at the magazine. Both *Spice it Right* and *Cooking With Color* were instant best sellers that continue to serve as great assets to thousands of kosher cooks. When *Mishpacha* magazine launched *Kosher Inspired*, Estee headed the team as editor, and the food magazine was hailed as a major success among its readers and fans. A year-and-a-half later, *Kosher Inspired* morphed into an online magazine called KosherScoop.com. Estee serves as the site's editor and contributes recipes and photographs on a regular basis. Believe it or not, Estee never uses cookbooks. Her love of new things ensures that she is always original and creative in the kitchen. Estee lives in Toronto with her family. She can be contacted at estee@kosherscoop.com.

David Blum

David began his career at the age of 16, working in Toronto's kosher restaurant scene. His love of food sent him to the Jerusalem Culinary Institute, where he received his chef's certificate. Following this, he graduated George Browns' Food and Beverage Management program. Immediately after completing his college studies, he made aliyah to Israel, the mecca of kosher chefs. After five years of working in some of Israel's best restaurants, including RYU of Jerusalem and Messa of Tel Aviv, David returned to Toronto with his wife Racheli and their daughter Ella.

David's style of cooking is best described as clean, light, and modern with Israeli/Mediterranean and Asian techniques and influences. His three years as a sushi chef are evident in his food presentation and finishing touches. Currently, David is Executive Chef of Hartmans of Toronto, and can be found in either of their two retail locations.

Dina Cohen

Dina is a registered dietitian nutritionist (RDN) with a Master of Science in Human Nutrition. Dina provides medical nutrition therapy and counseling for a variety of nutritional concerns, including diabetes, cardiovascular disease, PCOS, weight management, and eating disorders. She is a member of the Academy of Nutrition and Dietetics, the Academy for Eating Disorders, and the International Federation of Eating Disorder Dietitians. Dina enjoys helping her clients develop an appreciation for nourishing, delicious food and a mindful approach to eating that facilitates their physical and emotional wellbeing.

Faigy, The Baker's Daughter

As the daughter of a baker, a full-time mom, and a part-time baker herself, Faigy is always on the lookout for new and exciting ideas. To help with portion control, she focuses on developing recipes for bite-sized cookies with big flavor. Faigy's kids are her biggest critics—only recipes that get their approval are passed along to readers.

Chaia Frishman

Chaia works as a writer and owns Fruit Platters and More, a business based out of her Far Rockaway, New York, home. Her husband, Eliahu Frishman, works "behind the knife," creating stunning fruit displays and vegetable crudité platters while also making hearty soups, savory dips, and delicious salads and sorbets. (The Frishmans eat well!)

The marriage of her two professions is what spurred Chaia to write KosherScoop's "Best in Season" musings about fruits, vegetables, and the karma they bring to life.

With their daughter and three sons, the Frishmans promote healthy eating while beautifying the Shabbos, Yom Tov, and simcha tables of Far Rockaway, the Five Towns, and surrounding areas. View their work and products at www.fruitplattersand-more.com.

Norene Gilletz

Norene Gilletz, one of Canada's leading kosher food writers and the owner of Gourmania Inc., is crazy about food and her world revolves around recipes. Norene received her initial culinary training in her late mother's kitchen, where she was taught the creative art of recycling leftovers! Today, Norene divides her time between her work as a freelance food writer, editor, food consultant, cooking teacher, and culinary spokesperson.

Norene is a Certified Culinary Professional with the International Association of Culinary Professionals and a member of the Women's Culinary Network of Toronto. She performs cooking demonstrations and lectures for various organizations, including hospitals, food services, and charitable fundraising groups. Norene is passionate about healthy cooking and living and has expertise in a wide variety of health concerns and special diets. Her motto, "Food that's good for you should taste good," has been a core principle guiding her culinary career.

Norene's previous titles include *The Food Processor Bible, Norene's Healthy Kitchen,* and *Healthy Helpings,* and she is a freelance columnist for KosherScoop.com. Born and raised in Winnipeg, Norene raised her family in Montreal and now lives in Toronto, Canada. She has three children and five grandchildren.

Eileen Goltz

Eileen is a food writer born and raised in the Chicago area. Eileen graduated from Indiana University and the Cordon Bleu Cooking School in Paris. She currently lives in Fort Wayne, Indiana, where she writes for the Orthodox Union (OU), publishes a weekly column for the *Journal Gazette,* and freelances for various Jewish newspapers, magazine, websites, and blogs throughout the United States and Canada. Eileen blogs at cuisinebyeileen.wordpress.com.

Brynie Greisman

Brynie Greisman's passion for the culinary arts has been evident ever since she was a teenager collecting cooking magazines. After attending culinary school and honing her skills, Brynie eventually developed her own series of professional cooking courses. She teaches cooking courses for teenagers and girls in her home, and delivers baking and cooking workshops at the Israel Center. Brynie is also a recipe writer for *Mishpacha* magazine, where the challenge of developing original recipes keeps her creative juices flowing. She also owns Tasty Lo-fat Creations, a home-based business that sells over 50 flavors of whole wheat, low-fat muffins, biscotti, cakes, and all sorts of desserts to her many satisfied customers. She can be contacted at greisman.b@gmail.com.

Rabbi Tsvi Heber

Rabbi Heber is the Director of Community Kosher for COR, Toronto's community kashrus organization. In this role, he is responsible for all of COR's community kashrus operations, community education initiatives, and community interaction. Learn more about COR at www.COR.ca.

Sam Kanner

Chef Sam Kanner currently owns and operates Pantry Foods and Catering, a café and catering company in Toronto, Canada. Sam uses seasonal ingredients and fresh flavors from around the world to create delicious vegetarian and dairy delights. Sam's cooking style is straightforward fresh food with a creative twist. Visit Sam's website at pantryfoods.ca.

Levana Kirshenbaum

For more than thirty years, Levana Kirschenbaum has been teaching people how to cook healthy and nutritious meals. When she opened her eponymous restaurant with her husband and two brothers-in-law in the late 1970s on New York's Upper West Side, all of them were perfectly aware they were facing a hard sell: introduce fine kosher dining to the kosher public, which until then had been content either eating at home or grabbing a bite in the rare joints that served institutional, old-world treats. The general prediction was that the presumptuous idea would fall flat on its face. Undaunted by being the trailblazers of the trend, Levana and her partners surrounded themselves with the best chefs, developed the most delicious dishes, and waited patiently until the idea of upscale kosher caught on. The rest is history: the kosher food and wine market has experienced a veritable explosion and occupies pride of place among the most prestigious competitions.

Many luxury kosher restaurants have opened and thrived since Levana's pioneering days, bearing out the dictum that imitation is the greatest form of flattery. Levana still happily gives cooking demos regularly in her New York classroom and across the country. She is also the author of *Levana's Table: Kosher Cooking for Everyone, Levana Cooks Dairy-Free!,* and a book-DVD set based on her demo series called "*In Short Order.*" Visit her website, www.LevanaCooks.com.

Shani Malka

Previously a cooking instructor, Shani Malka is a mom who wishes she could spend more time tinkering and experimenting in her kitchen. In the small amounts of time she does devote to cooking, Shani creates some exquisite, family-friendly foods that are popular with all. Shani lives in Lakewood, NJ, with her husband and family.

Sari Matias

With a background in diet and nutrition, Sari has successfully helped hundreds of people, providing support as she teaches her clients the healthiest way to eat. Adamant on allowing a full range of food without depriving anyone of their favorite dish, Sari places great emphasis on providing her clients with a full menu to go along with their diet. Sari is constantly coming up with great new recipes, a few of which she has published in *Mishpacha* magazine.

Sharon Matten

Sharon lives in Chicago and is a freelance pastry chef, kosher food writer and blogger, cable TV guest chef, Wilton Cake Instructor, cookbook contributing editor, electrical engineer, wife and mother (not listed in order of importance!). Sharon blogs at www.koshereveryday.com, where she writes about cooking kosher with a family and a busy life. Visit her site to get great recipes, to view tempting food photos, and to learn more about her work.

Chanie Nayman

Chanie is the food editor for the weekly magazine *Family First.* Whether she's playing around with an old recipe or creating a new one, she says that learning how to taste test and spice up her usual fare helps her develop the recipes she shares with her readers. Chanie lives in Detroit, Michigan, with her husband and children, whom she calls "the best tasters ever."

Esther Ottensosser

Esther is a food stylist whose work has been featured in *Mishpacha* magazine and various other publications. Whether it's food design, unique craft creations, demos, or recipes, Esther takes simple, everyday products and transforms them into an extraordinary presentation. Many of her creations are featured on her blog, estherodesign.com. Esther lives in New Jersey and can be contacted via email at info@estherodesign.com.

Daphna Rabinovitch

A classically trained chef and pastry chef, Daphna Rabinovitch started her career working in Italy alongside Lorenza De Medici at her ancestral home, Badia A Coltibuono, teaching classic Tuscan cooking to traveling groups of North Americans and cooking privately for family and social events.

Upon her return to Canada, Daphna worked as a pastry chef for a well-known upscale gourmet food store and catering company. From there, she became Director of the Test Kitchen at *Canadian Living Magazine.* Over the course of her 10 years there, Daphna supervised the testing of over 500 recipes a year and penned countless articles herself. Daphna was also the editor of *Canadian Living Cooks Step-By-Step,* a compendium of how-to recipes that won the Cuisine Canada Culinary Book Award in 1999. A successful stint as co-host of the popular "Canadian Living Cooks" on the Food Network followed, with the show airing for four seasons.

After a two-year stint as Director of Product Development and Innovation for a large baking manufacturer, Daphna has now returned to her consulting business, writing for food periodicals and websites across North America, teaching, food styling, acting as a spokesperson, consulting with and creating recipes for different national food companies, updating restaurant menus, and editing cookbooks.

Paula Shoyer

Paula is the author of The Kosher Baker: 160 Dairy-Free Desserts From Traditional to Trendy. The Kosher Baker has been featured in newspapers, magazines, websites, blogs, and on radio and TV all over the United States. Paula is a pastry chef who owns and operates the Paula's Parisian Pastries Cooking School out of Chevy Chase, Maryland. She teaches scheduled and custom-designed classes in French pastry and Jewish cooking in the Washington, D.C. area and all around the country. Paula has appeared on Food Network's Sweet Genius, WGN's Lunchbreak, WUSA9 Washington, San Diego Living, NBC Washington News 4 at 4, and Martha Stewart Morning Living on XM Sirius. Paula believes that everyone deserves a delicious dessert, no matter what special diet they are on. She develops dessert recipes that are dairy-free, sugar-free, gluten-free, and vegan. Paula shares new recipes along with personal stories of her travels and events on her blog, www.kosherbaker.blogspot.com. Visit her website, www.paulaspastry.com, for both sweet and savory recipes.

Alexandra Zohn

A food writer, pastry chef, and instructor with a degree in nutrition and a master's in Food Studies, Alexandra Zohn Cepelowicz is the New York-based baker behind Three Tablespoons' wholesome and allergy-friendly treats, and the blogger living, writing, cooking, photographing (and cleaning up) using fresh, seasonal, kosher and all-natural ingredients. Alexandra blogs about super foods, motherhood, cooking, life, and trying to remain positive while balancing it all at www.ironyofbaking.blogspot.com. She can be contacted at ale@threetablespoons.com.

Index